Northwest Vist
Learning Resou
3535 North Ell
San Antonio, Texas 78251

New Woman and Colonial Adventure Fiction
in Victorian Britain

UNIVERSITY PRESS OF FLORIDA

Florida A&M University, Tallahassee
Florida Atlantic University, Boca Raton
Florida Gulf Coast University, Ft. Myers
Florida International University, Miami
Florida State University, Tallahassee
University of Central Florida, Orlando
University of Florida, Gainesville
University of North Florida, Jacksonville
University of South Florida, Tampa
University of West Florida, Pensacola

New Woman and Colonial Adventure Fiction in Victorian Britain

Gender, Genre, and Empire

꙰

LeeAnne M. Richardson

University Press of Florida
Gainesville · Tallahassee · Tampa · Boca Raton
Pensacola · Orlando · Miami · Jacksonville · Ft. Myers

Parts of chapter 4 originally appeared in *Silent Voices: Forgotten Novels by Victorian Women Writers*, edited by Brenda Ayres. Copyright 2003 by Brenda Ayres. Reproduced with permission of Greenwood Publishing Group, Inc., Westport, Conn.

11 10 09 08 07 06   6 5 4 3 2 1

A record of cataloging-in-publication data is available from the Library of Congress.
ISBN 0-8130-2944-9

The University Press of Florida is the scholarly publishing agency for the State University System of Florida, comprising Florida A&M University, Florida Atlantic University, Florida Gulf Coast University, Florida International University, Florida State University, University of Central Florida, University of Florida, University of North Florida, University of South Florida, and University of West Florida.

University Press of Florida
15 Northwest 15th Street
Gainesville, FL 32611–2079
http://www.upf.com

Contents

Acknowledgments

I need to thank several eminent Victorianists for their assistance, beginning with Andrew Miller, who guided me through every stage of the initial drafting of this book, offering his insights, sharing his knowledge, and making numerous suggestions that strengthened my arguments and my prose. Pat Brantlinger, Jim Adams, and Joss Marsh also made important suggestions in the early stages of this project.

The two readers for the University Press of Florida offered invaluable suggestions for the final revisions of this book. To Sally Mitchell and Linda Hughes, I am exceedingly grateful.

Georgia State University awarded a summer Research Enhancement Grant as well as flex time to assist me in completing revisions for publication. The GSU Department of English Works in Progress reading group commented thoughtfully on a draft of the introduction; I want especially to thank Michael Galchinsky, Paul Schmidt, Randy Malamud, and Stephen Dobranski for their comments.

I must express my gratitude for the libraries whose collections of nineteenth-century and feminist texts made this study possible: the Women's Library at London Metropolitan University, which has an impressive collection of New Woman (and related antifeminist) texts; the Indiana University Herman B. Wells library and Lilly rare books library; and the Stockwell-Mudd Library at Albion College, where John Kondelik and Carolyn Gaswick allowed me access to their collection of nineteenth-century journals at a key stage of this book's composition.

There is no way adequately to thank Jim Diedrick for his contributions to this book. His editorial eye, unstinting attention, and unfailing support have been vital to the completion of this project.

Introduction

In a 1931 address to the Women's Service League titled "Professions for Women," Virginia Woolf represents the female writer's life as an action-filled adventure in which she must slay the phantom of domestic duty. This phantom—the Angel in the House—haunts her quest to become a professional writer, putting obstacles in her path and in the way of her best prose. Woolf says she "acted in self-defense" when she killed this phantom, who, much like the cannibalistic tribesman of a Rider Haggard story, "would have plucked the heart out" of her writing. Instead of warring against this specter, Woolf would have preferred studying Greek or "roaming the world in search of adventures" (151). So despite her later repudiations of Victorian fiction, Woolf takes her terms here directly from two competing subgenres that emerged in late-century Britain: New Woman novels, typically featuring a professional woman (often a writer or artist) opposing the limits imposed by narrow-minded but powerful conventions; and colonial adventure fiction, focusing on a brave man encountering inferior but powerful vestiges of early human history. As Woolf's imagery indicates, these two ostensibly dissimilar subgenres of Victorian fiction interacted in profoundly suggestive ways—formally as well as ideologically.

At first glance, these subgenres are antithetic in their purposes and interests. The adventure novel, written from the perspective of the authoritarian, culturally dominant male, often justifies the subaltern's subordinated status, both by displaying the "obvious" inferiority of the African or Indian native and by demonstrating the superiority of the British male through his victories over "savage" landscapes, animals, and peoples. In contrast, New Woman fiction presents narratives written from below, interrogating the inequities of a system that assumes and asserts the very things adventure novels champion: male superiority, the right to dominate and rule others, paternalistic ideology. So why yoke them together? Because both genres were responding—not symmetrically, but in equally engaged ways—to a complex of cultural forces typically identified (depending on one's vantage point) as "cultural decline" or "cultural evolution." Moreover, reinserting them into literary history in tandem illuminates the terms of the gender debate and imperial politics in late-century Britain.

To be sure, gender and empire have together received much critical attention in the past decade. This book, however, introduces a new element into this gendered discourse of imperialism: the specific genre categories of masculine adventure fiction and New Woman novels. Bringing these subgenres into direct contact allows us to see the degree to which attitudes toward empire are gendered and engendered by cultural debates in the metropole. Bringing these two subgenres together illuminates both the development and interdependence of gender politics and imperialism in late-Victorian Britain. While it is a commonplace of postcolonial criticism that the British novel discursively engendered British imperialism (a position most broadly articulated in Edward Said's *Culture and Imperialism*), my study argues that late-century gender trouble, most clearly embodied in New Woman novels, profoundly influenced both concepts of imperialism and the novels that most fully represent them. Not only does gender become troubled in late-century male adventure fiction, where attempts to reproduce conservative gender politics in the colonies often backfire, but the New Woman novels appearing at the same time also alternately appropriate and challenge imperial structures in their representations of contested gender norms. By focusing on the interrelationship of these subgenres, this book demonstrates the ways in which they register and enact cultural conflict in late-nineteenth-century British culture: specifically the ways in which gender, empire, and genre strikingly and unexpectedly converge.

While critics like Anne McClintock and Sally Ledger have brought gender relations into focus through the lens of imperialism, I seek to demonstrate the ways in which both gender and imperialism are represented and contested in the two most popular late-century fiction subgenres. One expects the empire-builder to speak of enlarging his territory and creating a wider sphere of action; yet the New Woman uses the same metaphors for her excursions out of the domestic sphere. One anticipates that women might exploit their gendered authority in the domestic sphere to bolster their assertions of authority elsewhere; yet the colonial adventurer likewise manipulates the rhetoric of "natural" fitness to oversee others as a way of justifying his excursions into the colonial realm.[1]

This book demonstrates a conjunction beyond parallelism, however, for even parallel moves invoke the binary thinking that has characterized most considerations of these late-century novels. Rather, these subgenres are in an active dialog that results in their convergence around key discursive sites, tropes, and themes. Indeed, it is often impossible to separate the interests and the methods of these two subgenres. Rather than two distinct and separate subgenres, New Woman and colonial adventure fiction often present themselves as hybrid forms. It is telling that Olive Schreiner's *The Story of an African Farm* (1883)—considered the first New Woman novel—is set in an Africa more familiar to imperial adventurers than to nascent feminists.

Schreiner's literary followers often do more than replicate her heroine's longing for a wider sphere of action and a sound education; authors like Flora Annie Steel also adopt Schreiner's mix of exotic locale and feminist plot. Similarly, the master of the colonial adventure genre, H. Rider Haggard, often writes adventure plots inflected with New Woman characters and themes. His 1887 novel *Jess* is a rewriting of Schreiner's *African Farm*, featuring two English sisters (instead of cousins), in the care of their uncle (instead of their aunt), who struggle for survival amid the Boers and Africans of the karoo. Jess is the analog of Schreiner's Lyndall: an interesting woman who is not conventionally beautiful but who attracts men with her intensity, intelligence, and passion. One man, John Niel (the analog of Schreiner's Gregory Rose), falls in love first with Bessie, and then with Jess. Jess is "an odd woman" (49), but instead of the higher education, self-development, and independence that the proto-New Woman Lyndall seeks, Jess embraces the conventionally feminine values of "love and self-sacrifice" (36). What the novel lacks in New Woman credentials, however, it makes up for with adventure motifs: a wildebeest hunt, battles between the Boers and the English, wild rescues, and grueling treks.

Even when the two subgenres' typical plot elements are not so thoroughly entwined that they exist within the same novel, colonial adventure novels and New Woman fiction present intertwined ways of responding to cultural forces, and bringing them together produces a richer picture of late-century concerns than when they are analyzed separately. A time of imperial expansion and unrest, the fin de siècle period also saw women's issues come to the forefront of the national consciousness: the leading magazines addressed the "proper" position of women, universities confronted the fitness of women for higher education, and commentators formulated epithets like Wild Women and Shrieking Sisterhood, explicitly linking feminist women with unruly natives. Thus changing ideas about sex and gender are implicated in imperial discourse, and "dangerous" ideas are linked to the genres that helped engender them. The relationship between the women who imaginatively ventured into the territory of feminine emancipation cannot be studied separately from the men who imaginatively adventured into the outreaches of empire.

Viewing these subgenres as an integral part of a larger literary history also alerts us to the major role they played in the development of the novel. Lyn Pykett has already argued that the New Woman novel (along with the sensation fiction of the 1860s) contributed to the development of the novel generally. I argue that the imperial adventure novel is the twin star of the New Woman novel: that both revolve around one another, affected by the other's gravitational pull as well as by the influence of larger ideological constellations, from governmental action on emigration policy and property rights to personal attitudes toward race, nation, and motherhood.[2] I also want to rescue these works from the condescension that the designation "sub" in subgenre implies. They are no less important than the creations of Oscar Wilde or Thomas Hardy—nor are they somehow marginal to the "major" writers' concerns.

Indeed, a third figure walked the late-Victorian literary landscape with the New Woman and the colonial adventurer: the dandy. Linda Dowling has argued that the dandy and the New Woman were allied in the minds of their contemporaries because "Both inspired reactions ranging from hilarity to disgust and outrage, and both raised as well profound fears for the future of sex, class, and race. . . . [They] were widely felt to oppose not each other but the values considered essential to the survival of established culture" (436). Stephan Arata, who seeks to "bring seemingly unlike thinkers into productive conversation" (5), has explored the link between decadent literature and colonial adventure fiction. Both decadence and jingoism, he writes, were used by "medical specialists and cultural critics alike to designate forms of degeneracy. Yet it also became clear that, from the perspective of contemporary observers, jingoist imperialism seemed to have been called into existence by decadence, as a counterweight to aesthetic excess" (6). At times the dandy is more closely allied with the New Woman, and at other times with the colonial adventurer. Like the colonial adventurer, the dandy explores realms of hidden or forbidden knowledge: Dorian Gray's forays into the opium dens of south London are not only reminiscent of dangerous travel into the untamed jungle, they bring him into contact with a variety of colonial types as well: "Malays" (202), and a "half-caste, in a ragged turban and a shabby ulster" (203). And like the gruff and hyper-masculine heroes of Rider Haggard novels, decadence often manifests a misogynistic outlook:

dandies often are found in purely masculine company and have little regard for women's political action, which is typically denigrated as "ugly." But like the New Woman, the dandy contests gender roles and definitions: Dorian Gray is womanlike in his beauty and grace; the dandy's interest in his clothing and appearance, moreover, allies him with characteristics conventionally associated with women. The dandy is the implicit third term in this book, interacting in significant ways with both New Woman and colonial adventure fiction.

This study rose out of an attempt to understand the temporal history that New Woman and colonial adventure fiction share: both flourished beginning in the mid-to-late 1880s and largely died out—or mutated into other forms— by the turn of the century. Why would these two genres emerge when they did, and end when they did? Why was there an upsurge in feminist argument and concerns in the pages of over one hundred novels between 1883 and 1900? Why would colonial adventure fiction, admittedly committed to a politics of co-optation, rise up beside these novels of liberation? These questions must be answered together, because these subgenres developed relationally—in reaction to one another, as well as in response to cultural anxieties. More than this, they are formally, structurally, and ideologically complementary.

Despite recent critical attention to colonial and gender discourses, scholars have paired colonial adventure and New Woman fiction only to note how some imperial romance heroines incorporate characteristics of powerful, self-possessed New Woman heroines, most notably H. Rider Haggard's She-who-must-be-obeyed and Bram Stoker's Mina Harker. To be sure, the persistent feminization of the other in colonial adventure fiction has alerted readers to the way that sexual desire constitutes the narrative engine of these novels. But colonial adventure fiction and New Woman novels, like colonial and patriarchal discourses, are part of a cultural history in which more than shifting gender boundaries was at stake. Irish Home Rule, women's suffrage, the expanding empire, and a growing human rights movement (especially in response to the Belgian Congo) brought matters of autonomous self-rule to the fore. The intersection of these genres merits further investigation into the specific ways they concurrently register these pressing cultural debates, explore the dynamics of personal and political power, and re-imagine social relations.

Women's relation to empire cannot be reduced to the simple binarism of colonizer and colonized, and New Woman novels do not exist in uncomplicated opposition to colonial adventure fiction. Because white women are of the powerful and "superior" race, they share certain assumptions and privileges of authority; because women are not fully empowered, they share certain hallmarks of subjection. No disempowered subjects have an unambiguous relationship to empire, but because women were non-voting, primarily non-property-holding citizens, they may well have had a more complex understanding of the systematic disempowerment of Africans and Indians than middle-class British men had. It is significant that when women writers exploit rudiments of the adventure genre, they nonetheless leave other fundamental elements behind: Steel and Schreiner do not make explicit statements about the inferiority of native people or import scenes of their massacre.

Explicit references in women's novels to the colonies, racial characteristics, or enslavement are often cited to support claims about women's relationship to empire—most notably in Susan Meyer's *Imperialism at Home*, Gayatri Spivak's "Three Women's Texts and a Critique of Imperialism," and Edward Said's *Culture and Imperialism*. While all three writers demonstrate that nineteenth century British culture is thoroughly inflected with colonial markers and metaphors, I specifically investigate how the two subgenres' use of similar verbal structures and tropes reveal their affinities. These subgenres demonstrate that imperialist and feminist discourses exist in tandem and often constitute a dialog that employs similar terms, tropes, and rhetorical devices. For example, the presence of colonial discourse in New Woman novels is mirrored by the appearance of domestic discourse in adventure novels, for aspects of the colonial experience often mimic the domestic situation. Adventure novels often serve to represent an ideal relationship between colonizer and colony, one that mirrors the relationship of benevolent (but dominant) husband to submissive (but loving) wife. Their attempts to impose a conventional British domestic trope on the colonies, however, are consistently undermined by the ways the colonial situation refuses to conform to British ideals of colonial acquiescence and compliance. Colonial adventure narratives thus are obliquely allied to the transgressive politics of New Woman fiction.

When we bring the two subgenres into productive dialog, we see not only that their concerns intersect but also that these points of contact are complex and vital. The trajectory of a character like Rudyard Kipling's Kim is instructive: he learns to assimilate into Indian culture, and to take on its language and customs, in order to survive as an orphan in the bazaar. He is recruited to use his knowledge of India to serve British interests, and thus begins an important shift. Kim as a child interacts with Indians as a pseudo-Indian to benefit both himself and his Indian cohorts; as an adult, Kim represents himself as an Indian in order to gather information for the Raj. The adult Kim's Indian helpers tend to be semicomic like Hurree Baboo, and a reader understands that despite all of Hurree Baboo's attempts to join the Royal Society and British culture, an Indian will always be the other of the British man. Flora Annie Steel's Kate, from *On the Face of the Waters*, follows a similar path. An Englishwoman in India, Kate learns Indian ways and customs in order to survive as an unprotected white woman during the Mutiny of 1857. Like *Kim*, this novel instructs the reader about British and Indian culture, but instead of stressing the essential and insurmountable differences between Indians and the British, Steel's novel comments on the ability of women to care for themselves, to adapt to unfamiliar situations, and to use their intelligence *and* their capacity for human sympathy to learn from and work with others (whether they be black or white). Exploring the ways in which New Woman fiction enters into a dialog with imperialist "structures of feeling" (to paraphrase Raymond Williams) as this structure is inscribed in colonial adventure fiction provides a way of understanding the complex interdependencies of empire, gender, and genre in late-century England.

The chapters that follow bring genre and discourse into dialog in order to further explore the complex dimensions of this dialog. These novels intersect in a number of realms and in various ways—from their use of similar metaphors, modes of narration, and participation in larger public debates, to their similarly contested cultural status—so I employ a number of critical approaches in the following chapters. Nonetheless, the entire study is built on the foundation of genre theory and discourse, a dialectical pair whose opposing but interdependent ways of analyzing a text can together produce a richer understanding of the interplay between ideology and literary form. Genre is primarily a formalist literary term, while discourse takes precedence in cultural studies, but both are devices to categorize, shape, and better comprehend strands of cultural production. Because discourse analysis often elides genre categories, it can be useful in seeing things against the grain of genre studies. Likewise, genre provides a way of historically and formally categorizing modes and approaches not available to most discourse analysis. Just as the postcolonial notion of hybridity has helped to illuminate the margins where cultural differences come into contact and new subjectivities are formed, the dialectic tension produced by combining genre and discourse analysis allows us to identify new ideas and entities emerging from the interaction of disciplinary methods.[3]

Chapter 1, "A New Battle of the Books," demonstrates how the debate over the genres of realism and romance became gendered and thus extended a larger cultural debate about the changing roles of women. In a wide range of Victorian periodicals, romances—especially those set in India or Africa—were seen as revitalizing the male, whose virility was threatened by the usurpations of the New Woman's new roles. When these same periodicals began to align the New Woman's realist novels with naturalism, the definitions and associations of the naturalist mode changed from highly masculine and progressive to effeminate and degenerate.

Discourse, power, and subjectivity are the concerns of chapter 2, "Do we speak the same language?," which analyzes how discourses of power shape subjectivity, what is knowable, and what is known. Both subgenres were widely seen as constituting as well as representing new ideals of manliness and womanhood. As I note in chapter 1, critics identified a new British manliness emerging out of renewed interest in romance. Tacit in critical essays about the New Woman is that the novels *produced* New Women; if New Women appeared *first* in fiction and only later in reality, it was easier to categorize the social movement as unnatural, imported, and imposed on the "naturally" domestic British woman.[4] What Homi K. Bhabha has posited in regard to colonial relations—that speech is a political act and that discourse is an apparatus of power created to justify conquest and establish systems of administration—is true as well in the context of patriarchal relations. This chapter examines the discourse patterns of two colonial adventure novels—Joseph Conrad's *Heart of Darkness* and Rider Haggard's *King Solomon's Mines*—and places them into relief through comparison with George Gissing's New Woman novel *The Odd Women*. This comparison highlights the degree to which both subgenres converge around discourses of domination and use them to similar effect: to sustain one's own point of view, whether feminist or imperialist, and discredit the views of the other.

The next two chapters engage the interconnections of genre and ideology, first in the adventure novel's appropriations of New Woman figures, then in a feminist re-thinking of the adventure novel. Chapter 3, "Staking Claims," shows how masculine adventure novels that exploit the figure of the New Woman (like *Dracula*) both stake a claim on the New Woman's territory and attempt to drive a stake through the heart of the New Woman's feminism. Chapter 4, "'Aboriginal' Interventions," refutes William Barry's claim that the "unfeminine" women authors he deplores are not creatively original but atavistically "aboriginal" by demonstrating how Flora Annie Steel's feminist re-imagining of the adventure genre can be progressive for both women and colonized others. These chapters present novels that are hybrid forms, revealing the extent to which the same terms, tropes, and structures are at play in both subgenres.

Chapter 5 analyzes how discourses of possession and property play out in adventure novels where possession is, quite literally, nine-tenths of the law, and in New Woman novels where possessive individualism defines autonomous subjecthood (and where representations of marriage call attention to the legal possession of women by men). But as the chapter's title, "Unhand her!," suggests, changing laws—most particularly the Married Women's Property Act of 1882—complicated the status of marriage and initiated changes in discourses of possession.[5] Mona Caird's *The Daughters of Danaus*, for example, presents a rich and complex range of attitudes toward feminist self-possession. Not only does Caird depict the injustices suffered by the woman who is literally dispossessed by marriage laws and metaphorically dispossessed by the selflessness required by filial duty, she presents those who restrict women's actions as fully human and often honorable as well. Rather than demonizing the people who oppress women, Caird exposes the system that engenders injustice. Haggard's *Allan Quartermain* demonstrates the transferability of domestic terms to colonial situations by projecting the possession of women in marriage—the very thing Caird rails against in England—onto the African natives Quartermain encounters. Like Caird, Quartermain disparages the practice, although he distances his culture's treatment of women from the "marriage market" he depicts as an exclusively African custom.

Literary agitation was inseparable from late-century social agitation. A time of literary experimentation and change (in genre, in reading publics, in forums, in marketing), the 1890s boasted aesthetes, decadents, adventure novelists, naturalists, New Women novelists, as well as traditional realists writing triple-deckers. Yet both New Woman novels and imperial adventure romances have been considered, for the most part, outside this larger literary context. The conclusion, "The Territory Ahead," looks at colonial adventure fiction and New Woman novels alongside decadent prose, science fiction, and finally modernist works, to see both where these subgenres come from and where they go. The New Woman novel greatly influenced the work of modernist writers like Woolf, and adventure novels laid the groundwork for science fiction. Woolf's *Mrs. Dalloway* and H. G. Wells' *The War of the Worlds* share a focus on seeing and being seen, and each explicitly muses on the relation of vision to subjectivity. Examining how point of view follows the dictates of genre, this chapter concludes that ideas, modes of expression, and demands for power, understanding, or reconsideration circulate throughout the disparate subgenres of turn-of-the-century Britain, extending and expanding the dialog between New Woman and colonial adventure fiction.

"A New Battle of the Books"

Genre, Gender, and Imperialism

Writing against the grain of the decadent disregard for social utility that characterized the preface to *Dorian Gray*, the aesthete and cultural critic Vernon Lee insisted on the need to link art to social progress. In her "Gospels of Anarchy" (1898) she argues that "we stand in need of a new science of will, thought, and emotion" (723). Instead of rules of conduct, societies need to develop and encourage "a habit of feeling and thinking, an attitude" (728), and they develop these needful things in large part through literature. Poet and literary critic Richard LeGallienne also implicitly argues that literature is central to social development. As he wrote of Grant Allen's *The Woman Who Did*, "In form a novel, in reality it belongs to our noble series of change-demanding pamphlets. As literature it has small value; as a brilliant noise on behalf of human progress it means a great deal" (18). But in what ways was British culture to be influenced by these unacknowledged legislators? In what directions should British authors move British culture? And how best to represent the values that the British public needs?

Andrew Lang entered this debate in his 1887 essay "Realism and Romance." "In English and American journals and magazines a new Battle of the Books is being fought," Lang wrote, and it is over "the question of Novel or Romance—of Romance or Realism" (683) that the battle lines are being drawn. More than a public forum on literary merit, however, this generic dispute expanded to encompass all manner of social concerns: degeneration, domesticity, progress, and the empire. New Woman and colonial adventure novels are central to this debate, because the former was often taken to represent 1890s realism while the latter typically embraced romance. Despite their different generic affiliations, however, these subgenres share qualities and concerns that demonstrate their dialogic engagement with these larger cultural debates.

Because it is anti-intuitive to think of colonial adventure novels and New Woman novels as sharing fundamental formal and ideological concerns, this chapter will begin by describing the social conditions that shaped these sub-genres' interactions before investigating some of the formal characteristics they share. My goal is to demonstrate how the late-century aesthetic debate over *genre* simultaneously registers late-century *gender* debates. The late nineteenth century is known as a time when the Woman Question dominated public debate; what is less well understood is how completely the Woman Question colonized all arenas of public concern, and how thoroughly questions of genre are implicated in it. These subgenres' convergent ideological concerns demonstrate the degree to which questions of genre, gender, and imperialism infiltrated the late-century political consciousness.

Moreover, the dialogic relationship of these subgenres speaks volumes about the development of the novel in the latter half of the nineteenth century. Nancy Armstrong, in *Desire and Domestic Fiction*, advances a narrative of the novel's history wherein women's political power is represented as do-mestic virtue. But what happens when women's political power is no longer masked and legitimized by its association with the cult of domesticity? In the New Woman novel, behavior is emphatically both sexual and political: politics is no longer necessarily a metonym for sex. Sex and gender drive the political economy as women work and struggle—with men, with parents, with children—for autonomy; sex and gender drive the literary economy as New Women writers struggle with male adventure novelists for supremacy. In the debates over the relative merits of these novels, it becomes clear how gender differences interact with political and literary realities, and how late-nineteenth-century feminists worked to exploit ruptures in the system of rep-resentation. The New Woman writer recognizes that gender differences *are* political differences and not merely natural, while male adventure novelists attempt to reassert the discourse of "natural" gender divisions.

The congruity among formal, structural, and ideological aspects of these subgenres is part of a larger dialog on gender, empire, and literature in Brit-ish culture. The Woman Question debate revealed the extent to which social and political power structures were based on the separate spheres ideology. Women were both at the center of British culture, in that they were central to the imagined constitution of social relations, and marginalized by it, in that they were largely excluded from exercising political power. Judith Newton's "Making and Remaking History" describes the culture of manliness that developed in the later part of the nineteenth century as a counterpoint to the mid-century ideology of domesticity. From the 1860s on (when women became both more vocal and more visible in public life), masculine ideals constituted themselves in opposition to female culture. Thus, a new male elite emphasized separation from women rather than appropriation of their virtues (133–34). The New Woman, however, brought men and women back together, as it were, by appropriating masculine values. But in the eyes of conservative cultural critics, women who resisted their roles as passive beings were accused of turning themselves into men and abdicating their feminine responsibilities.

Debates on New Woman literature and the phenomenon that inspired it were pervasive, heated, and fully cognizant of the radical challenge posed by the New Woman: she denaturalized normative sex roles. The New Woman is "new" because she redefines the category of "woman." Any adult female who embraced one or more of the feminist ideas that constituted the larger-than-life image of the New Woman could be, depending on the speaker's politics, derogatorily or admiringly labeled a New Woman.[1] The image of the New Woman is unified only in that all her facets threaten the status quo. She was held by leading conservatives to represent laxity, immorality, over-reaching ambition, and any number of "unnatural" activities (such as going to university). In the words of Eliza Lynn Linton, one of the leading voices of resistance to the New Woman, "The wealth of a country is its population; and the finer and healthier the children of to-day, the stronger and nobler will be *the men* of tomorrow and the grander the destinies of the empire. Whether the new woman with her unhoned habits and manly ambitions, her overtaxing Higher Education and that deadly spirit of rivalry to men can fulfill either of these great duties of her sex . . . remains to be seen" ("Nearing the Rapids" 385; italics mine). She suggests that the New Woman's "manly ambitions" will lead to the downfall of the British Empire. True women, she argues, engender empire by rearing boys who will become imperialists.

By wanting the same education and the same employment opportunities, the same rights of citizenship, and even the same access to sexual expression, women challenged the basis of patriarchal power, rooted in a vision of women as fundamentally different from men: purer, simpler, weaker, and requiring men's tutelage, supervision, and protection. The logic of complementary thinking dictates that when women take the active role, men are necessarily rendered passive, displaced from their masculine responsibilities. This binary view of male and female characteristics is so firmly embedded that challenging it often causes a *reversal* rather than a *reconsideration* of ascribed traits. For instance, in Herbert E. Brown's antifeminist *Betsey Jane on the New Woman* (1897), when Betsey Jane's children return home from college proclaiming "advanced" ideas, they reveal a topsy-turvy world where women take on men's business and men acquire the feminine graces. Her son reports that "he had given way to the 'new woman,' and Alice [his sister] had fallen in line with the whole female population and was fitting herself for one of the professions and occupations that was just being opened to the women. At the colleges the young men were being taught to cook, sew, do house work and such light and graceful duties" (28–29). In Brown's vision, it is not possible that men and women both might occupy the professions; separate spheres ideology is so firmly entrenched that instead of redrawing boundaries, gender roles are merely inverted.

Accordingly, women who throw off the mantle of domesticity do not merely leave the home: they throw the social order into disarray. Kathleen Spencer notes that "more and more women insisted on leaving the house of which they had been appointed angel. . . . [I]n the eyes of most Victorian men, for women to deny their traditional role was to deny their womanhood, to challenge the distinctions between women and men upon which the family and therefore society depended" (206). This social instability generates fears of political unrest. As Judith Halberstam argues in relation to *Dracula*, "Mina and Lucy, the dark and the fair heroines of Stoker's novel, make Englishness a function of quiet femininity and maternal domesticity. Dracula, accordingly, threatens the stability and, indeed, the naturalness of this equation between middle-class womanhood and national pride by seducing both women with his particularly foreign sexuality" (89). Hence the imbrication of women with national security, of domesticity with imperial politics, of motherhood with nationalism.

Women's agitation for social and political rights thus impinges on empire in several ways. For one thing, women were fighting for emancipation from patriarchal oppression just when colonial oppression was at its height. Much has been written on the metaphoric relationship between colonized people and women: the lack of rights, the cultural and legal insistence on obedience, the oppressors' conviction (or delusion) that their actions are for the good of the oppressed. The so-called civilizing mission to bring light to benighted Africans closely mimics the patriarchal "care" of women—preventing them from overextending themselves by too much learning, preventing them from acting against their constitution by displaying too much will, keeping their pursuits in line with what is proper and prudent for their "natural" abilities. Indeed, English women's agitation for legal rights, which centered on their right to own property and thus exercise self-determination, served implicitly to highlight the very things colonizers deny to colonized subjects.

Moreover, the emancipatory rhetoric of the women's movement undermined the logic of the civilizing mission. What Carole Gerson terms the "illusionary duplicity of colonial freedom" (71) is evident in both New Woman fiction and in feminist rhetoric. As Frances Power Cobbe argues in *The Duties of Women* (1881), no one can improve the lot of a group of people except the people themselves: "Ours is the old, old story of every uprising race or class or order. The work of elevation must be wrought by ourselves or not at all" (10). Contrary to the workings of a romance plot, Cobbe argues that women will wait forever for a masculine hero to come and liberate them. And, she adds, if men did "liberate" women, women would not truly be free, because this would be proof of their continued dependence on men. Feminist skepticism about the ability to bestow freedom upon others reflected negatively on the civilizing mission. Thus, New Woman fiction and colonial adventure novels alike are responding to larger cultural struggles for autonomy. Women agitated for the power to decide their actions for themselves, and New Woman fiction is part of this agitation. The colonial adventure novel takes this power for granted, and exercises it to the exclusion of women and native others. Indeed, colonial adventure writers championed manly action in part to ward off the threat that "masculine" New Women posed, while New Woman writers asserted their autonomy from the structures of power championed by adventure fiction.

Submerged Similarities

Both colonial adventure and New Woman fiction were enormously popular; both caused enormous consternation to the literary-critical establishment. The New Woman novel and the fiction of imperial adventure alike became touchstones for cultural discussion on the fate of the empire, because both incited anxieties about cultural decline. The subject matter and style of New Woman and imperial adventure fiction challenged conventional concepts of reserve and taste, while their popularity undermined the power of the cultural establishment. Hugh Stutfield's essay "Tommyrotics" (1895) implicitly combines these two competing subgenres in one pejorative neologism in order to contest the appeal of both. While "tommyrot" is slang for "foolishness" or "nonsense," the added "-ics" gives the term an additional valence. "Tommy" refers to the common soldier (whom Kipling celebrated in his "Barrack Room Ballads" and in short stories), while "rotics" calls the supposedly neurotic and candidly erotic fiction of New Women to mind.[2]

While New Woman novels are generally character-driven and colonial adventure novels are typically incident-driven (hewing to the categories of realism and romance, respectively), both include narrators who are often ideologically driven and didactic. Critics generally identify an overtly political tone as the fundamental characteristic of the New Woman novel. From their emergence in the 1880s through the 1970s, New Woman novels were often considered "treatises first, novels second," mere "bald statements of problems" (Stubbs 117). New Woman novelist Sarah Grand unapologetically embraces the didactic dimensions of the genre, arguing that the frank discussion of sexual themes was necessary to the well-being and education of women. In a letter to her publisher William Blackwell defending her work, Grand asserted, "It was time someone spoke up, and I felt that I could and determined that I would" (qtd. in Kersley 69). The didacticism of adventure novels often took stridently pro-imperialist and pro-British forms. G. A. Henty, for instance, refers in *The Young Colonists* to "loyal Boers." These Boers are not loyal to the Dutch, however. They are loyal to *England*, although this requires them (from a less jingoistic point of view) to be *disloyal* to their country of origin. (This is not an anomalous formulation, for Rider Haggard's South African novel *Jess* does the same.) More than this, *The Young Colonists* is replete with long discursive sections, tangentially related to the plot, critically commenting on British governmental policy concerning relations with the Zulus and Boers.[3]

Both subgenres also typically embrace formal closure: the colonial adventurer concludes his quest and the New Woman, in her own way, finishes hers. (New Woman novels, however, while certain about the fate of their particular heroines, leave open the possibility of subsequent social change.)[4] The sense of inevitability that accompanies the generally resigned, if not tragic, end of New Woman novels is congruent with the sense of destiny in colonial adventure fiction. The former realistically reflects the fate of the uncommon woman in a social setting that refuses to accommodate her aspirations; the latter serves ideological ends, suggesting that foreign land is meant to be colonized, that "lesser" races need British intervention, that the fittest men are fulfilling a biological law by not only surviving but also conquering.

Moreover, both New Woman novels and novels of empire bring about closure without recourse to a marriage ceremony and generalized contentment. Adventurous men are "supposed" to be self-sufficient and not in need of women; New Women do not need men, and if they do, they are willing to sacrifice the financial security, emotional comfort, and companionship of a husband to attain independence. Both subgenres thus write against the grain of the traditional marriage plot. Mary Cholmondeley's *Red Pottage* (1899) ends with "two brides and two bridegrooms, all in one day!" as Mrs. Gresley exclaims, noting that it "is like the end of a novel" (374). But the brides are not the two heroines Rachel and Hester, and the grooms are not the male protagonists Hugh and Dick. Instead, four minor, conventional characters are married in an authorial gesture meant to show what sort of novel this is *not*. Mrs. Gresley is wrong about how novels end—at least how New Woman novels end. *Red Pottage* is emblematic of the genre, which refuses to gather the loose ends of its heroines' lives into a marriage knot. Likewise, the colonial adventurer, although he often meets with beautiful native women, remains primarily a lone actor, separated from those around him. The reason these characters remain unmarried is admittedly quite different. The New Woman generally fears losing her autonomy in a traditional Victorian marriage; the colonial adventurer asserts his supremacy over native women but fears miscegenation and racial degeneration.[5] Nonetheless, their generic divergence from the traditional realist novel is symmetrical.

One sign of the deeply intertwined nature of these two subgenres is the frequent appearance in each of scenes generically characteristic of the other. Robert Louis Stevenson's *The Ebb-Tide* (1894), the tale of three drifters in the South Sea Islands, is in many ways a classic adventure novel. The men use their wits to exploit their one chance at great wealth; their success involves their mastery over native islanders; they become "co-adventurers" (37 passim). But on their way to adventure, Stevenson's characters pass through a scene familiar from the domestic realm. Captain Brown needs to convince Herrick to go along with his scheme of stealing a schooner and its cargo; Herrick objects to the theft and the way Brown's plan impinges on his own autonomous action. Because all three men must participate for the plan to work, Brown does what is most expedient. First he plays on Herrick's emotions: "I tell you, Herrick, I love you" (33). Then, as if Herrick were a wifely angel, Brown appeals to Herrick's sense of duty to loved ones and to his power to save and redeem. (Ironically, participation in crime becomes a redemptive act, for with the money Brown "earns" from the schooner, he will be able to start anew and support his family in America.) Brown's accusation that to refuse would be to "desert me in my hour of need" (34) is reminiscent of the closing of Ella Hepworth Dixon's *The Story of a Modern Woman* (1894), where the New Woman Mary Erle encounters the same ploy to convince her to do something against conscience. Her former lover, who marries a wealthy American instead of returning to Mary as promised, tries to persuade her to be his mistress by drawing on notions of "being a true woman" (253): true, that is, to her supposed need for self-sacrifice in love. He suggests that Mary would be "giving up something for the man you love" and that her renunciation would "inspire me to noble things" (253). The typical appeal to a woman's need for love, to socially validated self-sacrifice, to putting the needs of others before one's own, is surprisingly transferable across these subgenres.

The key characteristics of the protagonists are also remarkably similar. While New Woman novels stress the heroine's intelligence, and colonial adventure heroes tend to have "smarts" or cunning,[6] the creative brainpower of both types of hero is equally valorized. Indeed, despite the differences in the *types* of action, both subgenres stress the need for action and decision on the part of their protagonists. For instance, George Gissing's *The Odd Women* (1893) disparages Virginia and Alice Madden because they wait for something to happen rather than making things happen (like the heroine Rhoda Nunn). The defining trait of both subgenres' protagonists, though, is autonomy and independence. Martin Green describes the colonial adventure novel as a narrative containing a series of events, remote from the domestic world, which constitute a challenge to the central character. His triumphs over adversity demonstrate his courage, fortitude, cunning, strength, leadership, and persistence (23). In Kipling's "The Man Who Would Be King," for instance, the imagination and drive of Daniel Dravot and Peachy Carnehan propel them beyond even India, which, in their estimation, "isn't big enough for such as us" (224). The British government has imposed regulations that prevent individual actors from prevailing in India, so Dravot and Carnehan go beyond the compass of the queen's laws and customs to make themselves rulers instead of subjects. The New Woman novel, as well, is characterized by the heroine's desire to exceed existing boundaries. While agitators for women's rights in the nineteenth century disagreed about which aspects of feminist ideology were primary, New Woman agitation generally stemmed from the fact that women had limited rights once married and were treated under British law as were—notoriously—idiots, the insane, and children. Women were arguing for their right not to marry, their right to own property and earn money, their right not to be legally beholden to any man. In essence, women agitated for the right to see truths and judge for themselves, without intervention of state, father, husband, or brother.

Both of these subgenres also concern themselves with the debate over degeneration, which intensified in Britain after the 1895 translation of Max Nordau's sociological study by the same name. Eliza Lynn Linton, ever the voice of antifeminist sentiment, directly relates the New Woman to evolutionary degeneration in her "Wild Women" essays that appeared in *The Nineteenth Century* in 1891–92. The Wild Women have not "bred true" (79); thus their wild savagery reflects not their actions but their birthright—one out of step with the rest of progressive industrial England. And, as is always the case with Linton, the New Woman's real threat is her unnatural "grand aim": "to directly influence imperial politics" (79). Mona Caird, in response to Linton, deploys evolutionary language to opposite ends. Women who are *not* wild, she claims, are "half-developed" ("A Defense" 813); it is an instance of "artificial selection" (815) that keeps them in submission to men. Caird rehearses the familiar argument about women's liberty—"if modern women are lapsing from the true faith, if they are really insurgents against evolutionary human nature . . . then their fatal error will assuredly prove itself" (817)—only to suggest that conventional notions require women to degenerate to the level of barnyard animals. The "time-honored argument that nature intended . . . woman to be a mother, and nothing else" (817), if taken to its logical conclusion, means that, since nature intended heifers and ewes to be mothers, "the nearer a woman can become to a cow or a sheep the better" (818). New Women, she stresses, "have risen above the stage of simple motherhood" (818).

New Woman writers often saw degenerate men (like Mosely Monteith or Major Colquhuon of Sarah Grand's *The Heavenly Twins*) as causes of woman's, the family's, and society's decline. Women, for them, become a sign of evolutionary progress, and they posit the need for a similar evolution in men so they can join women in the struggle. But degeneration in men is implicitly embraced by conservative cultural critics. When not positing women generally as less evolved than men, or accusing New Women specifically of engendering degeneration by neglecting the duties of motherhood, antifeminists posit atavistic males as an antidote to social ills. These potent primitives will return England to her glory days of conquering and ruling. In the romance genre, as well as in imperial ideology, empire wards off degeneration and renews civilization by engendering freedom from feminizing civilization, from confining social norms, from the effete life of the leisured classes. Haggard's *Allan Quartermain* begins with Allan's lament over the placidity of his life in the three years since he returned from King Solomon's Mines. He declares that no man can "go coop himself in this prim English country, with its trim hedgerows and cultivated fields, its stiff formal manners, and its well-dressed crowds" (22). For a true man, "prim," "trim," "cultivated," and "formal" England does not allow enough scope for manly action, except perhaps for the "superfine cultured idler" (22): a decadent dandy, to be sure.

Rider Haggard writes that colonial adventure fiction keeps men manly; it also works to entertain the modern reader, to take him out of his ordinary, workaday world into exotic locales. New Woman fiction, of course, is not meant to feminize its readers, or to reinforce ideas of masculinity and femininity. Rather, it seeks to demonstrate the limitations of traditional roles. This different orientation, however, leads to a similar place: both subgenres are set against the rigid rules of "civilization." Linda Dowling claims that the decadent and the New Woman are coupled because of the way the establishment was "perceiving in the ambitions of both a profound threat to established culture" (435); similarly, the adventure novelist and the New Woman are unexpectedly allied in their refusal to conform to certain dictates of contemporary culture. The difference lies in the way each type of novel defines civilization and culture.

Even the modes of discourse in the two subgenres are built on similar foundations. Colonial discourse, as Homi K. Bhabha argues, functions to justify conquest, establish systems of administration, and construct a reality for the European in the colonies. Colonial discourse helps define who white men or women are and how they relate to nonwhites. This discourse is ambivalent, though, because if authority were secure and identity unproblematic, complex definitions and justifications would be unnecessary. New Woman discourse (or antipatriarchal discourse more generally) functions to justify women's claims to what had been exclusively a male sphere. New Woman novels provide a model of how female independence can be accomplished (by representing educated, professional, unmarried women) and help construct a new reality for women. But the ambiguity present in colonial discourse holds true, as well, for antipatriarchal discourse. It is constantly aware of and riven by an internal recognition of patriarchal counter-discourse, which protests that changing women's roles is against social norms, against God, and against nature.

As Mary Ellmann points out in *Thinking about Women,* stereotypes of the other often collapse into their opposites. Thus, the Angel in the House can also be the sexual demon; the pious woman can also be earthbound and materialistic; the inscrutable female is also completely knowable and known by men. This holds true as well for the colonized native: he is both warlike and lazy; wily and stupid; savage and noble; uncivilized and uncorrupted by society. The strict binaries of colonized and colonizer have never been secure, because the definition of the colonized has never been stable. Colonial discourse's insistence on white superiority, on British dominance, on the civilizing mission, on godly sanction—all are fantasies of how the world should be (in the imperialist ideology) masquerading as the reality. Similarly, Valerie Sanders notes that the "separate spheres" ideology has never been the dominant reality but rather an ideal and a fantasy of how the gendered world should be ordered. Thus, each of these subgenres internally broaches the manifest concerns of the other.

At times, these subgenres stand in starkly antithetical relation to the same central concern. In many ways, these two subgenres represent opposing responses to the pressures of modernity. The New Woman embraces education, technology, writing, and representation, for these modern modes empower her. New Women novelists stress the opportunities provided by an era which has mechanized much toil: women become functionally the equal of men, as capable of many forms of employment and eligible for previously masculine training. Colonial adventure fiction represents a negative reaction to this "somewhat prosaic and machine-made epoch" (as Grant Allen called it in "The Romance of the Clash of Races" [71]). Haggard laments that the Victorians "macadamized all the roads of life" ("About Fiction" 174) and, like the degeneration theorists Cesare Lombroso and Max Nordau, sees the masculine attributes of bravery, strength, and protectiveness threatened by effeminacy. Thus these genres become ways of entering a cultural debate and registering competing cultural claims.

In addition, these two subgenres are in dialog with each other in ways that reveal how imperialist attitudes vied with progressive political movements for supremacy in the late century. Analyzing the ideological work of imperial discourse in Victorian culture at large, Jose Harris notes that "imperial visions injected a powerful strain of hierarchy, militarism, 'frontier mentality,' administrative rationality, and masculine civic virtue into British political culture, at a time when domestic political forces were running in quite the opposite direction, towards egalitarianism, 'progressivism,' consumerism, popular democracy, feminism and women's rights" (6). Imperial adventure novels and New Woman novels constitute significant and often nuanced contributions to this ideological struggle.

Realism and Romance

The aesthetic arm of this cultural debate was carried out as a controversy over the associations and merits of realism and romance. The periodical literature of the day, especially the way it registered and represented arguments about romance and realism, helps illustrate the ideological stakes implicit in the ways the two genres intersected, interacted, and contested one another. In his 1887 *Contemporary Review* essay "About Fiction," Haggard extols the merits of the romance genre. Indeed, it is "a matter of fact" that "really good romance writing is perhaps the most difficult art practiced by the sons of men" (172). For the author of *King Solomon's Mines* (1885) and *She* (1887) to posit the "true ends of fiction" (173) as romance writing is unsurprising. It is a surprise, however, when Haggard ends his essay by proclaiming Olive Schreiner's *The Story of an African Farm* (1883) one of only two profoundly interesting books to "have been published within the last five years" (180). W. T. Stead, in an 1894 review article on "The Novel of the Modern Woman" calls *African Farm* the forerunner of all New Woman fiction. New Woman novels competed for market share with the late-century male adventure romance and served as their ideological foils. Why, then, would Haggard celebrate Schreiner's feminist novel?

A closer look at the terms of Haggard's praise proves that his esteem is qualified in ways that relate to a larger cultural debate. Haggard singles out Schreiner's *African Farm* and the anonymous *My Trivial Life and Misfortunes* for their power, which has its source in the method of composition. They "are written from within, and not from without; both convey the impression of being the outward and visible result of inward personal suffering on the part of the writer" (180). The drawback of such writing "from within," however, is that once the experience is written, the author has nothing more to write. With the experience of the heart already on the page, the authors will have to write "from the head and not from the heart, and they must then come down to the use of the dusty materials which are common to us all" (180). Thus Haggard anticipates the criticism of New Woman novels that was to become common in the 1890s: the New Woman author merely records her personal experience; she is not a true artist because she does not create.[7]

Rather, it is the male romancers—Haggard mentions the authors of "Arabian Nights," "Gulliver's Travels," "Pilgrim's Progress," "Robinson Crusoe," and "other immortal works"—to whom the "lasting triumphs of literary art belong" (180). Although he pretends to deprecate the "calm retreats of pure imagination," it is clear that for Haggard this is where true art lies. That this is a gendered distinction is evinced by Arthur Waugh's statement: "the man remains an artist so long as he holds true to his view of life, the woman becomes one as soon as she throws off the habit of her sex, and learns to rely upon her judgment, and not upon her senses" (210).

Haggard also asserts that when the appeal of naturalism and William Dean Howells has faded, romance will still speak to all men. In this statement, Haggard shifts the terms of his argument, substituting "naturalism" for realism while implicitly equating the two terms. This rhetorical move, also present in Lang's "Realism and Romance," exploits the British suspicion of French novels and the supposed indecency of Emile Zola, and thereby negatively codes all realistic novels by associating them with naturalistic ones. This allows Haggard not only to marginalize all New Woman novels by associating them with degenerate French eroticism but also to associate romance with imperial Britain itself. In a theoretical narrative much like one of Haggard's own adventure plots, romance prevails over the forces that repeatedly threaten its superiority. Haggard's coding of the superiority of romance over naturalistic realism has a distinctly imperialist tone.

Before continuing, it is important to note that although romance was allied with colonial adventure novels and naturalism with New Woman novels, these designations conform more to nineteenth-century *assumptions* about these novels than to their reality. We must also note, following Northrup Frye, that "'Pure' examples of either form are never found; there is hardly any modern romance that could not be made out to be a novel, and vice versa" (7). Indeed, each of these subgenres encompasses examples that are, at best, mixtures of realism and romance. Conrad's *Heart of Darkness* (1902) is both a realistic psychological portrait and an adventure novel, blending development of character with the touchstones of colonial adventure: travel from

England to colonies, encounters with dangerous natives, struggles against disease and natural forces in the uncivilized world, a brush with savagery, and a successful return. Harold Williams's *Modern English Writers* (1918) identifies the mixed form as characteristic of Conrad: "Although Mr. Conrad sets nearly all his tales in an atmosphere of romance and rough seafaring he is not merely the romantic chronicler. . . . The romance of adventure, as it was written by Scott, Stevenson, and Dumas, he does not write. He blends with seafaring experience the psychology and theory of fiction evolved by the author of *What Maisie Knew* and the result is not seldom curious and incongruous" (389). About Schreiner's *The Story of an African Farm* he writes, "The title is scarcely a guide to its contents. It is not the story of adventure, nor of pioneer life" (427); despite its setting in the wilds of Africa it addresses the "question of woman's place in society" (429).

Moreover, "realistic" is most certainly misapplied to a New Woman novel like *African Farm*; *African Farm* is far too impressionistic, psychological, and allegorical to accommodate this label. Carolyn Burdett suggests that the mixed genre of Schreiner's novel is due to its unusual mix of feminism and colonialism: "neither realism nor romance is a fully adequate fictional form in which to represent the farm inhabitants' peculiarly colonial plight" (30). Naturalism is also not a logical narrative choice for feminist New Woman novels: naturalist style is too deterministic and leaves too little scope for free will and the power of individual effort to enact change. But the association of the New Woman novel with naturalist forms helps explain the novels' pessimistic endings; New Woman novels are "real," so the protagonists most often do not live happily ever after. In a world where conditions are more restrictive and consequences more severe for females than for males, such an ending would be highly improbable.[8] Nonetheless, almost all New Woman novels intimate future amelioration, and New Woman writers could thus use naturalism's "scientific rigor" (Zola 219) to their advantage. If a naturalist author, as Zola claimed, "is simply an observer who sets down facts" (197), the hopeful notes at the ends of New Woman novels could be understood as a factual deduction supported by the scientific method.

Despite the impurity of the generic designation, however, we need to think of these subgenres *as genres* because an understanding of genre influences every act of reading. Readers, writers, and critics each make instrumental, if sometimes unconscious, use of genre in understanding and interpreting texts. Genres—and systems of classification more generally—organize one's relationship to the text and its system of signification. We can begin to understand why each of these genres parallels the other's development when we realize that both are constituted by and contest late-century assumptions about masculinity and femininity.

In the 1880s, the ideological valences of realism and romance were in flux. Their strong gender associations were incipient but not yet firmly entrenched. Henry James, in his "Art of Fiction" (1884), writes that "the only obligation to which in advance we may hold a novel . . . is that it be interesting" (170), and an author can accomplish this in "innumerable" ways (170). James goes on to disparage classification into "the novel of character [or realism] and the novel of incident [or romance]" (174) because "these clumsy separations appear to me to have been made by critics and readers for their own convenience" (175). "There are bad novels and good novels" (174), and neither gender nor genre determines literary value. Even though Stevenson's "A Humble Remonstrance" (1884), written in reply to James, reasserts the classifications of novels into novels of adventure, novels of character, and the dramatic novel, he points out that all writers select their subjects from common elements of human life, so all novels are true in their way. Moreover, no novel is entirely true to life: "Life is monstrous, infinite, illogical, abrupt and poignant; a work of art, in comparison, is neat, finite, self-contained, rational, flowing and emasculate" (85). Even Lang, a staunch defender of romance, describes realism and romance as "two sides of the shield": "these two aspects blend with each other so subtly and so constantly, that it really seems the extreme of perversity to shout for nothing but romance on one side, or for nothing but analysis of character and motive on the other" (684). While Lang alleges that the intense analysis of character that typifies naturalism "makes one feel intrusive and unmanly" (688), he is still open to the merits of realism and to the vitality engendered by literary variety. Clearly "realism" and "romance" were not the battleground for gender ascendancy in the 1880s that they would become in the 1890s.

Indeed, the naturalistic impulses of New Woman novels were initially allied with the masculine recuperations of the adventure novel, as a symposium on "Candor in English Fiction" published by the *New Review* in 1890 demonstrates. Ann Ardis notes that "writers in this symposium contend that literature does not fulfill its cultural function if it misrepresents life. They insist that the cultural authority of the novel rests upon its truth-value, the accuracy of its representations" (33). This accuracy, coded as truth and fidelity, was allied with a sense of nationalism, with a manly facing of harsh facts, with victory over the forces of degeneration. Eliza Lynn Linton, who was also the most famous female opponent of the New Woman, associates naturalism with sexual virility in her contribution to the symposium. Like George Moore in his polemic essay "Literature at Nurse" (1885), Linton recoils at "the queer anomaly of a strong-headed and masculine nation cherishing a feeble, futile, milk-and-water literature—of a truthful and straightforward race accepting the most transparent humbug as pictures of human life" (qtd. in Ardis 33). Thus the naturalistic impulses of New Woman fiction—the frank depictions of unpleasant sexual truths such as Grand's treatment of syphilis in *The Heavenly Twins*—were initially allied with masculine strength and national virility. But because these expectations and conventions are socially constructed, they can change in response to cultural pressures.

When women began exploiting naturalism to expound feminist ideas, the valence of these definitions changed.[9] Even Hugh Stutfield, who rails against what he calls "the physiologico-pornographic school" has "no wish to pose as a moralist" ("Tommyrotics" 836). He finds the naturalistic works of Emile Zola and George Moore "shameless and disgusting" but not "precisely immoral" (836). He identifies the New Woman's variant of naturalism, however, as dangerous to "ideas of social order and decency" (843). He does not discuss male writers like George Gissing and Thomas Hardy who marry sexual candor with political agendas, but instead associates "Tommyrotic" fiction with women. Women are responsible for producing this fiction, because "Emancipated woman in particular loves to show her independence by dealing freely with the relations of the sexes" (836). (Stutfield allows that the recently imprisoned Oscar Wilde also discusses sexual relations, but says that Wilde represents "flabbiness and effeminacy" [843].) Moreover, women readers consume these novels, for "it cannot be denied that women are chiefly responsible for the 'booming' of books that are 'close to life'" (844). Stutfield looks to those who "cling to the old ideals of discipline and duty, of manliness and self-reliance in men, and womanliness in women" (845) to liberate British society from its hysterical embrace of "unnatural" representations.

Female hysteria is not the only cause for concern; the effeminacy of British men (resulting from the influence of naturalist literature) threatens the national health. The National Vigilance Association's pamphlet on "Pernicious Literature" (1889), which was a transcript of the parliamentary debate and trial of Henry Vizetelly for printing and distributing Zola's works, was pub-

lished to "sound as a note of alarm, and rouse the manhood of England to action" (351). Indeed, the debate in Parliament centered on the question of the
manhood of England, for immoral literature weakens "the race," a fact proven
by the condition of France, which, "suckled on Zola," is "now like Rome in
the last days of the Caesars" (355). In short, "such garbage was simply death to
a nation" (355). Naturalism is "a source of weakness to the nation" (356) and
only its abolition will preserve "the very root of the nation's welfare" (357).

Thus the discourse shifts from depicting naturalism as a source of manful
truth to viewing it as a scourge to the manhood of the nation, and frankness
comes under attack when the New Woman writer embraces it. Gail Cunningham notes that New Women's characteristic "plain speaking" struck
their contemporaries as "an almost terrifying frankness about sex" (47).
Waugh, in "Reticence in Literature" (1894), counts "frankness" as the defining characteristic of the British nation (202), but because of the new stress on
honesty in literature that rose out of naturalism, Waugh is at pains to regulate its use: "it will be clear, that this national virtue of ours, this wholesome,
sincere outspokenness, is only possible within certain limits, set by custom
and expediency" (203). He then outlines the modes of frankness current in
British letters: effeminacy[10] (associated with aesthetes and decadents) and
"brutal virility" (associated with naturalism). These are bad, "But the latest
development of literary frankness, is, I think, the most insidious and fraught
with the greatest danger to art. A new school has arisen which combines the
characteristics of effeminacy and brutality" (217): New Woman fiction. Indeed, "We are told that this is a part of the revolt of woman, and certainly
our women-writers are chiefly to blame" (218). Ironically, this assessment of
the New Woman appeared in the first issue of the *Yellow Book*—a magazine
whose art editor, Aubrey Beardsley, was not known for reticence in his art.
Moreover, the *Yellow Book* was a forum for many women writers, as Carolyn
Christensen Nelson notes: "The *Yellow Book* allowed many women, some
unknown at the time, to bring their work to public attention in a prestigious
journal . . . putting them in the company of well-known writers such as Henry
James, Arthur Symons, and George Moore" (xii). These male writers, though
often "frank," were not identified as a source of this problem. As Ardis notes,
critics responded to New Woman writing "by developing new standards of
literary value that delegitimized it" (45). *Female* candor needs to be limited
lest it endanger the British character.

This is the cultural climate that engendered Oscar Wilde's "The Decay of

Lying" (1891), which points out that the photographic, biographic, and ethnographic elements of modern fiction have claimed ascendancy to the detriment of pure fantasy and imagination. Wilde fears that fact is colonizing the fictional realm: "Facts are not merely finding a footing-place in history, but they are usurping the domain of Fancy, and have invaded the kingdom of Romance" (304). Defenders of romance like Haggard and Lang would argue that the best way to repel these invaders is with invigorating tales of imperial fantasy. Thus when Allan Quartermain, the hero of Haggard's *King Solomon's Mines*, tells "the truth" about his origins with "an imperial smile" (114), he in fact lies to the Kukuana tribe. Weaving his explanation from the cloth of pure imagination, he claims: "We come from another world, though we are men such as ye; we come . . . from the biggest star that shines at night" (114).[11]

Anxieties about the supposed effeminacy of naturalism and the danger it posed to British masculinity engendered ambitious conceptions of the cultural work to be performed by the romance novel. From the proper mode for boys, romance becomes the proper genre for men. Its champions stress how the adventure story can bring out the "old Berserker blood of Englishmen" ("The 'Imperialism' of Kipling and Stevenson" 466) and thus revitalize their over-refined sensibilities. Kipling's prose sounds as "a protest against [the] tameness, diffuseness, and the over-refinement of phrasing" (Bishop 476) associated with men like Wilde. Atavism in men, in this view, is regenerative rather than degenerative (since degeneration is now allied with the New Woman), and reviewers see a direct correlation between heroic characters in fiction and rejuvenated spirit in English men: "The impulse given by Stevenson to historical and heroic literature had its effect in the wonderful revival of the national spirit which characterized the later 80s. Englishmen were being daily educated into a knowledge of the glorious part played by their ancestors on sea and land" ("The 'Imperialism'" 466). Indeed, as the case of Kipling shows, literature itself can constitute a kind of imperial conquest. William Henry Bishop praises Kipling's authorial colonization of India: "India, quite untouched by the literary plough, was perhaps the last opportunity for a man to carve out a kingdom for himself in unknown regions" (477). Like the British Empire, Kipling is a force to be reckoned with because he seizes new territory and makes it completely his own.

Just as Romance and manliness are associated, realism and feminism are coupled. William Dean Howells became a common target for critics on both sides of the Atlantic because he was such a staunch champion—in the "Editor's Easy Chair" and "Editor's Study" columns he wrote for *Harper's New Monthly Magazine* from 1886 to 1892—of both women's rights and realism in fiction.[12] His "Easy Chair" column for February 1887 devotes half its space to the Woman Question, affirming that the "total surrender of the whole life to the commands of others, and . . . the sense of inferiority which is made to accompany it" are both the characteristics of married women's lives and "the characteristics of slavery" (479). Howells ends by connecting the modern woman with women in fiction: "the Easy Chair cannot agree with those who think that the more clearly and legally her rights are defined, and the more self-respecting because the more self-relying she becomes, the more the true womanly charm vanishes. The women of the old dramas and the old novels are not more womanly women than the tax-paying, self-supporting women of modern life" (479). His "Editor's Study" for February 1887 reviews literature by women and finds that "the sketches and studies by the women seem faithfuller and more realistic than those of the men, in proportion to their number" (485). For the era's most famous champion of realism and naturalism, this is high praise indeed. He approvingly quotes Thomas Carlyle in the April "Study": "the only genuine Romance (for grown persons) is Reality" (826).

Other journals, less consistent in their editorial stance, reveal the unsettled nature of this cultural debate by publishing essays that are radically at odds with one another, often in the same issue. *The Dial* for December 1893 contains an essay praising the formation of Radcliffe College from the former women's annex of Harvard University and calling for "the heartiest congratulations from all workers in behalf of the higher education of women" ("Radcliffe College" 380).[13] This essay commending Radcliffe is followed by Richard Burton's article on "The Persistence of Romance," in which he celebrates the "now palpable reaction from the realistic" (380). The same journal that champions the achievements of the New Woman also champions the literary genre that grew strong out of resistance to everything the New Woman represented. *The Fortnightly Review* from 1 January through 1 June 1889 features articles reviewing Henrik Ibsen, supporting women's suffrage, and favoring Home Rule for Ireland, as well as articles lauding the British South Africa Company, excoriating "The African Devil: The Soudan," and patronizingly describing "Eastern Women." If, as Linda Hughes and Michael Lund suggest, readers could view an issue of a literary magazine as a work by a single corporate author because articles appearing in the same issue become linked in the readers' minds (9), the "corporate author" of late-century magazines may be said to represent the self-contradictory thoughts of an individual British citizen living at a time of ideological agitation and instability.

New Woman and imperial adventure novels are similarly mixed in their associations and affiliations. Determining the New Woman novel's ideological stance is akin to deciding the dominant ideology of a colonial adventure novel like Kipling's *Kim* (1901), which itself has an ambiguous relation to imperial ideology. The strangeness of this novel inheres in the gaps between the respectful and sympathetic portrayal of Indian characters and the recurrent instances of Kipling's tautological Orientalism: Indians are lazy, lying, and mystical, *because* they are Indian. In this, as we shall see, *Kim* is like all the novels in this study, whose formal affiliations and ideological tensions embody the cultural imperatives they simultaneously register and seek to resist.

"Do we speak the same language?"

Contested Discourse at Home and Abroad

"I will answer you any question."
"That is spoken like a man. Tell me then—is there at this moment
any woman living who has a claim upon you—a moral claim?"
"No such woman exists."
"But—do we speak the same language?"

Everard Barfoot and Rhoda Nunn in *The Odd Women* by George Grissing

Although Rhoda and Everard literally speak the King's English, Rhoda rec-ognizes that something "spoken like a man" may resemble a foreign dialect to a woman's ears. Especially in the arena of "moral claims," the meanings and values assigned to words and ideas may vary widely. Because the dominant discourse[1] defines terms and manipulates ideas to the advantage of the domi-nant class (be it moneyed, gendered, or racial), a person from a subordinate class may misapprehend the answer to even a simple question. The power to direct the terms of the discourse, which is a function of physical strength, institutional authority, and social custom, becomes a tool to regulate cultural debates that erupt when a subject group questions the way it is defined by the ruling discourse.

Indeed, power is often couched in terms of language in not only New Woman but also colonial adventure fiction. In *King Solomon's Mines*, the Britons' strength resides in their guns—weapons never before seen by the Kukuana tribesmen. But this power is not represented in terms of advanced weaponry. Rather, Allan Quartermain tells the natives that guns are "magic tubes" which "talk with you loudly, and make you as sieves. Beware!" (118). The power to kill is represented as the power of speech. This is demonstrated to the natives when Allan shoots an antelope from a great distance, so that the sound is heard but the bullet is not seen. Allan "kill[s] it from here with a noise" (116) and says, "Ye see . . . I do not speak empty words" (116). His words, like his gun, are loaded and deadly.

The authority to represent—a weapon, a type of person, an immoral act, a natural event—is, in these subgenres, often the supreme power. The patriarch and the imperialist alike have the power to establish the terms of discourse; indeed, patriarchy provided the imperial system a ready-made language of rule, while the imperial system refined the discourse and gave the patriarch a supplementary vocabulary. Contests over the meanings supported by these discourses take place as actual debates in the pages of late-century magazines; authors refer to other articles and refute their conclusions. In novels, the same type of debate takes place internally and implicitly, signaled by attention to language use, to telling stories, to making oneself heard. This chapter will bring the twin discourses of patriarchy and imperialism to bear on one another in order to analyze their complex correspondences. Specifically, I will read George Gissing's *The Odd Women* (1893), which explicitly interrogates patriarchal power, alongside the imperial adventure fictions *King Solomon's Mines* (1885) and *Heart of Darkness* (1902) by H. Rider Haggard and Joseph Conrad, and situate all three in the context of the debates about the New Woman and women's roles in the imperial project that raged in popular magazines during the 1890s.

In each of these novels, a powerful "voice" (who speaks with the authority of the dominant discourse) stereotypes a subordinate who is then imagined as both completely other and completely knowable.[2] In all three novels under discussion, the ultimate impenetrability of the other indicates fissures in the dominant discourse that allow the voice of the racial or gendered other to be heard. The depth of these fissures is indicated by the important role white women play in the formation of both colonial and patriarchal discourses. All three novels, New Woman and colonial adventure alike, hinge on the position and role of women as moral center, as justification for male action, as provisional agent, as subject of discourse.

First, an important qualification. Because material conditions bear on all language formations, the conjunction of patriarchal discourse and colonial discourse had diverse effects on imperialists, patriarchs, women, and racial others. The wide gulf between white women and colonized people cannot and should not be elided. While patriarchal and imperial discourses informed each other in late Victorian England, imperial ideology was more unified and less subject to competing interests. Indeed, in *The Odd Women*, the young wife's proximity to the patriarch—her undeniable presence as a full human being—prompts a re-evaluation that would have been far less likely in the co-

lonial realm. As chapter 4 will demonstrate, the constant confrontations provoked by another's insistent claims to individual subjectivity eventually meet
with some consideration. The African native—who is more completely other,
whose difference is written all over his face, who literally may not speak the
same language as the white ruler—is much more easily dismissed. Language
barriers, racial prejudices, and geographic distance allowed colonial discourse
largely to drown out dissenting voices. When the voice of dissent was heard
in Britain, it generally emanated from white men or women speaking in the
terms established by imperialists: harsher or kinder measures toward colonized people were encouraged, but rarely with a view to a truly emancipatory
politics.[3] The history of native resistance was largely erased or re-told with
a British accent. Feminist resistance, in contrast, came from within British
culture, and when antipatriarchal writers were more widely read, feminist
agitators more visible in public places, and professional women increasingly
trusted in business, it became impossible to ignore feminist claims.[4]

In part, discourses of domination function by relying on stereotypes and
suppressing alternative representations. Colonial discourse, as Homi K.
Bhabha describes it, depends on fixed, static representation: "The objective of
colonial discourse is to construe the colonized as a population of degenerate
types on the basis of racial origin, in order to justify conquest and to establish systems of administration and instruction" (70). But Bhabha elides the
fact that these "systems of administration and instruction," the "production
of knowledges," and "surveillance" were perfected by patriarchs. Patriarchal
institutions, male-dominated government, and masculine knowledges have
their counterparts in imperial institutions, colonial government, and Orientalist knowledges. Thus, because patriarchal and imperial discourses inform
each other, feminist contestations of patriarchal discourse may well mirror
the ideological contests that took place in the colonial realm, contests that
have been drowned out by the voice of imperial history.

Colonizing Gender: The New Woman Debate

One major campaign in the war over words and ideology was waged in fin de
siècle periodicals, where debates about "odd women" became struggles over
terminology.[5] Single women were not only deemed "odd" but also part of
"the shrieking sisterhood" of women who publicly agitated for rights. Sarah
Grand countered this characterization in "The New Aspect of the Woman
Question" (1894) by labeling complaining men the "bawling brotherhood"

(660). The dialogical nature of these contests is illustrated by a series of articles appearing in the leading reviews in 1894. B. A. Crackenthorpe's "The Revolt of the Daughters" was the first of nine articles on the freedoms (and restrictions) necessary to the happiness and well-being of young women. Crackenthorpe begins by predicting an impending strike not by trade unionists but by "the daughters"—unless the elder generation renegotiates its social contract with the younger. Despite "the provocative nature, the egoism, the governing unreasonableness" (24) of the daughters' attitudes, Crackenthorpe sides with the daughters.

For their part, the daughters are not entirely pleased with their champion, who describes them as a "ruthless," "insensible," "self-centered" group whose main characteristic is "stubbornness" (26). Hence Kathleen Cuffe's and Alys W. Pearsall Smith's articles, both printed in the *Nineteenth Century* and each titled "A Reply from the Daughters." Cuffe agrees with Crackenthorpe's argument, but objects to her characterization of "revolt" as the daughters' aim: because the "so-called revolting maiden only asks for a small amount of liberty" (441), it is foolish to stir up the emotions with talk of "revolt."

The debate continued with Gertrude Hemery's *Westminster Review* article "The Revolt of the Daughters: An Answer By One of Them," Sarah M. Amos's *Contemporary Review* article "The Evolution of the Daughters," and Lady May Jeune's contribution (also titled "The Revolt of the Daughters") in *The Fortnightly Review*. Lady Jeune wonders if anyone would "wish to see our girls half men in theory and half women in inexperience and ignorance, with a superficial smattering of knowledge grafted on to the restless impulses and vague curiosity of youth" (275). To which Hemery replies that Lady Jeune "would have [women] sit down, with meekly folded hands, dutifully content with the success they have already won. It says much for the courage and determination of women that they refuse thus to stand still; that, having advanced so far and so well, they see no reason why they should not continue advancing and reaping fresh laurels" (679). Like Hemery, Amos appeals to progress and modernity, arguing that it is not revolution but evolution that is causing the social order to change. By shifting the terms from a social upheaval (revolution) to a scientific process (evolution), Amos suggests that those who oppose women's increasing liberation from the domestic sphere are working against the natural order and against British progress. Crackenthorpe's second article "The Revolt of the Daughters: A Last Word on 'The Revolt'" both acknowledges the daughters' dislike of the term "revolt" (she repudiates her original title) and imagines that it is possible to have the "last word" in a cultural debate. She is wrong. The article following hers in the *Nineteenth Century* is called "The Revolt of the Daughters: Daughters and Mothers," in which M. E. Haweis's words are literally "last" in this series of articles.[6]

Even the term New Woman became so loaded, so charged with contested meanings, that Grand wrote an article comparing "The New Woman and the Old" (1898), in which she transfigures the New Woman stereotype: the New Woman is not obsessed with sex and does not assume that all mixed gatherings are fraught with sexual tension, because her mind does not entertain impure thoughts. The Old Woman, by contrast, is always on the lookout for potential sexual danger, because sex is foremost in her mind. The New Woman's moral purity is further demonstrated in her continual progress toward higher goals. The Old Woman is content with her settled prejudices, assumed virtues, and outmoded customs. Grand's article is more than a tit-for-tat quarrel with antifeminists, for the ability to define what words mean is central to struggles for power. Conservative writers who seek to disrupt the New Woman's authority describe New Women as "maenads" (as in William Barry's "The Strike of a Sex").[7] Maenads, the female devotees of Dionysus, ripped men to shreds and then devoured their raw flesh; by appropriating this metaphor, Victorian antifeminists could cast women as the cannibalistic other of colonial discourse.

Colonial discourse and discussions of independent women converged in programs to send single women to the colonies. The 1860s witnessed a cultural panic instigated by W. R. Greg's *National Review* article "Why Are Women Redundant?" (1862) and by numerous responses to the "problem" of "redundant" women.[8] Greg found the solution to the problem of "Odd Women" in the colonies, where the male-to-female ratio was skewed in favor of men. Greg suggests government-sponsored emigration of women to drain "away the excess and special *obviousness* of this redundance" (452). Woman becomes an agent of empire, and in doing her duty to depopulate England of "excess" citizens, she becomes a force for colonial settlement.

The female emigrant "invaded" the outposts of empire in order to find benefits unavailable to her in England. Thus the female emigration schemes of the 1850s and 1860s followed those established for men earlier in the century, when the economic strife of the Hungry Forties caused men to seek a better life in the colonies. As Charles Dickens wrote in support of the Family Colonization Loan Society, it is wise to send "a steady succession of people of all laborious classes . . . from places where they are not wanted, and are miserable, to places where they are wanted, and can be happy and independent" ("Emigrants' Letters" 96). Dickens' charitable rhetoric overlays an underlying desire that the state-supported poor be exiled from England to a place where they can be "independent." Fallen women and prostitutes soon joined this group of abject others sent to Australia (like convicts) in order to be rehabilitated, as well as to rid England of nonproductive or unwanted bodies.[9]

After the 1851 and 1861 censuses, respectable women became the focus of emigration efforts because superfluous women were increasingly identified as a social problem. Greg writes sorrowfully and anxiously of the "hundreds of thousands of women . . . who have to earn their own living, instead of spending and husbanding the earnings of men; who, not having the natural duties and labors of wives and mothers, have to carve out artificial and painfully-sought occupations for themselves; who, in place of completing, sweetening, and embellishing the existence of others, are compelled to lead an independent and incomplete existence of their own" (436). The basis of Greg's anxiety remains largely unstated, but his discussion of female servants is telling. As single women who earn their own living, one might expect servants to be a large part of "*the evil and anomaly to be cured*" (440). But Greg asserts that "*Female servants do not constitute any part* (or at least only a very small part) *of the problem we are endeavoring to solve*" because "they fulfill both essentials of woman's being: *they are supported by, and they minister to, men*" (451). The problem of single women is not their loneliness, their poverty, their isolation, or their tribulations: it is that they are not serving men and the needs of the empire. Carmen Faymonville identifies the motive behind Greg's single-minded solution: "One way of dealing with the potential social and political 'waste' that 'redundant' women presented, however, was not to give these women what they wanted ["the vote, economic possibilities, and gender equality"] but to engage them instead in the consolidation of the British Empire" (64). The crux of the issue is not women's well-being (for many of the "beleaguered" souls Greg described *chose* to be single) so much as men's. Indeed, twentieth-century statisticians have failed to find the hundreds of thousands of superfluous women nineteenth-century demographers identified. The "superabundant female," writes Michele Ren, was "a necessary myth for the redirection of female usefulness to imperial goals" (46).

Many feminists used Greg's findings to very different effect.[10] In "What Shall We Do with Our Old Maids?"(1862), Frances Power Cobbe repeats his dire statistics: 30 percent of women in England never marry, leaving one-quarter of both sexes in a state of celibacy (236). These numbers, writes Cobbe, prove that we need "a revision of many of our social arrangements" (237), because we can no longer expect that women's sole destiny is marriage. Either educate women accordingly, writes Cobbe, or "promote marriage by emigration of women to colonies" (237). This would be an expedient, but not a moral, solution, for it would be "promoting sin" by endorsing "mean marriage of interest, a marriage for wealth, for position, for rank, for support" (237). For Cobbe, education of unmarried women does not make them un-natural, as Greg asserts. It saves them from the perversion of enforced mar-riage, thereby keeping both the women and the ideal of true marriages (those "founded on free choice, esteem, and affection—in one word, on love" [237]) unsullied.

As Cobbe knows, free choice in marriage is not an option for women who must marry because law, education, social prejudice, or upbringing prevents them from earning an independent living. This ideological double-bind— that a woman must marry to gain economic support, *and* that a woman must not marry for mercenary reasons—constitutes what Bhabha terms "sly civil-ity" (93) in colonial discourse. Marriage is the perfect example of sly civil-ity, as chapter 5 will more thoroughly illustrate: it is a seemingly beneficent relationship that strips away property rights, restricts female autonomy, and prevents the subject partner from terminating the agreement. And yet if a woman chooses not to marry, she has very few legal advantages and many social deficits (barred from professions, deemed unnatural for not perform-ing her God-given function, and left without a sanctioned social role). As Hadria, the heroine of Mona Caird's *The Daughters of Danaus* (1894), re-marks to her wooer's sister, "You who uphold all these social arrangements, how do you feel when you find yourself obliged to urge me to marry, not for the sake of the positive joys of domestic existence, but of the merely negative advantage of avoiding a hapless and forlorn state?" (129).

Race, Gender, and Adventure Fiction

Conservative cultural critics identified the New Woman novel with threats to patriarchal hegemony. Like the sensation fiction of the 1860s, New Woman novels were thought to engender rebellious sympathies in the women who read them. Written primarily by women, these novels "played a central role in the formulation and popularization of feminist ideology" (Showalter, *A*

Literature of Their Own 182). Colonial adventure fiction is no less ideological; its ideology is merely aligned with what was culturally dominant. The colonizer directs the novel's discourse and the colonized individual is represented in the colonizer's words. So even when they are as diverse as the unabashed apologist of empire H. Rider Haggard and the cosmopolitan protomodernist Joseph Conrad, colonial adventure novelists "speak the same language."

King Solomon's Mine and *Heart of Darkness* share many formal features. Both are first-person narratives in which an adventurer retrospectively retells the story of his greatest African adventure to an audience of English men. Both feature white men who awe the natives with their Western knowledge in the guise of supernatural powers. Both tellers, despite their protestations, have some trouble telling the truth. And the audience for the "tales-as-told-to" in both novels is exclusively white and male. Marlow relates his long tale to his former seafaring friends; Allan Quartermain writes his narrative as an entertainment for his son working in a hospital back in England. This strategy puts the female reader (and especially the female reader of color) in the role of interloper, eavesdropper, exiled from the site of privileged discourse and, as I will argue later, the means of representation.

Both *King Solomon's Mines* and *Heart of Darkness* purport to be true, historical narratives, if only as the true history of one man in an extraordinary situation. These memoirs serve to inscribe an image of the white man among the natives, the British subject in Africa. These representations finally caricature history, however, because their attempts to write a gilded version of British history in the colonies are consistently undermined by the narratives themselves. They need to represent the colony as fixed in time, in need of the progress the British can import, but also must acknowledge the *fact* of change.

Fixing a country historically denies the nation and its people process, change, growth. The West's Orientalizing impulse creates a static object of knowledge out of a changeable subject. A static object can be written upon, defined, *constituted* to serve the ruler's interest. It has its analog in the way patriarchal discourse denies interiority: if a wife is without subjectivity, her husband is not only able to define her but he is also *obliged* to do so, in order to give her direction, desire, decision. A "good" husband must extend his personality and beliefs to his childlike wife, just as the civilizing mission must bring Western knowledge and light to the benighted colonies. In both instances, however, the ruler can justify his actions only by asserting fixity despite his knowledge of flux.

Marlow's opening statement that England "has been one of the dark places of the earth" (9) seems a gesture of sympathy with Africa (the current "dark place"), but it is actually a rationalization. If the prehistory of England is the present history of Africa, then imperial brutality is justified, for Western civilization, British culture, and Marlow himself are the legacy of ancient Roman imperialism. To further bolster his moral position, Marlow offers another defense of British imperialism: it is different from Roman imperialism.[11] The Romans, says Marlow, "were no colonists, their administration was merely a squeeze, and nothing more, I suspect. They were conquerors, and for that you want only brute force" (10). Yet Marlow's experience reinforces the image of British as brutes interested solely in plunder. It is only the women who are silly enough to embrace "an unselfish belief in the idea" (10) of Western culture's benevolent mission. Marlow's attempt to represent Africans will always fail as history; the colonial body will never fully represent (because it is not white or British) or be represented by (because the story is white and British) this history.

Thus, the narrator of *King Solomon's Mines* can describe the "truly alarming spectacle" of an African king, Twala, in this manner: "The lips were as thick as a negro's, the nose was flat, it had but one gleaming black eye (for the other was represented by a hollow in the face), and its whole expression was cruel and sensual to a degree" (141). The only way for Haggard to represent this subject is as itself. The simile he constructs ("the negro was like a negro") both disavows any connection with the depersonalized African ("it" is described, not "he") and reinscribes a myth of an original African-ness which is like nothing but itself.

This colonized subject, with the "hollow in the face" where his eye should be, is an inversion of the British Captain Good. Good "always wore an eyeglass in his right eye" which "seemed to grow there, for it had no string, and he never took it out except to wipe it" (13). His "one shining and transparent eye" doubles Twala's "hollow in the face," but also fills the lack that hollow represents. Instead of a blank emptiness, the Good British man both reflects (is "shining") and reveals (is "transparent"). An Englishman who is beyond classification counters the fearful, despicable, and inhuman African who represents nothingness. It is the failure of the Africans to classify the three adventurers as merely human that saves the Britons from immediate death at the hands of the Kukuana tribe. The fortunate conjunction of the tribe's discovery with Good's ablutions causes this confusion. In a state of half-dress, half-shaved, with one "eye," and removable false teeth, Good becomes as a god to the Kukuanas with the supernatural power of variously growing and melting his own teeth. In this manner, the Britons save themselves from death and gain aid in crossing the desert (a potentially "unsound method" quite similar to the one Kurtz employs at the Inner Station).

But Twala is much like Good in appearance, a similarity that is emphasized when his eye is described as "gleam[ing] fiercely" (179). This constant movement toward and away from, this recognition and subsequent disavowal, represents a failure in representation. This failure disrupts the authority of colonial discourse and in fact reveals the failings of authority itself. When Twala (Good's double, or "mimic-man") represents nothingness and powerlessness, Good is tainted with these characteristics as well. Moreover, the very fact that the unclassifiable Good can be imitated reveals that he is not in a class by himself. The "menace" of this mimicry is that both the ordinariness and the constructedness of the British conquerors are exposed.

The desire to "fix" the native in one knowable subject position is the will to knowledge of colonial rule. In *King Solomon's Mines*, Allan Quartermain not only treats Sir Henry's servant as less than human (he resents the "certain assumption of dignity" [47] in Umbopa's manner), he assumes that other blacks will think this is natural as well. When the exploring party encounters the Kukuanas, Allan tells the natives that the strangers they see (including Umbopa) come "from the biggest star that shines at night" (114)—that they are all, in essence, colonizers from another world. Yet this other world repeats the existing one, the one he assumes is natural. He introduces Umbopa as his servant and addresses him "in a savage tone" as "you dog and slave" (115), as if the Kukuanas themselves would think it only natural for the black man to serve the white one. Allan simply cannot imagine any other possibility.

In fact, Allan consistently describes Umbopa as having Zulu characteristics, even though Umbopa is not a Zulu. Allan says, "I always called him a Zulu, though he was not really one" (67), ignoring the possibility that there may be differences among geographically and culturally dispersed natives. Moreover, even though he knows Umbopa is not a Zulu, Allan ascribes his actions to Zulu heritage and traits. For instance, immediately after telling his reader that Umbopa is not a Zulu, Allan goes on to say that Umbopa "went on with one of those strange bursts of rhetorical eloquence which Zulus sometimes indulge in" (67). Allan's Zulu stereotype fixes *any* colonial subject in an entirely knowable and classifiable position; and Allan continues to rely on stereotyped descriptions even when he recognizes their inadequacy.

The incompatibility of fixity (or stereotype) with history is made apparent when Conrad's Marlow reveals why he wanted to make the perilous journey to the Congo. Marlow famously remarks that his earliest desire was to go to the blank places on the map. The most desirable was "the biggest—the most blank, so to speak" (11) because it was still available to any identity. But Africa goes from blank to black; by the time Marlow arrives the space is filled in, represented. The change in historical representations denies an essential fixity of African identity; but the European ideological move simultaneously posits the representation of Africa as a discovery of its essence, its eternal qualities. Thus, any African can be a Zulu, for all Africans participate in the eternal African-ness of the continent as defined by the colonizers. Underlying all of these attempts to situate the other as unified and unchanging (the product of a desire that purity be possible) is a fear that the African is changing, hybrid—and that the stability the colonizers had posited for themselves is equally doubtful. The fear is represented in Twala's missing eye: instead of reflecting back or even registering European subjectivity, "it" (both Twala and his eye) shows the colonizer his own vulnerability to shifting definitions and changing social positions. Stereotype exists between opposing forces: the desire for stasis, identity, and domination on the one hand and the demands of change, history, and difference on the other.

In the passage that best reveals the splitting of colonial discourse, Marlow recognizes the "reality" of Africa but manages to ignore it by attending to the mere phenomena of his work. By concentrating on surface, he says, "the reality—the reality, I tell you—fades. The inner truth is hidden—luckily, luckily" (36). He follows this with a depiction of the reality he tries to push aside:

> The earth . . . was unearthly, and the men were. . . . No, they were not inhuman. Well, you know, that was the worst of it—this suspicion of their not being inhuman. It would come slowly to one. They howled and leaped, and spun, and made horrid faces; but what thrilled you was just the thought of their humanity—like yours—the thought of your remote kinship with this wild and passionate uproar. Ugly. Yes, it was ugly enough; but if you were man enough you would admit to yourself

that there was in you just the faintest trace of a response to the terrible frankness of that noise. (37–38)

The terrible reality is that these natives *are not inhuman.* Marlow does not say that they are human, merely that they are not inhuman (and this is but a suspicion). They are, in Bhabha's terms, "almost but not quite." Marlow does not quite acknowledge African subjectivity; rather there is a "remote" connection, a "faint trace" of recognition. It is disturbing, it is ugly, *and it is thrilling.* In the domestic realm, these competing desires and demands are mirrored in relationships between men and women. The analog in *The Odd Women* is Barfoot and Rhoda's excitement when one experiences opposition from the other. They argue, disagreeing utterly: "he read pleasure in her face, saw in her eyes a glint of merry defiance. And his pulses throbbed the quicker for it" (144).

Marlow's recognition of the African's humanity is marked by contradictory impulses of attraction and repulsion. The power to decide the terms of the discourse—to represent—allows the colonizer promptly to disavow his likeness to the "ugly," "horrid," yet "not inhuman" other. Consequently, speech is the supreme power in *Heart of Darkness.* Kurtz is a symbol of magnetic potency throughout the narrative, and Marlow says that "of all his gifts, the one that stood out pre-eminently, that carried with it a sense of real presence, was his ability to talk, his words—the gift of expression" (48). Because Kurtz "could speak English to me" (50), Marlow "became aware that that was exactly what I had been looking forward to—a talk with Kurtz. I made the strange discovery that I had never imagined him as doing, you know, but as discoursing" (48).

The kind of power Kurtz represents—the power of language—obscures the internal incoherence of colonial discourse. When Marlow recognizes the truth of his intimate biological connection with the natives, he responds: "[A man] must meet that truth with his own true stuff—with his own inborn strength" (38). But "his own inborn strength" is not enough: its nature is unclear, its efficacy unknown. Marlow continues: "An appeal to me in this fiendish row—is there? Very well; *I hear; I admit, but I have a voice too, and for good or evil mine is the speech that cannot be silenced*" (38; italics mine). Marlow is now able both to admit and to deny, and it is the power of his voice that will prevail. The natives may call to him from shore, but he can drown out their voices with his own. The power to represent oneself and to represent others gives agency and provides the fiction of a stable self that others can neither divide nor disturb. If the colonizer can shout his own words loudly enough, he can disavow an understanding of the colonized's subjectivity (which, in turn, makes conquering less personally disquieting).

With a strong voice of his own, Marlow is also safe from Kurtz's fate. Kurtz listened to the voice of the darkness, whispering "to him things about himself which he did not know, things of which he had no conception till he took counsel with this great solitude—and the whisper had proved irresistibly fascinating. It echoed loudly within him because he was hollow at the core" (57–58). Kurtz's power resided in his voice, but once he listened to the darkness, he "forgot himself" (56). The fragility of the European self is announced in broken English by the Manager's "boy": "Mistah Kurtz—he dead" (69). Kurtz's subjectivity was pure performance. There was no core; like Twala, he represented hollowness: "The voice was gone. What else had been there?" (69).

Nothing. Yet Marlow carries this nothingness back to England to make something of it. He brings this hollow colonial discourse into the domestic realm, where his meeting with the never named, always expectant Intended gives the lie to the civilizing mission. Although Marlow pronounces that "I hate, detest, and can't bear a lie . . . because it appalls me. There is a taint of death, a flavor of mortality in lies" (29), he also affirms that it is a lie that propels imperialism; one lies about it because colonization "is not a pretty thing when you look into it too much" (10). The civilizing mission obscures the brutal fact of expropriation, of "taking [land] away from those who have a different complexion" (10). Colonizers can tell themselves that they are bringing not just guns and disease, but also a higher order of humanity and a true religious belief (a belief also propagated by feminist proselytizers, as evidenced in *The Odd Women*). When Marlow continues his description of "the idea," the underlying delusion becomes clear; the idea is "something you can set up, and bow down before, and offer a sacrifice to . . ." (10). The civilizing mission is like a pagan ritual that requires one to keep faith and surrender reason.

It is women's supplementary mission to approve the lie on the domestic level and to ignore its implications for themselves. Because she was so "out of it" (87), the Intended embraces a foolish belief in Kurtz and a perverse blindness to his desire for dominion. Without establishing an overt connection, Marlow discusses the Intended, the air of death and lies around Kurtz, and the avarice that is the true impetus of imperialism: "You should have heard the disinterred body of Mr. Kurtz saying, 'My Intended.' You would have perceived directly then how completely she was out of it. . . . You should have heard him say, 'My ivory.' Oh yes, I heard him. 'My Intended, my ivory, my station, my river, my . . .' everything belonged to him" (49). For Kurtz, Africa is more than something to explore, to enlighten, or even to plunder. It is something to own. And his fiancée is among his conquests, his possessions. She represents the conjunction of patriarchal and imperial discourses: "My Intended, my ivory, my station, my river."

This intermingling of colonial and domestic images continues when Marlow associates the Intended's gesture of grief with the outstretched arms of the "savage and superb, wild-eyed and magnificent" African woman (60). Marlow actually establishes a *triple* relationship among Kurtz, African women, and English women: "I shall see this eloquent phantom [Kurtz] as long as I live and I shall see her too, a tragic and familiar Shade resembling in this gesture another one, tragic also and bedecked with powerless charms, stretching bare brown arms over the glitter of the infernal stream, the stream of darkness" (75). This ghostly trio is held together by Kurtz's lies—the evasions and ambiguities necessary to discourses of domination. And again, the truth unwittingly emerges out of the network of lies when the Intended says, "He died as he lived" (75). This is truer than the discomfited Marlow wants to admit, for Kurtz did die as he lived: weak, delusional, yet sure of his own power over "My Intended, my station, my career, my ideas" (67).[12]

Marlow claims that the African woman is "bedecked with powerless charms," but like the Intended, she fills the men who confront her with dread of her frightening powers. They fear her when, in her assumption of domestic roles, she most resembles idealized white women. Her standoff with the ship carrying Kurtz away demonstrates her fealty and her sense that her bond with Kurtz is something that no man can put asunder. Unabashed, undaunted, she faces the British steamer, British men, and British guns. Though she is unarmed, the Russian nervously declares, "If she had offered to come aboard I really think I would have tried to shoot her" (61). The Russian was similarly daunted by her domestic power when she challenged his right to care for her sick "husband." Seeing the African woman aligned with the ministering Angel in the House, the Russian might have been forced to recognize her humanity and her similarity to idealized white womanhood. Instead, he presents his discomfort as a language problem. He claims he was never able to grasp the woman's intentions because "I don't understand the dialect of this tribe . . . I don't understand. . . . No it's too much for me" (61).

Marlow is similarly unsettled by the Intended's power, by what he perceives as the authority of her "mature capacity for fidelity, for belief, for suffering" (73). These feminine virtues ought not be threatening, but Marlow feels "as though I had blundered into a place of cruel and absurd mysteries not fit for a human being to behold" (73). This "place of cruel and absurd mysteries" seems a description of the dark savage jungle, but this is the domestic heart of "a soul as translucently pure as a cliff of crystal" (70). The colonial realm continually shades into the domestic one. The home is savage, inscrutable. And without this home world—or at least the *idea* of it—colonial discourse breaks down.

Marlow agrees that it is impossible not to love Kurtz once one has heard him speak, acknowledging this to the Intended "with something like despair in my heart, but bowing my head before the faith that was in her, before that great and saving illusion that shone with an unearthly glow in the darkness, in the triumphant darkness from which I could not have defended her" (74). If it is right to preserve her "enlightened" illusion, why does doing so make him despair? The valences of truth and lie are reversed when Marlow decides the truth is "too dark—too dark altogether" (76). For whom would the truth be "too dark"? It is Marlow who emphasizes his need to lie, who is haunted by the memory of Kurtz, who says "my imagination . . . wanted soothing" (70). He knows that he cannot defend the Intended from darkness; in fact, he feels the darkness press upon him in her presence. It is for his own sake, for his own peace of mind, that he resists exposing the Intended to darkness. He is afraid of her weakness, and of her strength; he cannot reveal the truth for fear of what it might do to him. She, not recognizing his mental and moral crisis, has no solace to give him. They simply do not speak the same language.

Colonial Discourse in the Domestic Realm

George Gissing enters the Victorian debate on independent women and addresses the consequences of discursive power with *The Odd Women*, his novel of single women alone, by choice and by necessity, and their quotidian experiences. As Elaine Showalter defines her, the odd woman "was the one left over, the uneven number, the spinster who could not find a husband to pair off with her" (*Sexual Anarchy* 19). Of course, the very phrase "odd woman" posits single women as a problem, an anomaly. But Gissing's novel repudiates the uncomplicated stereotype of "the spinster" by representing single women with disparate attitudes and dissimilar lives: the feminist educator, the radical separatist, the unloved and unskilled spinster, the unmarried sisters, the fallen woman, the shopgirl, the flirt, the schoolteacher. Of these women, five are involved with men. Two die as a direct or indirect result, one is left to raise her child alone, one retreats "with honor," and one is happy.[13] Indeed, the odds are against women in relationships with men. In this light, it is not at all odd for a woman to choose to be an "odd woman."

The Odd Women is doubly implicated in the convergence of patriarchal and colonial discourses, for Gissing not only explores the world of women who live outside the protection of men but also invokes an imperialistic metaphor to explain the single woman's new role. Mary Barfoot, the proprietor of a business school for women, gives an inspirational address on the topic of "Woman as Invader." Establishing that they "live in a time of warfare, of revolt" (135), she stresses that woman "must become militant, defiant. She must push her claims to the extremity" (136). Her antagonistic language highlights the ferocity of the struggle. But unlike the masculine invaders that Mary takes as her model, women do not seek to take ground away from others; rather, women are fighting for ownership of their own ground, a space of self-definition outside of "that view of us set forth in such charming language by Mr. Ruskin" (135).

Because women are "enslaved by custom" (136), says Mary, they need strong, independent women to set a new example of emancipated life. She is willing to admit that when women gain territory in this systematic invasion, someone must lose ground. Women's new role as capable, independent income-earners means displacing some men from jobs (an implicit recognition that by working within the terms of the established discourse, a social revolutionary only repeats the injustices of the current system). Mary justifies her gendered invasion by asserting that women's interests are more important than those of a few men: "in the miserable disorder of our social state, one grievance had to be weighed against another, and Miss Barfoot held that there was much more to be urged on behalf of women who invaded what had been exclusively the men's sphere, than on behalf of the men who began to complain of this invasion" (135).

The imperialist underpinnings of this justification are made clear in a different context. "There's one advantage in being a woman," says Mary's associate Rhoda. "A woman with brains and will may hope to distinguish herself in the greatest movement of our time—that of emancipating her sex" (87). Mary agrees, answering: "You are right. It's better to be a woman, in our day. With us is all the joy of advance, the glory of conquering. Men have only material progress to think about. But we are winning souls, propagating a new religion, purifying the earth!" (87). This is the "civilizing mission" redux: missionary zeal effaces the injured parties and obscures the totalizing impulse behind the belief that the one true religion (in this case, feminism) will "purify the earth."

As an orator, Mary is ambitious and optimistic; but in her capacity as friend and advisor, she more realistically represents women's limited options. When Mary and Rhoda first meet an orphaned shopgirl named Monica, they agree that "Of course she must find a husband" (51) because "it seemed a great absurdity to talk to her about business" (51). Monica, too, feels the force of necessity. If she does not marry, she will be forever consigned to work as a shopgirl, a job whose long hours and poor conditions physically and mentally deplete her. She is morally degraded (according to Gissing) by working with vulgar, ill-bred women and associating with the kind of men who seek out shopgirls. So when, by chance, she meets a well-off bachelor, she marries him on short acquaintance despite her misgivings about his advanced age, retrograde attitudes, and jealous tendencies.

This supposed social good—an engagement even the feminist Mary Barfoot agrees is necessary—makes Monica sick: "With strange suddenness, after several weeks of steady application to her work, in a cheerful spirit which at times rose to gaiety, Monica became dull, remiss, unhappy; then violent headaches attacked her, and one morning she declared herself unable to rise" (106). The doctor cannot name the cause, but suspects some "trouble . . . weighing upon her" (106). Although Mary and Rhoda do not know it, the cause of Monica's "mental disquietude" (106) and subsequent sickness is Edmund Widdowson, who has proposed marriage. The supposed "solution" to Monica's shopworn health—a marriageable man—is even more detrimental than shop work to her well-being. The marriage solution is much like European plans to colonize, which ostensibly will solve the "problem" of African savagery and backwardness but will also bring military force, imposed rule, and economic exploitation. The difference is that Monica has a choice in the matter, although both of her options are stark: marry the imperious Widdowson, or live alone in poverty.

Living alone might not seem such a terrible option except that Monica's

models of single womanhood are her sisters, whose poverty-induced vege-
tarianism enfeebles them and further reduces their chances of remunerative
employment. They are "kind, innocent women; but useful for nothing except what they have done all their lives" (51)—teaching children at starvation
wages. Monica fears being in their situation, too feeble to earn a living wage
and too old to attract a husband to support them: "Whenever I think of Alice and Virginia, I am frightened; I had rather, oh, far rather, kill myself than
live such a life at their age. You can't imagine how miserable they are, really"
(111). Alice and Virginia are precisely the sort of women toward whom the
propaganda of groups like the Female Middle-Class Emigration Society was
directed, because they were respectable, "well-bred," but poor women with
little prospect for gainful employment or marriage in England.[14] For women
like Alice and Virginia, who live in a state of unrelenting penury, difficulties
abroad can be preferable to destitution in England. Indeed, almost anything
is better than the life they lead in England. In Virginia's dispirited worldview,
marriage to a stranger is better than no marriage at all. When she hears the
news of Monica's nuptials, "She laughed, uttered cries of joy, even clapped
her hands" (113) even though all she knows of this man is that he is a "private
gentleman" (113).

Monica's subsequent relationship with this stranger, however, is nothing to applaud. Widdowson tries to control his wife's life, her actions, her
personality, her daily activities. He is excessively jealous and thus feels the
need to monitor Monica's every movement. To maintain his sense of superiority he must interpret Monica only through the terms he already accepts
(196–97), and he adopts the language of imperialism and the ideology of
the civilizing mission to justify his domination: "I am no tyrant, but I shall
rule you for your own good" (224). Despite his limited experience with actual women, Widdowson is assured that he understands Monica because he
has assiduously absorbed patriarchal knowledge: books by experts—namely
John Ruskin—on proper wifely demeanor and woman's nature. They tell him
that women, like primitive people, "were simply incapable of attaining ma-
turity" and that he, like British imperial forces, "represented the guardian
male" (196–97). According to Ruskin's *Sesame and Lilies*, the "noble woman"
sanctifies the home and makes it "the place of Peace" (85). Monica's arguments and dissatisfactions, then, are deeply disturbing to Widdowson, for
they indicate that his house "ceases to be home" and that his Monica ceases to
be a "true wife" (Ruskin 85). Like Umbopa who, in Allan Quartermain's eyes,

is always a Zulu because Allan thinks of all dark-skinned people as Zulus, Monica as an individual personality never exists for Widdowson because he imagines all women conform to his idea of "Woman."

Part of Widdowson's difficulty understanding Monica is that he wants to understand "Woman" rather than one woman. His assumption is that "Woman" is a unitary category rather than a pluralistic one; thus he embraces a stereotype, which "produces the colonized as a social reality which is . . . entirely knowable" (Bhabha 70–71). When Monica declares her dissatisfaction with Widdowson's ideology and insists that he stop treating her like a wayward child, Widdowson is "baffled, and even awed, by this extraordinary revelation of a woman he had supposed himself to know thoroughly" (168). It is beyond his imagining that Monica might want more freedom, even though she tells him that his perception of her needs is wrongheaded, misguided, and based on preconceived notions. But Widdowson "was unconsciously the most complete despot, a monument of male autocracy. Never had it occurred to Widdowson that a wife remains an individual, with rights and obligations independent of her wifely condition. Everything he said presupposed his own supremacy; he took for granted that it was his to direct, hers to be guided" (152).

Indeed, Widdowson so thoroughly believes the Angel in the House ideology that he seriously views household chores as a woman's "privilege" (162). When Monica claims that domestic chores are "work" (162), Widdowson thinks her unnatural for not appreciating the sacred joys of caring for home and husband: "Widdowson, before his marriage, had never suspected the difficulty of understanding a woman; had he spoken his serious belief on that subject, it would have been found to represent the most primitive male conception of the feminine being. Women were very like children; it was rather a task to amuse them and to keep them out of mischief. Therefore the blessedness of household toil" (236). Not only is the "limited form of otherness" (Bhabha 78) that Widdowson allows Monica emblematic of the tendency toward stereotype in colonial discourse, the stereotypes of women and natives are expressed in similar terms (they are childlike, undeveloped, dependent).

As in colonial discourse, the "fetish" of patriarchal discourse is an open secret. Like the skin of the racial other, a woman's anatomy gives her away, makes her always other. Her body and, according to nineteenth-century science, her mind constitute an incontestable difference on which cultural and social oppositions can be based. Therefore, Widdowson's recognition that

"Women had individual characters" (237) has the force of a revelation to him. Indeed, it momentarily shakes the foundation of his patriarchal ideology by subverting his belief in the Ruskinian model of womanhood: "that discovery, though not a very profound one, impressed him with the force of something arrived at by independent observation" (237). But Widdowson suppresses his doubt, clutches his fetish, and holds onto his contradictory beliefs. His observations of Monica give him incontrovertible, empirical evidence of her separate identity and desires, yet "To regard her simply as a human being was beyond the reach of his intelligence" (237). While Widdowson at some level understands that Monica is an individual, he cannot treat her as such. Instead of accepting what his observation and his experience reveal, "He cast the blame of his difficulties upon sex, and paid more attention to the hints on such afforded him by his reading" (237). He goes back to the source of his difficulties—believing only what book-writing experts say about women—and resolves to watch over Monica with an even more vigilant patriarchal eye. After all, "Women—so said the books—are adepts at dissimulation" (237).

Widdowson thus sees regulation and control as the most effective way of managing his wife (for "His duty was to manage her" [239]). Monica, however, cannot be fully human under Widdowson's regime. She appeals to Widdowson's self-understanding and asks him to extend the same understanding to her: "You mustn't be afraid to leave me the same freedom you have yourself" (168). The result is that Widdowson "felt his passionate love glow with new fire. For a moment he thought himself capable of accepting this change in their relations. The marvelous thought of equality between man and wife, that gospel which in far-off days will refashion the world, for an instant smote his imagination and exalted him above his native level" (168). His momentary vision of Monica as human first and a woman second quickly dissipates and he is left with his preconceived notions. Continually forced to recognize Monica's claims, he later realizes that "The bitterness of his situation lay in the fact that he had wedded a woman who irresistibly proved to him her claims as a human being. Reason and tradition contended in him, to his ceaseless torment" (197). To rephrase Widdowson's sentiment in the language of colonial discourse, he is torn between a recognition of their likeness (his reason cannot deny "her claims as a human being") and a disavowal of this recognition (he cannot escape the force of patriarchal tradition).

The relationship between Rhoda Nunn and Everard Barfoot, infused with explicit discursive struggles and characterized by militaristic maneuvering for strategic position, would seem to expand on the struggle for autonomy in the face of a controlling male presence presented by Monica. When Barfoot thinks that it "would delight him to enrage Rhoda, and then to detain her by strength, to overcome her senses" (142), we are encouraged in this view. And although he admits "he was in love with her," he also believes "To obtain her consent to marriage would mean nothing at all; it would afford him no satisfaction. But so to play upon her emotions that the proud, intellectual, earnest woman was willing to defy society for his sake—ah! That would be an end worth achieving" (176–77). He is thinking like a man set out to win the Great Game: strategizing his strongest position, deliberating upon his opponent's weaknesses. Their encounters often are couched in this adversarial language of opposition and dominance.

But if Barfoot believed that women were naturally inferior, submissive, and subject to a man's will, there would be no triumph in subduing Rhoda. His success would merely be the workings of "natural law" (164), to quote Widdowson. The imperialist must rely on stereotype to fix the other in a controllable place. Barfoot, however, constantly recognizes that Rhoda eludes reductive categories. Again and again, he marvels that he has never known anyone like her: "It was so difficult to be sure of anything in regard to Miss Nunn. If another woman had acted thus he would have judged it coquetry" (139). Barfoot cannot decide what Rhoda's behavior might mean because he allows that she is not completely knowable and transparent to him, that she is different from other women. He grants her an interiority and complexity that a man like Widdowson is completely unable to grant a woman.

Moreover, Rhoda participates in and encourages this adversarial relationship. In fact, she takes on the adversarial role. After a conversation in which Barfoot declares that he would never marry because he believes in free unions, she considers convincing him to propose marriage: "The interest would only be that of comedy. She did not love Everard Barfoot. . . . But, if he loved her, these theories [of free union] would sooner or later be swept aside; he would plead with her to become his legal wife. To that point she desired to bring him" (148). Not because she wants to be his wife; rather, "To reject a lover in so many respects desirable, whom so many women might envy her, would fortify her self-esteem" (148). Just as Barfoot's ego would be gratified by having a "proud, intellectual, earnest" woman bow to him, Rhoda is gratified by Barfoot's eventual proposal: "She had gained her wish, had enjoyed her triumph" (186).

Their final set of negotiations is a tangle of pride and desire for stature in the eyes of the other. Barfoot recognizes the contradiction of his position: "Delighting in her independence of mind, [Barfoot] still desired to see her in complete subjugation to him, to inspire her with unreflecting passion" (261). Barfoot wants Rhoda to agree to a free union because "he must have the joy of subduing her to his will" (265), but he does indeed plan to marry her. This sounds base, but Rhoda, when wondering if she should accept his offer of free union, also considers her pride as much as her emotions: "The temptation to yield was very strong, for it seemed to her an easier and a nobler thing to proclaim her emancipation from social statutes than to announce before her friends the simple news that she was about to marry. . . . If it became known that she had taken a step such as few women would have dared to take—deliberately setting an example of new liberty   her position in the eyes of all who know her remained one of proud independence" (264).

So when they decide to marry in a rush of unconsidered sentiment, "neither was content" (268) because the desire for domination dominated both. Barfoot is in "a mood of chagrin" because "he had not triumphed. As usual the woman had her way. She played upon his senses, and made him her obedient slave" (268). Barfoot feels that "it would have been far wiser to persist in rejecting legal marriage, that her dependence upon him might be more complete" (268). From admiring Rhoda's independence to requiring her dependence, Barfoot reverts to the patriarchal ideal when faced with the actuality of Rhoda's equality. Because there is no model for this new type of relationship, Barfoot can only imagine the traditional marriage relationship in reverse. Instead of the husband directing the wife, Barfoot expects to be directed when he does not establish his own superiority from the start. So he imagines the worst: "a long, perhaps bitter, struggle for pre-dominance. . . . Need he entertain that worst of fears—the dread that his independence might fail him, subdued by his wife's will?" (268). He cannot imagine what an equal relationship would resemble, so he falls back on social norms.

William Barry's *Quarterly Review* article "The Strike of a Sex" (1894) identifies the source of Barfoot's discomfort. In comparing Mrs. Humphry Ward's *Marcella* (1894) with Sarah Grand's *The Heavenly Twins* (1894), the reviewer argues that Ward truly understands women and thus ends her novel with the chivalrous codes "we" all know and honor. He believes, however, that the New Woman exemplified by Grand would suggest a different ending:

If the New Woman were consulted, she would undoubtedly suggest as a novel but appropriate ending, "Queen castles and takes knight." The wedding ought to be a surrender on the part of the bridegroom, condemned henceforth to do his lady's will, to see with her eyes, and let her govern while he pretends to reign. . . . That, however, is not the philosophy of Marcella's biographer, to whom an equality of the sexes in this large revolutionary sense appears to be impossible. The knight, by sheer force of character, takes the queen, compelling her to own that he is worthy of her obedience as well as her love. (305–6)

That this sentiment is intimately connected with *Odd Women* is intimated by Barry's obsessive return to the idea of free love (even though the books under review do not mention free love, much less advocate it). New Women, in his mind, are inseparable from free unions and remaining single.[15] New Women are further connected by necessity with Odd Women, because no sane man *would* marry a New Woman, even if she could accommodate herself to the idea: "Who would bind himself to spend his days with the anarchist, the athlete, the blue-stocking, the aggressively philanthropic, the political, the surgical woman? And what man would submit to an alliance which was terminable, not when *he* chose, but when his comrade was tired of him?[16] Such are not the ideals to which he has looked up, or the qualities that win his affections" (317).

For her part, Rhoda "visited her soul with questionings no less troublesome" (269) than Barfoot's fear of waning manhood, even though "She had triumphed splendidly" (269). She, too, envisions a loss of status, fearing that Barfoot "had yielded, perhaps more than half contemptuously, to what he thought a feminine weakness" (269). There would be no triumph if Barfoot relented because he thought her weak and in need of propitiation. Again, the triumph is not of personal happiness and fulfillment, but a triumph "In the world's eye," a better match than anyone could have expected a "spinster" of thirty to make.

A marriage never takes place, because both wish to see the other subdued. This represents an advance on Widdowson's ideal marriage in which the husband is unilaterally in control; nonetheless, at this point marriage is impossible for Barfoot and Rhoda because there is no discursive context for understanding the kind of relationship they seek. They cannot overcome the dominant social discourse, which infuses marriage with notions that neither party accepts as valid.[17] Neither Rhoda nor Barfoot can precisely articulate the problem, but the impossibility of their relationship is based in the idea that a marriage relationship must have one dominating partner and one submissive partner. Each desires the other, but neither can escape the language of domination, and neither can accept being dominated. Moreover, when love relations are so thoroughly cast in terms of domination, both want the reassurance and surety that only the other's submission can bring.

At some level, Barfoot knows that domination is not what he wants, for he recognizes that what attracts him to Rhoda is her independence: "She feared nothing that he might say. No flush of apprehension; no nervous tremor; no weak self-consciousness. Yet he saw her as a woman, and desirable" (143). This "yet" is telling. It signals what Barfoot believes ought to be a contradiction: Rhoda is strong, assertive, *and* attractive, womanly. This new definition of womanliness, this new vision of womanhood, ought to generate a new conception of marriage. Barfoot recognizes the worth of a nontraditional wife, but he cannot escape the power of established discourse. His self-definition depends upon being master—at least for the moment—of the relationship.

Rhoda's wish to dominate Barfoot, as well as her resiliency when she finds they do not "speak the same language," is the result of her determination that woman must be the invader, the imperialist. She is acutely aware that she is unwilling to accept the role of traditional wife, and has dedicated her life to working for the independence naturally granted to middle-class men. Because she has means of supporting herself—educational, financial, and, perhaps as important, emotional—Rhoda can "retreat with honor" (the title of the penultimate chapter). She is chastened and saddened, but she has also gained strength and wisdom. When Barfoot and Rhoda are on the beach at Seascale, deciding whether to marry, he reassures her that no other woman exists for him, that no one else has a claim on him. Rhoda replies: "But do we speak the same language?" (263). This is a central question in all relationships where one party is more powerful than the other, especially when the dominant discourse is being challenged. Barfoot refuses to fetishize stereotypes about women, but he is unwilling to modify his social practices to accord with his broader understanding. The power of the stereotype (and the mastery it engenders) dominates late-nineteenth-century imperial and patriarchal discourse even among those who recognize its tyranny.

Staking Claims

Colonizing the New Woman Novel

This chapter focuses on three novels in which elements of New Woman and colonial adventure fiction uneasily co-exist: Bram Stoker's *Dracula* (1897) and H. Rider Haggard's *She* (1887) and *Mr. Meeson's Will* (1888).[1] The generic hybridity of these texts brings into relief both the constitutive elements of adventure novels and the cultural anxieties that often drive them. The narrative function of the quasi-New Woman characters in these novels highlights the fear elicited by the New Woman and the New Woman writer. Enlisted by men when they can serve their ends, excluded when they threaten the men's supremacy, these women share a kinship with the monstrous forces that threaten the novel's heroes. They are hybrids born of their creator's ideologically riven relationship to the gender trouble of the late century.

Like the monster she helps defeat, the heroine of *Dracula* seeks entry into the domain of power and knowledge occupied by the all-male Crew of Light. In fact, Mina Harker proposes that sharing knowledge across genders is the key to victory over the monster: "We need have no secrets amongst us; working together and with absolute trust, we can surely be stronger than if some of us were in the dark" (197). But the men oppose Mina's full entry into their domain; Dr. Seward's diary records the men's consensus that Mina, with her developed powers of insight and analysis, must "say goodbye to this work" because "it is no part for a woman" (207). He writes:

> Mrs. Harker is better out of it. Things are quite bad enough to us, all men of the world, and who have been in many tight places in our time; but it is no place for a woman. (225)

Their insistence that Mina be excluded from their project presages Marlow's more famous formulation in *Heart of Darkness* (1902):

> Did I mention a girl? Oh, she is out of it completely. They—the women I mean—are out of it—should be out of it. We must help them to stay

in that beautiful world of their own lest ours gets worse. Oh, she had to be out of it. (Conrad 49)

Marlow's speech gives the lie to the men's assertion that they alone are involved in empire, for his formulation of women's position moves from positive assertion ("are out of it") to judgment ("should be out of it") to tacit acknowledgment that women's distance from empire serves a specific purpose ("had to be out of it"). By willing their absence, these men are affirming women's presence—their conceptually central role in the ideology of empire.

Both characters in these passages employ slippery spatial signifiers: women need to be "out of it"; "it is no place" for a woman. But the "it" remains provokingly unspecific. What, exactly, is "it" that women need to be kept out of? On one level, these men are formulating a version of the chivalric code: women must be kept out of "it" in order to protect them from the corrosive effects of the masculine world. When women are in masculine places, it is men's duty to escort them out. But there is an aggressive and defensive edge to this rhetoric that belies its chivalric emphasis. "It" in these formulations comes to represent a masculine social and psychic territory that women are invading. By the end of the nineteenth century, women were assuming men's vocations and providing for themselves; in so doing, they threatened to abandon their supposed social and biological functions. New Women were colonizing masculinity by both questioning its basis in nature and assuming its mantle of power.

Why then would male adventure writers appropriate the New Woman character? At one level, they did so in response to market considerations, capitalizing on the popularity of the independent woman as heroine. As Chris Willis notes, novels with New Women figures "were not necessarily written by supporters of the women's movement: the New Woman had become a marketable novelty figure whose presence in a story increased its chance of good sales" (64). This strategy also served ideological ends; the writers sought to neutralize the threat of the New Woman writer. These fictions typically enact the ultimate exile of the New Woman from masculine spaces, both physical and psychic. This is achieved by allying the New Woman—and New Woman writers especially—with the forces of danger and degeneration. The New Woman novelist was an excellent target, for she embodied feminist ferment, provided a community for other questing women, and offered models of what seemed, to many men, like a distinctively masculine female identity.

Mina, with her "man's brain . . . and woman's heart" (207), exemplifies this dangerous colonizing of masculinity. What seems like a compliment—that Mina is a complement to the men—is actually the first step in her subjugation. It involves segregating her from the men's pursuits because "it is no part for a woman" (207). This story has a familiar ring. In Charlotte Brontë's *Jane Eyre* (1847), for instance, St. John Rivers argues that Jane must accompany him to India as his wife, so that she may be "influence[d] efficiently" (357). Jane replies that she has only sisterly regard for him, but he insists that her sex prevails over her intellect:

> It is known that you are not my sister; I cannot introduce you as such.
> . . . And for the rest, though you have a man's vigorous brain, you have a woman's heart, and—it would not do. (359)

St. John's explanation helps illuminate the fear behind the Crew of Light's desire to keep Mina out. St. John's first reason (that everyone knows Jane is not his sister) indicates his desire to keep his own sexual reputation unsullied. But he implies another reason. "The rest" is clearly love, because he worries that Jane's "woman's heart" will override her "man's brain": he worries that she will not be able to control her sexual feelings. Without a marriage tie to manage her sexual desire, a woman may "go native": after all, nineteenth century sexual science deemed women lower on the evolutionary scale, so they were already dangerously similar to the native others men felt fit to rule.

The alarm provoked by the New Woman is similarly allied with fear of their degenerative tendencies when they elude masculine control, as well as their ability to cause white men to devolve. In *Dracula*, Mina's temporary alliance with the vampire reveals the dangers lurking in the independent woman. Her writing, decisiveness, and powers of analysis help to defeat the monster, but they also endanger the British men around her by usurping their roles and their supposedly masculine abilities. While Ayesha in Haggard's *She* is not herself a writer, she has learning and education that, like the authority to write, give her power over her world, her circumstances, her people. *Mr. Meeson's Will* represents a more complex figuration of a similar outline. Like the other novels, it features a professional woman who writes; but Haggard explicitly allies himself with his scribbling heroine and her presence thus problematizes and threatens Haggard's masculine identity and narrative enterprise. Clearly troubled by this alliance, Haggard subjects Augusta to torture, hardship, deprivation, and loss of family—seemingly as retribution for emasculating her creator. Like Ayesha and Mina, Augusta suffers terribly for her arrogations of power, which defy both man and "nature," and endanger both men and the race.

When male authors bring New Woman characters into the masculine landscape of adventure narratives, then, they do so only to deny them full participation in the male quest. *Dracula, She*, and *Mr. Meeson's Will* enact distinct versions of this essential strategy. Each novel creates New Woman characters who are ultimately exiled from the narrative action; they are domesticated and returned to properly feminine activities so that they are no longer a threat to the existing social order. These novelists repeat Marlow's gesture: they invite women in to the adventure novel before judging that women "ought" to be out if it and then demonstrating why women "had to be out of it." And the reason women need to be out of "it" is that their autonomy allies them with degeneration: women writers, especially, reproduce monstrously; they are creative rather than procreative. In these authors' minds, women, writing, and degeneration are intimately and dangerously bound.

The Fear of Invasion by the New Woman

The New Woman, who prompted new ways of imagining women's social and increasingly political roles, engendered cultural anxieties that extended well beyond the Woman Question. The ideal of the domestic woman was a foundation stone of British patriarchy; as this ideal was increasingly disputed by actual women, the structure of power threatened to collapse in on itself. For when women are not "women" as previously understood, the definition of "men" is also put in question.[2] If women's actual subjectivity challenges patriarchal ideology, then the basis of men's social, cultural, and imperial power is also destabilized. New Woman novels, whose heroines are often writers or artists, both articulated women's desire to invade masculine domains and personified the forms these invading women would take. Hence, critics of naturalist writings, as I demonstrated in chapter 1, withheld approval of male naturalists but aggressively attacked female naturalists as dangerously atavistic.

Charles Harper embodies the extreme reaction against shifting female manners in his tract *Revolted Woman: Past, Present, and to Come* (1894). Not only are women "usurpers of man's distinctive dress" (31), but they also are so concerned with "the writings and doings of the pioneers of the New Woman" that they "forget that Woman's Mission is Submission" (2). Indeed, as women usurp man's dress and abandon the posture of submission, they become dangerously atavistic: "when women begin to talk of their Work with all the zeal and religious fervor that characterizes the attitude of the savage towards his fetish, it behooves us to inquire what that Work may be which arouses so much enthusiasm and is the cause of the cool insolence which is becoming more and more the note of the New Woman" (45). Paid work, which makes women savage fetish-worshipers, is dangerous because it "has nothing to do with the up-bringing of children or the management of the home" (45).

Harper targets women who pursue "the artistic and literary professions" (49), because "the woman's mind is normally incapable of rising to an appreciation of the possibilities of any medium" (49). In his chapter "Women in Men's Employments," Harper admits that women have "almost feminized" the field of new employments "evolved from the increasing complex civilization of this dying nineteenth century" (131). The acknowledgment of progress evident in his confidence about late-century complexity and economic expansion is countered by the note of decline in the phrase "this dying nineteenth century." It is women who engender his pessimism; occupations that should signal England's progress instead announce its colonization by the forces of femininity. While acknowledging that "these wage-earning women have proved their right to their new place" when small, quick hands are required, he nonetheless finds that "in the occupations of clerks, cashiers, telephonists, telegraphists, and shorthand writers they have sufficiently demonstrated their unfitness" (131). It is their femininity (not their feminism) that keeps them employed: women are hired because of "the sexual sentimentality which would rather have a pretty woman to flirt with in the intervals of typewriting than a merely useful and unornamental man" (131). The disorder of the professional world follows on the disorder of the domestic realm caused by women's refusal to accept that their "true profession is marriage" (130).

As women agitated for both freedom from domestic enclosure and power to earn a living, a complex of issues surrounding their mental and physical fitness arose. Long considered lower on the evolutionary scale than men, women who assumed power over men outside the domestic sphere gave rise to visions of savage rule.[3] For conservative cultural critics like James Ashcroft Noble, the woman/savage correlation was being played out in New Woman novels. His essay on "The Fiction of Sexuality" (1895) claims that the New Woman writers' willingness to discuss sex, their "lack of those pudencies and reticences," associates them with "primitive man." Reticence about personal issues, Noble claims, "becomes instinctive in the earliest developments of civilization" (494). By this logic, New Woman writers represent a form of cultural devolution.

In "Plain Words on the Woman Question," Grant Allen extends Ashcroft's claim about the New Woman writer's degeneracy when he argues that any independent woman represents an atavistic anomaly in the modern world. Advanced civilization supports women in their childbearing role; primitive societies make women work to support themselves. As Laura Chrisman has noted, Allen was not alone in his views. Contemporary discourses construed progress "as a consolidation and increased 'appreciation' of women's domestic status; in contrast, the system of 'primitive' culture turned women into 'drudges' by forcing them to undertake 'social'/manual labor" (43). "Advanced" women, therefore, should be content in the domestic sphere that ages of progress have created for them. Women who protest against their confinement in a "domestic cage" are throwbacks, primitives, savages.

Moreover, the savagely unfeminine woman was often suspected of causing men to lose their manly vigor; a woman's assumption of masculine independence makes men redundant. Thus, unnatural women are not only signs of degeneration but also producers of it. Harper's *Revolted Women* warns that "the New Woman, if a mother at all, will be the mother of a New Man, as different indeed, from the present races as possible. . . . [There is] the prospect of peopling the world with stunted and hydrocephalic children . . . and [the] ultimate extinction of the race" (27). These women are dangerous purveyors of degeneration. Count Dracula is, as Cannon Schmitt argues, a projection of the monstrous "new" mother: he uses his children to feed his blood lust, he destroys other children to feed his own, and he produces pale and sickly beings. As the progenitor of a terrible new species, Dracula embodies the threat posed by the New Woman.

Paradoxically, not only were there fears that New Women would bear children and produce a degenerate species of British child, there were also recriminations against the New Woman for refusing motherhood entirely and failing to propagate the species and repeople the nation. The New Woman's "masculine" desire to exist outside and beyond home and husband led critics to see her as a threat to all the British held dear: home, family, nation, empire. Grant Allen's "Plain Words" is adamant on the national responsibility of women. He contends that every woman must "use up the ten or twelve best years of her life" to bear "four or five children" (451) in order to maintain the

British population. In Allen's eyes, this is merely her duty. The connection with nation-building—and by extension the colonial mission—is clear when Allen adds that "if women realized how noble and important a task it is that falls upon mothers, they would ask no other. If they realized how magnificent a nation might be molded by mothers who devoted themselves faithfully and earnestly to their great privilege, they would be proud to carry out the duties of their maternity" (456). Mothers are integral to the nation and hence the empire. Those selfish women who do not wish to bear children are responsible for the degeneration of not only the race but also the nation and the empire.[4]

Emma Brook, a feminist involved with the Men and Women's Club, questioned the assertion that maternity is an essential component of woman's nature. If women themselves feel compelled to bear children, the question of women's fitness for other roles is moot: "The assumption of this strong Desire in Women for Children—so strong that it can only be compared to the mighty impulse of men towards women—is a *most* important one; because if such an imperial Desire exists there is an end to the Sex-question; what remains is a population-question" (qtd. in Brandon 52). If it is true that women feel an "imperial desire" to bear children, the question is merely how many children, and how often they should be produced. But Brook points out that this is an "assumption." Like J. S. Mill in "The Subjection of Women," Brook declines to assert what cannot be known; what is "natural" to women cannot be known within a culture that inculcates them into gender roles from infancy. Indeed, the meaning of "imperial" is at stake here, for she questions "imperial desire" itself—is it destiny, a force of nature not to be resisted, or a wish and an assertion by British men to aggrandize their own power?

Taking Women Out of "It": *Dracula*

The first item the reader of *Dracula* encounters, after the title page, is a paragraph informing her that the text has been assembled from various sources. It is evasive about who precisely is responsible: "How these papers have been placed in sequence will be made manifest in the reading of them" (5). What the reader soon discovers is that Mina is the composer of the narrative: what she does not write herself, she transcribes for male writers. Moreover, her decision to transcribe Jonathan's Transylvania trip diary along with her own diary of Lucy's sickness empowers the vampire hunters by providing crucial information about Dracula's movements. Mina also asserts her authority by typing out Dr. Seward's phonograph diaries. When Seward objects to the public dissemination of his personal diaries, Mina overrules him: "they must!" she says, "Because it is a part of the terrible story . . . because in the struggle which we have before us to rid the earth of this terrible monster we must have all the knowledge and all the help which we can get" (197).

Mina's interventions represent an invasion of the masculine psyche that extends well beyond the figurative. Not only does Mina read Jonathan's diary but she also listens to Seward's diary, including the portions "personal to me" (196). This ability to get inside the heads of the men gives her power: she is "master of all the facts" (194), so much so that Godalming voices the ladylike attitude that "all I can do is to accept your ideas blindfold and try to help you" (203). Mina is the only one (among five men) to realize that "if we get all our material ready, and have every item put in chronological order, we shall have much done" (198). Her mastery of the technology of writing is married to her journalistic memory (163) and her "masculine" powers of deduction.

This latent masculinity makes Mina a threat akin to Count Dracula himself. Mina's—and the New Woman's—likeness to the vampire is first evoked when the three vampire women approach Jonathan in Castle Dracula. Jonathan is sleepily musing in the ladies' library, thinking of the gentle women who wrote letters there. The vampire women, however, are not "ladies" in the traditional sense; as Carol Senf claims, "Their aggressive behavior and attempt to reverse traditional sexual roles show them to be New Women . . . and Harker is openly ambivalent about this role reversal" (40). These dangerous women seduce and thereby feminize Jonathan: he subsides into a passivity that will literally and figuratively drain him. These women leave him weak in mind, powerless in body, reduced to the thrall of the supposedly weaker sex.

This scene is mirrored in the scenes leading up to Mina and Jonathan's wedding. Although Mina mockingly records in her journal that "Some of the 'New women' writers will some day start an idea that men and women should be allowed to see each other asleep before proposing or accepting" (87), she in fact enacts this radical notion. She sees her husband sleeping before they are married, and she initiates a reversal of sanctioned roles when she and Jonathan wed. She takes the active role in their wedding because Jonathan is bedridden with neurasthenia, a typically feminine affliction. He is "thin and pale and weak-looking" (99). Womanlike, "the resolution has gone out of his dear eyes," and Mina thus fears "tax[ing] his poor brain" (99). Reliant on Mina's determination and strength, Jonathan abdicates the man's role and merely responds to Mina's proposals. Indeed, it is Mina who "asked Sister Agatha to beg the Superior to let our wedding be this afternoon" (100). Jonathan is completely out of the decision in so far as he sleeps through it: "We are to be married in an hour," writes Mina to Lucy, "or as soon after as Jonathan wakes" (100).

These images of powerful women, however, are misleading. Indeed, Stoker insists the women do not have any real power; they are pawns in men's imperial struggle. Dracula subjugates women, strips them of individual volition, and makes them "my creatures, to do my bidding" (267). When Mina drinks Dracula's blood, she is further enslaved: "When my brain says 'Come,' to you," says Dracula, "you shall cross land or sea to do my bidding" (252). In his appropriation of female bodies, he is aligned with the British men, and, as Stephen Arata argues, this behavior is entirely familiar in the Victorian context: "Just as Dracula's vampirism mirrors the domestic practices of Victorian patriarchs, so his invasion of London in order to 'batten on the helpless' natives there mirrors British imperial activities abroad" (119).

Women are the ideological foundation on which male power—especially imperial power—is built. Colonizers gain power over native men by regulating native women. *Dracula* enacts this dynamic by representing the transmission of male power through control of women: be it Van Helsing and his men or Dracula himself, their struggles with each other are represented by their control of Mina and Lucy. Although women are absent from Dracula's recital of his ancestors and their exploits, just as they are largely absent from official British imperial history, in *Dracula* the possessor of women possesses the nation. Thus Dracula colonizes England by colonizing English women's bodies.

Dracula enlists Lucy and Mina both to mortify the men and, ultimately, to transform them into his minions. As Dracula taunts, "Your girls that you all love are mine already; and through them you and others shall yet be mine— my creatures, to do my bidding and to be my jackals when I want to feed" (267). *Dracula* shows how regulating women keeps men in power; women are the battleground of power struggles among men.[5] To subdue Dracula, Van Helsing, Seward, Morris, and Godalming undertake the ritualized killing of the vampiric Lucy; it is only by destroying a woman who has joined the ranks of the "enemy" that they regain control.

If knowledge is power, it is clear that *Dracula's* Englishmen prefer their women ignorant. The women's very lives depend on knowing who and what

Dracula is, but the men consistently withhold information. (Mina is an exception, but the men seek to restrict her to transcribing and compiling information and thus to being a medium of exchange.) The men do not tell Lucy or her mother what Lucy's illness is, and both therefore do things that further endanger Lucy's life. Late-century texts, like Sarah Grand's *The Heavenly Twins* (1893) and George Egerton's story "Virgin Soil" (1894) often illustrate the real dangers of keeping "girls" in ignorance—the foolishness of imagining that ignorance is a young woman's best protection. Egerton's Florence blames her mother "because you reared me . . . ignorant of everything I ought to have known. . . . You sent me out to fight the biggest battle of a woman's life, the one in which she ought to know every turn of the game, with a white gauze . . . of maiden purity as a shield" (157). Similarly, the men's blundering attempts to "protect" Mina actually make her more vulnerable to Dracula's attack. Moreover, they ignore the signs that Mina has Lucy's "sickness" even though both women manifest the same symptoms: pallor, fatigue, and fear of sleep.

Initially, the men are helpless against what seem like Dracula's evolutionary advances. He is not restricted to the human form. Appearing as a bat, a wolf, a mist, or as elemental dust, he can "come out from anything or into anything, no matter how close it be bound" (211). He has human strengths—the ability to reason and learn—but not human weaknesses: he is immortal, he can grow younger; he has superhuman strength, and he can even see in the dark. Yet these supposed advances are proven to be vulnerabilities, and he is defeated by mortal men. He is not evolved, we find, but primitive. Mina, too, devolves from a modern woman, who seems superior to "ordinary" women, into an atavistic anomaly. She almost willingly drinks Dracula's blood (247), for "strangely enough, [she] did not want to hinder him" (251) when he bites her neck. "Unclean, unclean!" (248) is her continual refrain, because she is tainted with the mark of the ancient and barbaric vampire ritual. She thus becomes the savage sidekick of the colonial adventure novel: helpful in understanding the dangerous primitives the white men hunt, but too closely allied with the primitive herself to be fully trusted, to be "one of the boys."

Indeed, Mina's greatest promise lies in the boy she bears after she withdraws from the male domain. Her son is born on "the same day as that on which Quincey Morris died" (326). What Jonathan (who narrates this postscript to the novel in Mina's stead) fails to mention is this is also the day Dracula dies, and thus the day Mina is freed from her association with the monstrous.

The birthday of Mina's true womanhood is also "the same day as that" on which her son is born. The woman who was not only the genius behind the narrative but also the spur to solving the mystery and defeating the monster does not finish this novel. Instead, her reassimilation into the feminine fold is marked by the laying down of her pen (and other tools of composition) and the birth of the baby who bears the names of all the men she once wrote about. Jonathan gets the last word and Stoker reasserts the masculine writer and his ability to reclaim his role as narrator, originator, and author of British society.

The New Woman as Monkey: *She*

A traditional quest romance full of masculine swashbuckling, H. Rider Haggard's *She* nonetheless revolves around a powerful woman; a generic feminine pronoun is all that is necessary to represent the alluring and dangerous (anti-) heroine Ayesha. As in *Dracula*, degeneration, feminine power, and the New Woman are inseparably combined in her. Moreover, women's writing provides the impetus of this narrative, just as Mina is responsible for assembling the Dracula papers.

The shard of Amenartas, an ancient potsherd inscribed with a directive to her male heirs to seek out and destroy Ayesha, is at the heart of this story. Without its matrilineal bequest, the story would have ended with the first son's attempt to avenge his father's death at Ayesha's hand. (Married to Amenartas, Kallikrates refuses Ayesha's offer of love and eternal life. Enraged, Ayesha strikes him dead. Amenartas escapes back to Egypt, bears Kallikrates' son, and begins the cycle of vengeance that continues for two thousand years and into the present of Haggard's story.) Not only are Amenartas' words central to the narrative, they are obsessively repeated, translated, and translated again as well. From modern English, to uncial Greek, to cursive Greek, to an "ancient black-letter translation into medieval Latin" (41), and an expanded medieval Latin version, Amenartas's writing occupies a status to which Haggard's own writing can only aspire. Her message has lasted for centuries, been treated seriously by scholars, and influenced the lives of many men. To be sure, the woman who writes this "marvelous composition" (31) is herself Haggard's invention; nonetheless, he puts the essential chronicle into a woman's hands.

The only other writing on the outer surface of the shard is also a woman's: a doggerel couplet by Dorothea Vincey. "In earth and skie and sea / Strange thynges ther be" (35) also takes pride of place on the title page of the novel; like Amenartas' script, which provides the impetus for Haggard's plot, a woman's words precede the masculine narrative. It is not until Holly and Leo turn the shard over that they find evidence of male activity; the reverse is "covered from top to bottom with notes and signatures" (35) by various men who have attempted the quest. Although consigned to writing on the other side of the shard, the male heirs soon become preeminent. As Patricia Murphy argues, Amenartas' consignment to the "other side" reveals the masculinity of this history—and of history more generally conceived: "A woman's tangential participation in that history places her in a double bind, as Amenartas's fate reveals, for she is either a vessel whose words are expropriated and reinterpreted or a potentially disruptive source of inaccuracy" (39). Each man writes "to my son" (36) and signs his name, effectively bequeathing the quest for Ayesha in his own name and thereby usurping Amenartas'.

Once women have established the narrative and generative lines of the novel and its characters, they are entirely marginalized.[6] Amenartas is never heard from again, and Ayesha's role for the next two thousand years is waiting "in her living tomb ... for the coming of her lover" (*She* 295) while the Vincey men continue to progress through history. Moreover, Amenartas' potsherd is passed down to all the *sons* of the Vincey family; only men are heir to this narrative of Western civilization (the very history Leo studies at Cambridge). The shard aligns the Vincies with Western civilization (Arata 100), leaves Amenartas a figure of the past, and Ayesha alive but stranded outside of history, disengaged from the British and male narrative of progress. Like Mina, whose life is occupied with care for her child and whose writing is left for her husband to bring to closure, Amenartas loses her power to create words after she has created a son.

The New Woman—and the education and authority that characterize her—is similarly pushed aside in this narrative. Despite Ayesha's familiarity with chemistry, eugenics, and philosophy, she nonetheless wants her man, not her independence (like Victoria, another white queen with imperialist impulses, who advocated traditional gender roles despite her powerful position). Although she seems a self-supporting and independent ruler who needs no manly aid, Ayesha reveals that she merely "wait[s] for him I love" (150). When Kallikrates returns (in his reincarnated form: as Leo), she becomes submissive, humble, intent on handing her power to her husband. During their improvised wedding ceremony, Ayesha's "first most holy hour of completed Womanhood" (284), she promises to be a good and conventional wife: "I will be ever guided by thy voice in the straightest path of Duty. I swear that I will eschew Ambition" (284). She concludes her vows, saying, "I humble myself before thee. Such is the power of Love, and such is the bridal gift I give unto thee, Kallikrates" (285). She-who-must-be-obeyed promises to love, honor, and obey, and to give up her New Woman ambitions for command.

Just as Bram Stoker and Grant Allen envision New Women as truly ata-vistic, Haggard's narrators often find that women have more affinity with the savage than men.[7] Allan Quartermain reports that, as much as *man* longs for "savage" adventure, it is women who most strongly bear the marks of moder-nity's evolutionary past: "my dear young lady, what are those pretty things round your own neck?—they have a strong family resemblance, especially when you wear that *very* low dress, to the savage woman's beads. Your habit of turning round and round to the sound of horns and tom-toms, your fondness for pigments and powders, the way in which you love to subjugate yourself to the rich warrior who has captured you in marriage. . . . [I]n the fundamental principles of your nature you are quite identical" (*Allan Quartermain* 22). For Haggard, it is not merely "new" women whose civilization is quite thinly "silver-gilt"; all women, even more than men, are savage at heart.

The primitive element in Ayesha becomes apparent when she attempts to demonstrate her advanced knowledge. The flame of life, she says, will give "life and youth that shall endure . . . and with it pomp, and power, and wealth" (*She* 239). But when Ayesha steps into the flame of life, the power she anticipates becomes a mockery of progress.[8] Haggard graphically portrays the devolutionary horror lurking underneath the advanced woman's assured exterior: in the words of the serving-man Job, "she's turning into a monkey!" (293). She devolves before the men's eyes into a primitive being. This particu-larly gruesome form of retribution against the powerful woman is not merely masculine wish-fulfillment, Haggard stresses; "it was an awful and unparal-leled fact!" (295). Moreover, it is a blessing in disguise, for "it requires no great stretch of imagination to see the finger of Providence in the matter" (295). A "strong and happy" Ayesha "would have revolutionized society, and even perchance have changed the destinies of Mankind. Thus she opposed herself against the eternal Law, and . . . was swept back to nothingness . . . with shame and hideous mockery!" (295).

Despite her declarations of wifely sentiment and her disavowal of ambition, Ayesha never promises nor intends to bear Leo a child. She offers, instead, to make him live forever by taking him into "the very womb of the Earth" (286). Thus Ayesha, like the degenerate New Woman, relinquishes her reproductive power. The conjunction of Ayesha's degeneration into "a baboon" (294) with her sterile intrusion on a feminized Earth mother who "doth conceive the life that ye see brought forth in man and beast" (286–87) is not coincidental. Ayesha is negatively contrasted with this Earth mother because Ayesha does not bear life within her; she only observes the creation of life from the outside.[9] Although she gives Leo "a mother's kiss" (291), the true mother—the mother who "doth conceive the life"—reveals Ayesha's sins against man and nature as the Flame of Life causes her to devolve into a creature "no larger than a big monkey, and hideous—ah, too hideous for words. And yet, think of this—at that very moment I thought of it—it was the *same* woman!" (294). The *same* woman who had just moments before seemed a model of feminine advancement becomes a biological throwback, defeated by the forces of motherly creation she had foolishly eschewed. Not only is Ayesha punished, but also men can be assured that any future feminine menace who opposes "the eternal Law" will be avenged by Nature for her unfitness, her inferiority, her atavism.

Conscripting the New Woman: *Mr. Meeson's Will*

H. Rider Haggard's *Mr. Meeson's Will* also features the spectacle of a woman's immolation, although this one is figurative. Augusta Smithers, a novelist, endures "torture for something like five hours" (139) from the slow burn of the tattooer's crude instrument, a procedure that indelibly marks her as the subject of a man's script and a savage plot. In this novel, male anxiety about the New Woman, female authorship, and authority is literalized. Augusta, a fully modern independent woman and successful author, is clearly a New Woman figure, and—like Mina and Ayesha—she embraces marriage. Unlike these two, however, Augusta promises to continue working and writing even after her wedding. More surprisingly, Haggard's imaginative identification with his writer-heroine obviates any conclusive suppression of her agency or vocation, destabilizing the narrative and frustrating his attempts to constrain female agency.

The novel begins as a New Woman narrative, but Haggard's caustic send-up of late-Victorian publishing practices is the liveliest and most original aspect of this novel, indicating that it will not remain one. The villain is Jonathan Meeson, the head of a ruthless publishing house where "tame authors" are paid a pittance to toil all day in the "hutches," grinding out unoriginal prose. At Meeson and Company, employees are known only by number, "personalities and personal responsibility being the abomination of the firm" (20). In his remorseless quest for profits, Meeson preys on naive authors in financial straits: he offers a single low payment for an initial book and a contract that requires the author to become "a literary bond-slave for five years" (32). Augusta, an author with "genius—true genius" (55), has been trapped by Meeson, having sold the copyright to her novel for fifty pounds. An impoverished orphan supporting herself and an ailing sister, she applies to Meeson for more money after seeing that her book has sold sixteen thousand copies and earned the publisher over a thousand pounds. In a scene reminiscent of *Oliver Twist*, Meeson explodes with anger, incredulous at her audacity in seeking more. Meeson's nephew and only living relative, Eustace, observes the whole scene. Because Augusta is beautiful, Eustace takes an extra interest in the proceedings, and after she is dismissed without satisfaction, he tells his uncle that his business practices are corrupt. A powerful man who cannot bear to hear the truth, Meeson disinherits Eustace on the spot.

Unlike most New Woman fictions, which remain centered in England,[10] Haggard has the distraught but dauntless Augusta journey to New Zealand to start over. She sails on the *Kangaroo* and finds that the elder Meeson is also aboard. The captain, a fan of her book, seeks her out, moves her to a first-class berth, and introduces her to Lord and Lady Holmhurst, colonial governor and first lady of Australia. Augusta reveals Meeson's business practices, and he is ostracized by all despite his fortune. Her honesty, independence, and intelligence win people to her cause. Moreover, she is the belle of the ship, and every man is in love with her; one wealthy colonist even makes her an offer of marriage.[11]

Thus the New Woman plot quickly degenerates into a sentimental romance. Augusta soon "found herself the most popular character on board," and because of her "youth, her beauty, her talent, and her misfortunes . . . Augusta was all of a sudden elevated into the position of a perfect heroine" (84). She is a "popular character" and the "perfect heroine"—but not for a New Woman novel. This subgenre having foundered at sea, Haggard reverts to an adventure plot. Poetically cooperative, the ship also founders: the *Kangaroo* hits a small whaling boat and tears a hole in its own hull. The ship has one thousand people aboard and lifeboats for only three hundred. Panic ensues, but Augusta clearheadedly goes below, saves the Holmhursts' son, and gets into a lifeboat.

Augusta is cast adrift with young Dick Holmhurst, two sailors, and Mr. Meeson. The lifeboat arrives at a small, rainy, deserted island, where Meeson is on the verge of death. Repenting his treatment of his only relative, Meeson wishes to make a new will. But there is no pencil, no paper, not even a scrap of linen to write on. The men eventually decide to tattoo the will on Augusta's back, and Augusta's submission to this painful procedure is rewarded. Although Meeson dies, and the two sailors stumble to their deaths during a night of debauchery, Augusta and Dick are soon rescued. Back in England, Augusta returns Dick to his mother (who also miraculously survived), becomes a national celebrity, and meets with Eustace again, who admits that he fell in love with her the first time he saw her. He proposes; she accepts. They file a suit to override the previous will and the last third of the novel becomes a courtroom drama.

Mr. Meeson's Will, like *Dracula* and *She,* represents the figure of the New Woman without her feminism. Augusta, like Mina and Ayesha, is intelligent and resourceful and can fend for herself when it is necessary. But Haggard goes to great lengths to show that an independent woman cannot truly be happy. Indeed, it is presented as a kind of "eternal Law" (*She* 295) that "the reluctance that some young women show to talking of the possibility of their marriage to the man they happen to have set their hearts on, is only equaled by the alacrity with which they marry him when the time comes" (*Meeson* 157). Indeed, marriage "would be an end to all her worries and troubles. . . . Woman, even gifted woman, is not made to fight the world with her own hand" (90). Like Grant Allen, Haggard finds it unnatural for a woman to choose to live alone. She "is not made" for it.

Augusta's attempt to override the mandate of feminine "nature" leads to her own degeneration: she is "tattooed like a savage" (133). Despite her other appropriately feminine spiritual qualities, this tattoo keeps focusing attention on her savage body. Augusta is presented as Meeson's last will and testament to the Registrar for "inspection of the document" (210). With some consternation, realizing that it "is a painful matter, very, to a person of modest temperament" (211), the Registrar shows Augusta to a small closet where she can "make the necessary preparations" (211). When she begins removing her jacket in front of him, he reacts by thinking: "I supposed she is hardened. . . . I dare say that one gets used to this sort of thing upon desert islands" (212). The hardened woman, undaunted by appearing naked in front of men, is more like a savage than a respectable British lady. Or, rather, she is like a hybrid of the two: Augusta's tattoo is high enough on her back to be visible when she wears a low-cut evening dress.

This hybridity is one of many similarities between Haggard's and Stoker's heroines. Both male authors give over the writer's role to their heroines, and both effect a subsequent narrative attack on her. Mina is branded by the vampire's teeth and by "the mark of shame upon [her] forehead until the Judgment Day" (Stoker 259). Likewise, Haggard constantly stresses the permanent "disfigurement" (253) of the tattoo: a "blot upon her beauty" (261), the tattoo will leave Augusta "scarred for life" (169). The difference is that Mina's "mark of shame" will disappear as if it never existed. Quincey Morris sacrifices himself to take away Mina's scar. His last words, "It was worth this to die!" (326), demonstrate that Mina is returned to a properly "feminine" role—that of a woman who needs a man's protection. His death coincides with Dracula's, and Mina's "mark of shame" vanishes. The subsequent birth of Quincey Harker is evidence that Mina was worthy of the sacrifice; Mina the mother is a true woman and a legitimate recipient of masculine protection. No one sacrifices himself for Augusta, so she is marked forever by the tattoo and by her status as a New Woman. She does not give up her writing the way Mina does (Augusta assures Eustace that a happy marriage is conducive to good work and that "if I can, I will show the world that you have not married a dullard" [267]), and no child arrives to absolve her of her sins of independence.

Garrett Stewart, in *Dear Reader*,[12] argues that Haggard implicitly declares the supremacy of male writing: "After having lashed us to the mast of attention with his shipwreck saga . . . the ranking purveyor in his day of male bravura and masculinist bravado seems almost to bait the reader: So you still want to read a *woman, do you*?" (163). But I read this novel quite differently. For one, *Meeson* does not lash the reader "to the mast of attention" the way *She* does. Moreover, even though Haggard clearly thinks of women's writing as different from men's, he consistently identifies himself with Augusta and her writing. Masculinist bravado thus coexists with "feminine" domesticity, sympathy for women writers alternates with denigration of women's writing, and women's autonomy is affirmed even while its effects are resisted. The result is a narrative whose ruptures register a crisis in gender relations.

Haggard's focus on a woman writer ultimately unmans him, for he increasingly identifies with his "authoress." In several passages, Haggard's omniscient narrator muses on authorship, and it is fairly clear that Haggard is talking about his own career as much as Augusta's. When Haggard writes that "the average Briton has, at heart, a considerable contempt, if not for literature, at least for those who produce it" (66), the reader can almost hear the personal resentment and the still-fresh wound of public disparagement. Despite his great popularity with mass audiences, critics excoriated Haggard's style. Especially after *She* was published (the year before *Mr. Meeson's Will*), critics mocked Haggard's "slipshod and vulgar writing" (A.M.F.R. 72). Augustus Moore asserted that *She* had "no imagination at all, and only bad constructions, bad English, and an idea 'older than any history that is written in any book'" (514). Moore then ridiculed Haggard for having a Cambridge don as the narrator of *She*, pointing out Haggard's meager vocabulary and the fact that Haggard had never attended university.

Accused of plagiarizing the main idea of *Meeson* after its publication in the Summer Number of the *London Illustrated News* (1888), Haggard composed a preface to the bound volume to defend his authority. His anxiety about originality simultaneously registers uneasiness about decadence; Haggard presents a world of exhausted ideas and enervated emotions: "at this period of the world's history, absolute originality has been a little difficult. There's no such thing as a new passion or even a new thought" (xi). In the novel, Haggard soothes his unease about authorial decline by shifting responsibility for literary exhaustion to the publishing industry. Because the "public don't like genius," because "they like their literature dull and holy" (32), publishers grind the originality out of their authors in a quest for profits. Even a promising young author like Augusta is nearly a casualty to this practice.

One might imagine that Haggard would ultimately suppress Augusta and her vocation by having her conform to middle-class dictates about married women's employment—especially since women authors competed directly with Haggard. But in this text consumed by anxiety about authorship and writing, Augusta functions as Haggard's authorial alter ego. Augusta's plotline is Haggard's professional history. Haggard's description of Meeson's predatory practices was also a retaliation against J. and R. Maxwell, with whom he had unknowingly signed an agreement to publish all of his books for five years.[13] (He nullified that agreement, in lieu of litigation, by allowing them to publish *Mr. Meeson's Will* and *Allan's Wife*.) Instead of "out of it," Augusta needs to be in the thick of "it" in order metonymically to set the publishing world, which has unmanned Haggard, to rights. She fights the fight Haggard will not, wins the public and critical support Haggard does not, and writes the novel that Haggard cannot.

And so, Haggard explicitly figures himself as a "lady novelist." Meeson, on his deathbed, makes Augusta into his confessor; he is going to relate all of his misdeeds through his twenty years of rough dealings in the publishing business. But Haggard's narrator intervenes, writing:

> Asterisks, so dear to the heart of the lady novelist, will best represent the confession that followed; words are not equal to the task.
> (141)

*   *   *   *   *

The fact that Haggard says asterisks are "dear to the heart of the lady novelists," and then proceeds to use them, is telling. The phrase itself demeans women writers, implying they write by whim and fancy rather than by reason and adherence to literary standards. Why then would he apply to himself the very tactic he ridicules? He is not ironizing the practice, for he uses asterisks two chapters later as the way to "best represent" Augusta's time aboard the rescue vessel en route to a safe port. And twice again later, asterisks hold the place of events happening off-stage.

Fredric Jameson has described the ideological function of romance fiction this way: "Romance may be seen as an imaginary solution to a real contradiction, a symbolic answer to the question of how my enemy can be thought of as evil (other than me, marked by absolute difference) when what so characterizes him is the identity of his conduct with mine—in points of honor, challenges, tests of strength, he presents a mirror image" (118). Romance as a form accommodates and enables the split ideological affiliations that mark *Mr. Meeson's Will*. Haggard wants to keep the lady novelist "out of it"; after all, she is the competition. But woman has so thoroughly invaded Haggard's psychic territory that he has internalized her. If she prevails, so does he.

Indeed, in this novel, Haggard is as "domestic" as any "lady novelist," having departed almost entirely from the adventure narratives that made him famous. The most exotic character we meet is the outrageously selfish and venal Meeson. The most exotic locale is Kergulen Land, an island characterized by its dismal and rainy (that is, British) climate. True, the castaways survive on penguin eggs, but the potentially exciting and romantic penguins are never physically described, and are represented as so harmless that Dick, a boy of five, can gather their eggs. Moreover, *Meeson* is predictable. From the moment Eustace is first entranced by Augusta's lovely eyes, the "discerning reader" (66) assumes that a marriage is immanent. Except for the wonderfully sardonic treatment of Meeson and the diabolically imaginative depiction of his business, the style of the novel is prosaic. Haggard is too contemptuous of a heroine who is "like all women" to write a New Woman novel and too tied to this image of women to write a woman-centered adventure novel. An adventure heroine "should" be having adventures—meeting strange creatures and overcoming obstacles by cunning and strength—but Augusta is telling stories to a little boy and roasting eggs. Her triumph inheres in her survival, including enduring the mutilating marks of men. *Mr. Meeson's Will* fails as both a New Woman and an adventure narrative, but its failures are deeply suggestive.

Haggard takes and inflicts great pains to subvert the feminism of the New Woman in the novel. The legal document tattooed on Augusta's body marks the end of her independence and the beginning of her service to masculine interests. Instead of an independent agent, she becomes the site and sign of male business transactions. Before the tattooing, she struggled against male domination. Now she agrees to make her latent subjection manifest; she becomes a blank page inscribed by male authority. It is almost as if Haggard needs to punish Augusta for engendering his own decadent decline when he identified with a woman writer. As in *Dracula* and in *She*, the usurping woman is eradicated and a rational male voice takes over. Indeed, even as Mina's and Amenartas's writing were appropriated by men for their own ends, Augusta's writing is channeled into a more acceptable and traditionally feminine avenue. Her final scene of writing involves another sacrifice to the interests of others: she decides to give away two hundred thousand pounds "to found an institution for broken-down authors" (285) and is seen at her writing table at work not on a novel, but on "that scheme [which is] . . . such a boon to the world of scribblers" (286).

In his reading of the novel, Stewart also focuses on the writings of and on Augusta, on the way this popular novelist is quite literally "read" in Haggard's rendering. Stewart suggests that the interested readers of Augusta's tattoo metonymically represent the interested readers of Haggard's novel. Thus Stewart sees Haggard's creation of Augusta as a protofeminist move that explores "the ways in which the female figure in fiction is often reduced to the inscribed body of simulated (because still only textual) spectation, [a] material exhibit for the deciphering masculine voyeur" (157). In other words, "the writing woman as popular novelist finds herself denuded and reduced to the mere figure of public reading" (161).

This is true enough, but Haggard's punning on "will" alerts the reader to a supplementary reading. Haggard most clearly plays with the various meanings of "will" when he has the counsel for the defense allege that "the will had herself procured the will, by an undue projection of her own will upon the unwilling mind of the testator" (221). Here "will" signifies autonomous action, a legal document, feminine ambition, and male resistance. By displaying the complex of meanings bound up in one term, Haggard is staging the disjuncture between social norms and legal rights.

Meeson's male characters and its narrative logic consistently take away Augusta's will while affirming masculine will. Eustace is a worthy hero, despite his mundane job and accomplishments, because he has will—volition. When he sensed "that a great crisis in his fortunes had come"—even though this crisis is when to propose to Augusta—Eustace realizes that a man can employ his resolute will or be a failure as a man: "There are some men who rise to an emergency, and some who shrink from it, and the difference is that difference between the man who succeeds and the man who fails in life, and in all which makes life worth living" (186). But Augusta, after enduring the impress of Mr. Meeson's will, loses her will to follow through with the legal action: "'I do think it is a little hard,' said Augusta, with a stamp of her foot, 'that, after all I have gone through, I should be taken off to have my unfortunate neck stared at by a Doctor some one or other'" (206). She then loses her will altogether and allows herself to be presented *as* the will: "notwithstanding her objections of the previous day, she had at last consented to go" (208).

The law and its fair-minded representatives, however, assert the parity of women's will as a matter of justice. Augusta must have as much right to speak and be heard as any man, because to refuse her, says the judge, would "be contrary to equity and good policy, for persons cannot so lightly be deprived of their natural rights" (245). A woman's right to equality under the law is again affirmed by Doctor Probate, who must rule on how Mr. Meeson's unusual will can be filed. In his decision, he affirms that "it is clear that I cannot put any restraint upon the liberty of the subject. . . . I doubt if it would be possible to do so by any means short of an Act of Parliament" (213).

The unprincipled counsel for the defense, however, argues that Augusta cannot testify in court because she is merely a document to be read: "A document is a thing which speaks by its written characters. It cannot take to itself a tongue and speak by word of mouth also; and in support of this, I may call your Lordship's attention to the general principles of law governing the interpretation of written documents" (244). The defense, however, loses its case. The judge refuses to accept that "the personality of Miss Smithers" is "so totally lost and merged in . . . her documentary capacity as to take away from her the right to appear before this Court like any other sane human being" (244). Augusta *is* a document, to be sure, but she nonetheless retains her individuality. *Mr. Meeson's Will* continually plays on the various meanings of will (Augusta signed the contract with Meeson "of [her] own free will" [27], for instance), so it is significant that even though she is a will, her status as a human with a will of her own is repeatedly recognized. Nonetheless, Augusta also has a man's will indelibly marked on her. And in the end, the man's will is stronger.

Thus do male adventure writers take the New Woman in and swallow her whole, absorbing all that can be converted to their own use and eliminating all that is toxic to their sense of self. These authors are colonizing the New Woman in order to conquer her savage nature. Like the strong but barbarous primitive, a woman with authority menaces masculinity and imperils imperialism. These male authors thus play the part of the missionary who will welcome the outsider in to his religious rites, but only for the purposes of conversion. The other must accept his doctrines and recite his creeds; the woman must consent to domesticity and bear a child.

Because adventure tropes are so thoroughly naturalized in the nineteenth-century imaginary (of course the men work to protect Mina; of course they have full confidence in their knowledge systems; of course they stake Lucy through the heart, cut the heads off three other vampire women, and hunt down Count Dracula even after his return to Transylvania), it can be hard to imagine an alternative. As Rhoda Nunn and Everard Barfoot discovered in *The Odd Women*, cultural scripts are difficult to rewrite. But Haggard's and Stoker's narrative interpellations of the New Woman do not represent the only possibilities for generic boundary crossing. As we will see in the next chapter, Flora Annie Steel blends New Woman ideology with adventure tropes to create a New Woman adventure novel—a novel that puts these tropes in the service of feminist ideals.

"Aboriginal" Interventions

The New Woman Adventure Novel

A review of Flora Annie Steel's *In the Permanent Way*, a collection of stories published one year after her best-selling novel *On the Face of the Waters* (1896), asserts that "No writer—not even Mr. Kipling—knows the life of the mixed population of the Anglo-Indian empire better than the author of *On the Face of the Waters*" (398). The evocation of Rudyard Kipling here is predictable and unsurprising, but the assumption of equal familiarity with Steel's work speaks volumes about the effect of canon formation on literary history. While Kipling has become virtually synonymous with literary representations of British colonial rule, Flora Annie Steel (1847–1929) has all but disappeared from the canon of writers on empire. And yet no writer—not even Mr. Kipling—can tell us as much about the ideological work of competing fin de siècle literary genres, the intersection of colonial and patriarchal discourses, or the conflicted role of white women in the imperial project. This chapter will focus on the first of these issues, with frequent references to the latter two. Most commonly classified as an adventure novel, *On the Face of the Waters* demonstrates the confluence of late-century popular genres by embracing Indian romance, colonial adventure, and New Woman tropes. Steel's novel not only ranges beyond the boundaries of adventure fiction, but New Woman concerns ultimately trump adventure ideals in it. Indeed, *On the Face of the Waters* becomes a New Woman novel by co-opting adventure novel tropes: the protagonist Kate becomes like Kipling's Kim, in disguise, speaking Hindi, mixing with Indians—but in order to effect feminist rather than imperial understanding.[1]

In the last chapter, we saw how male adventure novelists appropriated New Woman tropes and themes to produce a hybrid genre that ultimately served masculine interests. *On the Face of the Waters*, which represents Steel's fraught negotiation of the models presented by colonial adventure writers and New Woman novelists, has more complex affiliations than *Dracula*, *She*, or *Mr. Meeson's Will*. The reviewer for the *Pall Mall Gazette* writes of *On the*

Face of the Waters that "Mrs. Steel has beaten Mr. Kipling on his own ground, India." The martial metaphor implies an adventure novel plot, which is driven by the need to subdue a competitor and conquer another's territory. *The Daily Chronicle*'s effusion that "Mrs. Steel gets fairly inside the Indian's skin, and looks out upon the life of that troublous fiery time through Indian eyes" indicates the conflicted interests produced by the novel's generic hybridity.[2] Getting inside the other's skin represents an extreme form of colonization—colonizing the other's body, his very self. In contrast, looking through Indian eyes subordinates Steel's English eyes and her necessarily partial, partisan point of view. It represents a profound attempt at understanding, a way of putting one's self in another's place.

Genre affiliations are thus central to an analysis of Steel's significance. *On the Face of the Waters* is set in India at the time of the Indian Mutiny of 1857, and features exotic situations, brave soldiers, and daring heroes. The dashing Jim Douglas, with the aid of his Indian servant Tara and her brother Soma, protects Kate Erlton in besieged Delhi. Kate's philandering husband has seen his mistress Alice Gissing killed by an Indian religious fanatic, and he waits on the ridge above Delhi with the army for the opportunity to retake the city in a final climatic battle. But *On the Face of the Waters* is not quite an adventure novel. While it resembles Kipling's *Kim* (1901) in important ways—Jim is a spy with a gift for disguise; Steel, like Kipling, describes Indian life close-up—it lacks a single protagonist who is identified as the locus of adventure, of power, of Western values. Moreover, many of Steel's women characters are like New Women: independent, rebellious, critical of prevailing gender and sexual codes (although, since the novel is set in 1859, they are not so named).

Genre Trouble Before Steel: *The Story of an African Farm*

The generic complexity of *On the Face of the Waters* can be understood by comparing it to its more famous counterpart and predecessor: Olive Schreiner's *The Story of an African Farm* (1883). *African Farm* is in many ways an adventure novel. As in most colonial romances, Schreiner literalizes a topology of adventure: the majesty of the South African karoo reflects Lyndall's striving spirit; its isolation reflects her singularity; its desolation reflects the hardships she undergoes. The novel is also very much a quest: it is the story of Lyndall's struggle to achieve autonomy. Like the traditional adventure hero, she is a lone actor who must go her own way regardless of the dictates of conventional society. Lyndall's superiority to her peers does not, however, involve the bloodshed and warfare that the traditional adventure hero experiences. More typical is G. A. Henty's Dick Humphries in *The Young Colonists* (1880), who becomes involved in the 1877–78 skirmishes that accompany Britain's annexation of the Transvaal; or the heroes of Rider Haggard's *Kings Solomon's Mines* and *Allan Quartermain*, who incite civil war; or the heroes of *She*, who kill natives with guns, spears, and—when necessary—their bare hands.

Classifying *African Farm* solely as a tale of adventure, however, fails to account for its complexities. While adventure novels typically focus on a larger-than-life hero, *African Farm* is not restricted to a single sensibility: Schreiner focuses on Waldo's existential crises as much as Lyndall's emergent feminist consciousness. By means of these multiple perspectives Schreiner resists the tendency of the colonial adventure novel to unite its characters in ideological solidarity. Indeed, Schreiner's characters do not necessarily identify with the British public and British pride.[3] Lyndall does not hunt wild beasts or kill Africans; but by going off to school, traveling, and becoming romantically involved with a man without her guardian's consent, she is undertaking an adventure. Jan Cohn argues just this point in her analysis of women's popular romance novels: "it is possible and useful to see the romance heroine as the 'hero' of a particularly contemporary form of traditional romance, a form produced specifically to answer the otherwise unanswerable questions posed by women as a subordinated class. Popular romance, from this point of view, is the story of the heroine's quest" (19). Things men take for granted—freedom to travel unchaperoned, freedom to flout the conventions of society, freedom from the sexual double standard—constitute adventure for women who are generally much less free than men to do as they please.

Because of Lyndall's extraordinary character and strength of mind—those qualities that help make her an ideal adventure heroine—she has no need of great physical strength. She possesses a certain unexplained moral power. Tant Sannie ceases beating Em when Lyndall lays a restraining hand on her; and when Lyndall demands that Blenkins move aside, "Bonaparte the invincible, in the hour of his triumph, moved to give her place" (57). This power is not necessarily *racial*, for Em does not share it. Nonetheless, Western racial hierarchies obtain: even Em, with her poor self-image, her vulnerability to Tant Sannie's rages, and her grotesque body, does not share the subject position of the Kaffir woman. The poorest white woman has opportunities the native does not. If nothing else, she is immune from the inborn debilities that accompany dark skin in the eyes of the Boers and the British.

Like most male adventure writers, Schreiner is unconcerned with representing "native" subjectivity. When natives do appear, they are presented as utterly different from the whites. Lyndall is elfin, beautiful, intelligent, independent, articulate. The "Kaffir woman" (52), the "herd's wife" (50), remains unnamed: her identity is restricted to her race or her position in the patriarchal structure. A "sullen, ill-looking woman, with lips hideously protruding" (52), she is nothing more than a spectacle, a naked "black body" without insight, emotion, or humanity. Otto is the only white who treats her as a human being, for it "was not his way to pass a living creature without a word of greeting" (53). Discovering the exiled herd's wife, he offers his own coat as protection from the cold and gives her his remaining food. But unlike the virtuous Lyndall, who rails at the injustice Tant Sannie inflicts on Otto, the Kaffir woman turns against him, laughing at his misfortune (which echoes her own: both were exiled from the farm by Tant Sannie) and encouraging Tant Sannie in her harshness: "Give it him, old missis! Give it him!" (56). The text then glosses the Kaffir woman's thoughts: "It was so nice to see the white man who had been master hunted down" (56). Here it is revealed that colonizing practices themselves make the woman so unfeeling. When the "master" is himself mastered, she hopefully imagines that the master's masters may one day also be overthrown.[4]

To a degree, Lyndall can understand the oppression of the native African, for she too feels oppressed by Tant Sannie and Blenkins. This understanding makes her a champion of the powerless, a protector of the weak. Chafing under Blenkins's domination, she declares that one day, when "I am strong, I will hate everything that has power and help everything that is weak" (59–60). Her child's mind does not register the contradiction: when she has strength enough to help the weak, she will be among those she professes to hate, those with power. Lyndall's conceptual difficulties exemplify the position of women in empire-building. As women they occupy the place of the weak in the patriarchal system; as colonizers, they are themselves the hated power.[5]

Schreiner represents, without resolving, the double bind experienced by English women under the rule of empire and patriarchy. But her sympathetic portrayal of female agency led antifeminists like William Barry to liken the New Woman to the primitive "other" in need of colonial control. Writing in the *Quarterly Review*, Barry argues that New Women novelists "betray the savage element glorified by Diderot" (295), and describes feminism and atavism as intimately intertwined "instincts" (296). Indeed, writes Barry, the New Woman's sentiments are not so much "original" as "aboriginal" (295). "Aboriginal" becomes Barry's epithet for those who would challenge the traditional roles of women, an ideological move that mirrors the adventure novelists' objectification of New Woman characters as "savage." What Barry does not ask about their "aboriginal" claims is how they are related to the claims for independence made by native peoples colonized by British imperial forces. This relationship is central to *On the Face of the Waters*.

Reading and Misreading Genre

Although *On the Face of the Waters* does not quite fit the profile of a colonial adventure novel, recent criticism claims it does, which leads to charges that Steel's novel is not only imperialist but also racist. If Jim were the hero in a colonial adventure novel, then the criticisms of Benita Parry, Nancy Paxton, and Rebecca Saunders would be credible. But Steel's novel does not support these readings. Fredric Jameson usefully cautions that "genre is . . . immanently and intrinsically an ideology in its own right" (141) and categorizing a literary work as "wholly this" or "wholly that" represents a *decision* to define a text in opposition to other genres (142). These categories are useful only as long as they are understood as provisional and constructed. When the category becomes reified, the ideological dictates of the genre can obscure other competing voices and ideological forces. Readers expecting a colonial adventure novel are unable fully to understand Jim, for adventure novels tend to be unsubtle in their ideological affiliations, and they seldom require the reader to analyze and judge statements made by their heroes. Jim Douglas functions the way an unreliable narrator would: he says things that are sometimes accurate, sometimes self-serving; he expresses contradictory convictions; he often gives explanations of events that are partial, limited by his viewpoint and subject position.

Benita Parry demonstrates how the adventure paradigm can colonize a reader's reactions to a novel when she claims that the struggle in *On the Face of the Waters* is "between 'aimless, invertebrate discontent' and 'law and order,' as savagery challenges civilization" (119). To be sure, Jim does use the offensive description "aimless, invertebrate discontent" to refer to the sepoys' (in)actions. But the novel's events prove not only that his characterization of the Indian soldiers is wrong, but that his analysis of how events will play out is mistaken as well. Moreover, Jim's harsh words refer to a specific situation, not to some conception of the Indian national character. He is annoyed at being proved wrong, and he repeatedly responds with invective when angry. He had told the British commanders that they had not yet seen a serious insurgency because India's Hindu and Muslim populations were so divided against each other that they would not unite against a common enemy. But the beef and pig tallow rumored to be in the new gun cartridges were abhorrent to members of both religions, and Jim is sure that this development will bring on a mutiny (141). This is why he declares it "d—d inconceivable folly and tyranny" (170) on the part of the British leadership when eighty-five sepoys are put before the court-martial and sentenced to ten years hard labor for refusing to fire the new cartridges.

The eighty-five are shackled in front of the assembled native troops, however, and still the sepoys obey their British officers. Jim's initial anger is at the British army officers: "this business has strained the loyalty of the most loyal to the uttermost; and we deserve to suffer, we do indeed" (171). The insistent superiority of the generals infuriates him: "Why can't we admit boldly . . . that the cartridges are suspicious? That they leave the muzzle covered with a fat, like tallow?" (171). Though Jim himself indulges in this British superiority when he calls the Indians "children—simple, ignorant, obstinate" (192), this is not an example of Steel's racism; it illustrates her continual emphasis on his mistaken judgments.

Jim's sympathy for the sepoys turns to anger at them when they "fail" to react to injustice the way he would. The troops quiescently watch their comrades being shackled; they march the prisoners off toward the stockade without incident. When they reach the jail without an uprising, Jim is disgusted:

> If this intolerable tyranny failed to rouse action there could be no immediate danger ahead . . . he felt that a handful of resolute men ought to be able to hold their own against such aimless invertebrate discontent. He felt a vague disappointment that it should be so. . . . They were a poor lot who could do nothing but talk! (173)

At this moment, his assessment appears high-handed. But it ultimately reflects back on the British. The sepoys do rebel[6] and the British fail to act for several days. Instead of fighting the rebels, British officers sound the retreat in order to insure the safety of the European cantonments. All is quiet there, but the British soldiers remain on the parade ground all night (200). The men talk of action, but they do not act; their officers will not permit it, even refusing requests to ride the thirty miles to Delhi to give warning of the unchecked rebellious sepoys headed their way. We discover that it is the British who are "a poor lot who could do nothing but talk!"

With no information about the state of affairs in Meerut, the British army in Delhi "was paralyzed by that straining of the eyes for a cloud of dust upon the Meerut" hoping for help or news. Kate, a "mere woman," is "weary of the deadly inaction" (251), and the British men fail to act on their opportunities: "the long hours had dragged by uselessly" (253). Indeed, when troops are finally assembled to retake Delhi, it is nearly *four months* after the initial uprising at Meerut. Even at the end of the century, this was not the accepted version of events. A. C. Lyall's *Edinburgh Review* essay castigates Steel's fictional account of "serious history" because it is not flattering to the British national character: "She very plainly intimates that nothing but culpable inaction and want of energy prevent instant pursuit by a force from Meerut of the mutineers" (430).

Steel's narrative strategy is especially evident in a passage where she refers to British "Men" and Indian "Murderers." The narrator relates how the British troops finally attack Delhi after having the city under siege for four months: *"to the three thousand marching upon Delhi that cool dewy night . . .* there were but two things to be reckoned with in the wide world: Themselves—Men. Those others—Murderers" (307; italics mine). Steel clearly indicates that she is recording the thoughts of *"the three thousand marching upon Delhi,"* but she is often misunderstood because she employs free indirect discourse. Benita Parry quotes this "men/murderers" section to prove that Steel believes that the mutineers are savage, aggressive criminals (120). But again, this is not Steel's viewpoint, nor does she represent it as a justified, virtuous, or commendable one. Steel's intention is dialogic; she orchestrates multiple voices, or, to use the metaphor she adopts in her introduction, she is the recording camera rather than the partisan analyst.

Saunders suggests that passages such as these reveal "the lurid quality of Steel's writing" (314). The passage Saunders highlights, however, represents the anguished thoughts of the young soldier Mainwaring at Alice Gissing's death. Steel demonstrates that Mainwaring (who naively believed Alice a model of angelic virtue) feels the need to avenge Alice's death; but Steel herself is not advocating revenge. She continually stresses that atrocities are committed on both sides. Patrick Brantlinger avoids these bald misreadings, noting that "Steel enters into the thoughts and feelings of a variety of characters, both British and Indian, often without maintaining a distinct narrative voice. It is therefore not always possible to separate her judgments from those of her characters" (*Rule of Darkness* 220–21). But reading with an eye toward other genre affiliations makes it possible to read Steel's representations of opposing views as part of her narrative strategy rather than a narrative defect.

Steel's harshest critics seek proofs of her imperialistic tendencies in two nonfictional sources: her autobiography *The Garden of Fidelity* and the co-authored *The Complete Indian Housekeeper and Cook, and Practical Recipes for Cooking in all its Branches* (with Grace Gardener). But the deployment of this evidence often betrays insensitivity to genre. A book that proposes to promote understanding between the races will not have the same tone or intentions as one purporting to help Anglo-Indian women manage their Indian servants. That Steel recommends a "high-handed dignity in dealing with those who for thousands of years have been accustomed to it" (*The Garden of Fidelity* 133) does not reflect well on Steel, but neither does it provide sufficient evidence that Steel's *novels* recommend a "high-handed dignity" with Indians.

Rosemary George discusses the female Indian romances as if they were ideologically and generically identical to Steel's novels. Her primary argument is that the "lady novelists" of India— she singles out Maud Diver, Alice Perrin, and Steel—represent women's complicity with the imperial project through their authoritative tone and their characters' racial superiority:

> What is remarkable about these novels and guidebooks is the confidence of the female authorial voice. The ideological proximity of this genre with the other discourses of imperialism constructs 'the Englishwoman'—a female subject who is firmly anchored as a 'full individual' through her racial privileges. . . . [T]heir writing represents a coherent, unified bourgeois subjecthood. (61)

But are other novelists less confident? Does George Eliot have a less authoritative authorial voice? Edward Said, in *Culture and Imperialism*, extends George's argument to novels in general: "imperialism and the novel fortified each other to such a degree that it is impossible . . . to read one without in some way dealing with the other" (71) because of the "convergence between the patterns of narrative authority constitutive of the novel . . . and . . . a complex ideological configuration underlying the tendency to imperialism" (70). Steel's novels are imperialistic in the sense that the novel's narrative mode encodes imperial precepts, and they represent a "unified bourgeois subject-hood" to the same extent as most nineteenth-century novels do.

Steel's representations of racial difference are actually *less* mired in images of British superiority and dark-skinned degradation than a novel like William Makepeace Thackeray's *Vanity Fair*. *Vanity Fair's* casual racism, its way of expressing racial stereotypes to comic effect, its Sambos and Schwartzes, represent a level of British imperial racism far beyond that of *On the Face of the Waters*. Steel's novel is, unarguably, compromised by her limited vision of other races, her Western perceptions of Indian philosophy and society, her pride in the work of empire to educate, to influence, and to effect what she saw as progress. But Kate's subjectivity is less "firmly anchored" in her identity as a British woman who is superior to women of color than George suggests. Her coming to full consciousness of her powers is based in her interaction *with* Indians, not in her control *over* them.

Enlisting Nancy Armstrong's assertion that "such writing as the [eighteenth-century] conduct books helped to generate the belief that there was such a thing as a middle class with clearly established affiliations before it actually existed," George argues that reading the following century's Indian romances and guidebooks establishes that "the modern *politically authoritative* Englishwoman was made in the colonies: she was first and foremost an imperialist" (37). In essence, because she represents herself as such, the memsahib in India *is* politically empowered and authoritative. This is a problematic assertion, however, because women had no institutionalized political power, they were largely dependent on their husbands, and the freedoms of Anglo-Indian society also involved a great deal of constraint.

Antoinette Burton points out that one of the tropes that British feminists invoked to demonstrate Indian women's debasement was the zenana or harem: "Seclusion was thought to be the equivalent of degradation, and harem life 'dull and vacuous to the last degree'" (66). Ironically, British women were in their own kind of zenana, secluded from Indian society, shuttled off to hill stations in hot weather, barred from mixing in general Indian society. The stereotypical image of the memsahib is a "small-minded, social snob who tyrannically rules over a household of servants and refuses to associate with Indians" (Sharpe 91). British men, in striving to protect "their" women from

Indian culture, confined women to the home with little to do (without even children to care for) and thus impelled them into the superficial, flirtatious, frivolous behaviors for which they then criticized the stereotypical memsahib for exhibiting. Like the supposedly "dull and vacuous" Indian women, British women in India were said to spend their days with other women in intrigues, idleness, and gossip. Whatever authority over Indians they possessed was accompanied by a great measure of imposed restriction.

We can gain a clearer picture of Steel's aims by focusing on what is generally absent from both New Woman and colonial adventure fictions: native women, and the Englishwoman's relationship to them. Steel's treatment of the Indian widow Tara Devi, as Sharpe argues, proves that she is too involved with Western feminism's idealization of individual agency. Sharpe claims that Tara, as subject of sati, occupies the "space of death," while the British women who survive the Mutiny come through that space of death to find agency and empowerment. Sharpe writes that "The tropological value of sati lies in its efficacy as an icon for domestic subjugation. It permits Steel both to establish English woman's agency and to protect the domestic model through which the racial superiority of the colonizers was reaffirmed" (102). To be sure, Western women tend to see power in terms of individual power, agency in terms of individuation. But Steel does not point out parallels with all women's "domestic subjugation" only to prove that British women are superior. Indeed, Steel demonstrates a broader basis for their joint action.

British and Indian women share a similar ideologic function in relation to men. Jenny Sharpe notes that notions of women's honor are central to both cultures, and that both reflect on masculine identity: "Both British and Hindu codes venerate womanhood as an institution to the extent of devaluing women's lives" (102). British ideals of death before dishonor and the Hindu practice of sati means that women prove their worth—and the nation's valor—by dying. Indeed, to a lesser extent, Kate sacrifices herself to her husband in order to conform to the ideal of feminine domestic virtue. Ironically, British domestic virtue produces what amounts to a pagan religion, one that is not god-centered but husband centered. Kate's "cult of home was a religion to her" (22), but she does not even have the satisfaction of truly believing in it. Her salvation, her way of coping with her intolerable situation, is her attempt to convince herself that she does believe. The "civilized" pressure to conform to social customs is as strong as the supposedly savage pressure that compels

Tara to burn on her husband's funeral pyre. The disjuncture between women's actions and their beliefs is embodied in Tara's willingness passively to accept her fate as sati only because she is drugged by her family. Jim Douglas pulls her off the pyre, however, and she suffers the same longstanding torment of daily life that Kate Erlton does. She stifles all emotion and thought of a future in order to live through the present.

Tara and Kate have more in common than their self-abnegation. Most critics, however, claim that Tara and Kate function as opposites, with Tara's Indian sensuality playing off Kate's British reserve. Saunders's comment that "In contrast to Tara's sexuality is Kate's transcendence of it" (312) is misleading, because Steel goes to great lengths to demonstrate how alike Tara and Kate are in their repressed sexuality. Tara is largely desexualized: as a widow, she remains true to her husband's memory by denying herself. Like Kate, who "refused to admit the claims or rights of passion" (234), Tara's "cry of suttee" is her call to self-repression. Tara can quell the desire roused by the lovemaking between Jim and his Indian wife Zora with this cry; she can deny passion easily.

Steel's Indian women are not uniformly obsessed with sexuality and passion (as her critics charge). But Tara does find it difficult to distance herself from the companionship, comradery, and easy contact between Jim and Kate. Zora never engaged with Jim "as an equal," as Kate does. "And, strangely enough, the familiar companionship—inevitable under the circumstances— roused her jealousy more than the love-making on that other terraced roof had done. *That* she understood. *That* she could crush with the cry of suttee. But *this*—this which to her real development seemed so utterly desirable; what did it mean?" (347). Tara's heart aches at her separation from male companionship, when it did not ache at her lack of physical passion. Tara's sexuality is not so much at issue here as is her desire to transcend it.

The eventual emergence of Kate's sexuality (long denied due to her abhorrence of her husband) shifts her symbolic affiliation from Tara to Zora. Jim's plan is for Kate to "pass as his wife—his sick wife, hidden, as Zora had been, on some terraced roof" (281). Although she initially balks at his request to wear Indian dress and jewelry, her connection with Zora is established as soon as Jim puts one of Zora's bracelets on her: he attaches a "gold fetter" to her wrist and she feels an "odd thrill" (285) of sexual attraction. Jim recognizes an affinity with Zora in Kate's interest in dress and appearance. She "wished so much for a looking-glass just now, to see how I looked in" native dress that Jim "felt an odd resentment in recognizing that Zora would have said the words as frankly" (284). The women are so alike in some respects that he has a "vague feeling he had done all this before" (284).

Alice Gissing, too, is likened to Zora. Both lose a child in its infancy, both are sexually uninhibited, and both are "bought" by men. Zora is literally bought by Jim from "a house of ill-fame, as he would have bought a horse, or a flower-pot, or anything else which he thought would make life pleasanter to him" (28). Alice found "wealth in the person of Mr. Gissing" (53) after the death of her first husband, whom she chose for the "good looks which had attracted her" (53). Alice, like Zora, cannot understand the social dictates that admonish her for employing her "knack of making most men happy" (229). She remains "strangely, inconceivably unsoiled" (56) by the so-called sin in which she participates; Zora, unmarried but sexually active, "was a good woman for all that" (285).[7]

Saunders writes that Alice must be killed because "Steel here is as much the tool of imperialism as any memsahib. Alice is sacrificed to women's larger role of helping Englishmen control Indians. The sacrifice of Alice shows an urge for women to deny their victim status and identify with men" (314) rather than celebrate their personal freedom. But actually, Alice is sacrificed to prove that she is, and always has been, a good woman (despite what conventional morality might deem her). Her death further suggests that her culture cannot accommodate the new morality suggested by her character. Although she is a married woman, pregnant by another woman's husband, she is not portrayed as evil, morally corrupt, or contagious. There is no course of action she can take without causing damage to some innocent party, however. Like many New Woman novels, social attitudes conflict with new roles, so there is no "happy" ending possible for women who defy conventions.

On the Face of the Waters effects a brutal representation of race relations, but Steel's perspective is realistic rather than racist: she acknowledges the seemingly insuperable racial conflict between the British and the Indians. Erlton, when out driving with Alice, accidentally strikes and kills an Indian child with his horse. Alice responds that she "should have been much sorrier if it had been a white baby" (63). When the doctor withholds assent, she replies, "People say, of course that it is wicked not to feel the same toward people whether they're black or white. But we don't. And they don't either" (63). Alice cuts off his "sententious" (64) answer, asking "I wonder what your wife would say if she saw me driving in your dog-cart?" (64). The doctor is stymied, because "The one problem was as unanswerable as the other" (64). Sexual associations, like racial prejudices, are fraught with contradiction and self-deception. The doctor's attempt to deny the racism that underlies British-Indian relations is as deluded as a claim that a woman with Alice's reputation is fully accepted by the other British women. Steel does not see a solution on the horizon, although her quest for mutual understanding, respect, and toleration will go a long way toward realizing the goal of racial and sexual equality.

Even Jim Douglas, flawed as he is, realizes that differences between the British and the Indians are cultural rather than racial. He wants to father a white boy not because the child will resemble him physically, but because it will resemble him culturally. A white boy would be educated in English institutions, mix in English society, and would thus "inherit familiar virtues and vices, instead of strange ones" (357). Jim knows full well that both nations have their full share of virtues and vices. The British are not superior in their behavior; their behavior is merely familiar.

On the Face of the Waters as Adventure Romance

White women's relationship to empire is at the heart of recent discussions of Steel's *On the Face of the Waters*, and the question of genre, which these discussions oversimplify, is central to understanding this complex relationship. The vast number of late-century Indian romances, written mostly by women, represent India as "an exotic backdrop to tales of love and improbable adventures" (Parry 70). Bhupal Singh, in *A Survey of Anglo-Indian Fiction* (1934), notes that the Indian romance, a "novel of Anglo-Indian life" (2), features a female protagonist who arrives in India, has picturesque escapades in the Indian landscape, becomes involved in the machinations of Anglo-Indian society, and achieves an end to her travails "in a happy marriage" (2).[8] Like a New Woman, the heroine of the Anglo-Indian novel is "spirited," "courageous," and "can talk well" (3). But this heroine is generally "a mere puppet" (3), because the real interest of the story lies not in her character but in the depictions of Anglo-Indian society.[9]

On the Face of the Waters shares a focus on love and adventure with the Indian romance novels popularized by Maud Diver, Alice Perrin, Mrs. F.C.F. Penny, Mrs. B. M. Croker, and I.A.R. Wylie, but it does not otherwise conform to the dictates of the genre. Benita Parry discusses the "Indian Romancers" and denigrates their writings to such a degree that she usually refers to their works as "novelettes" rather than as novels (70 passim). Significantly, she separates Steel's works from the "novelettes," despite her distaste for Steel's "confident and opinionated voice," her "assured self-righteousness," and "her obsessions about Indian sexuality and the pervasive weirdness of ordinary life in India" (102). Unlike most Indian romances, *On the Face of the Waters* makes India the focus of the story and foregrounds the lives and actions of Indian characters. Rather than dwelling on Anglo-Indian society and the romantic intrigues of the hill-station, Steel highlights the relationships between Indians and the British.

    On the Face of the Waters displays the hallmarks of an adventure novel in its setting as well as its battle scenes—featuring bloody skirmishes, cannon fire, and the brave exploits of soldiers trying to hold the fort. Moreover, the male protagonists love battle for battle's sake: like Rider Haggard's heroes, they feel that fighting and prevailing is what men do. When immortal Ayesha, anxious to protect her mortal lover, suggests that Leo stay safe at home while Holly goes out to fight, Leo is moved "to absolute rage" at the idea, because he is "a man brave to rashness, who, although he disapproved of it in theory, loved fighting for its own sake" (*Ayesha* 305). Likewise, *On the Face of the Water's* battles and struggles for survival test the mettle of the men—and women— just as adventure is supposed to do. (Indeed, because novels of the 1857 Indian Mutiny were so popular at the end of the century, there is an entire subgenre of colonial adventure devoted to this event.)[10]

    Like many colonial adventure novels that purport to be nonfiction, *On the Face of the Waters* makes claims to be a "scrupulously exact" example of "pure history" (v). Steel claims that "I have not allowed fiction to interfere with fact in the slightest degree" (v). Most claims of documentary fact in adventure novels are meant to assure the reader that the hero really *is* as stalwart as the narrative demands him to be, that his adventures are within the realm of the possible, and that the British national character possesses the mettle necessary to rule the empire. Significantly, Steel writes in her preface that her goal in writing from the historical record is to engender forgiveness: she has "tried to give a photograph—that is, a picture in which the differentiation caused by color is left out—of a time which neither the fair race or the dark race is ever likely to quite forget or forgive" (vi). Her hope is that the novel may bring each party understanding of the other, even if the events cannot entirely be forgotten.

Most adventure novels assume an exclusively British audience (with the possible exception of Kipling, whose audience was Anglo-Indian, rather than British or native Indian) and seek to educate the men of England in the responsibilities of rule. Haggard dedicates *Allan Quartermain* to his son "in the hope that in days to come he, and many others boys whom I shall never know, may, in the acts and thoughts of Allan Quartermain and his companions, as herein recorded, find something to help him and them to reach to what, with Sir Henry Curtis, I hold to be the highest rank whereto we can attain—the state and dignity of English gentlemen." But as the *Fortnightly's* reviewer cautions, the adventure novel's "gloating delight in details of carnage and horror and ferocity for their own ghastly sake" ("The Fall of Fiction" 325) might not provide the example all parents would want for their sons. This, however, was a minority position. In an article called "The 'Imperialism' of Kipling and Stevenson," a *Review of Reviews* editor argues that "the influence of the popular novelist in molding the public sentiment is usually underestimated" (466). The reviewer invests the adventure novel with profound cultural influence: "No other force in our time is so subtle, so powerful, and so far-reaching in causing millions of persons unconsciously to adopt the same ideals about certain courses of action" (466). Haggard and the *Review of Reviews* clearly see this as a good and just revival of the British fighting spirit. The audience of Englishmen-in-training, it seems, favored carnage and domination. Steel, who imagines Indians will read and appreciate her work, refrains from celebratory scenes of their massacre.

Generic Hybridity, Multiple Perspectives

Like *The Story of an African Farm*, *On the Face of the Waters* neither advances a specifically British authority nor focuses on one single character's consciousness. Steel tries to represent Indian subjectivity, an example of other-identification that contemporary reviewers often resented. Faulting Steel for "crowding her canvas" with Indians, one writer claimed that "their talk, their distinctive peculiarities of character and costume, their parts in the great tragedy which is taken as the ground plan of her story, are so abundantly described as occasionally to bewilder the inexperienced reader" (Lyall 428–29).

While this representation of Indian ways sets Steel apart from other adventure novelists, she nonetheless oscillates between racial pride and racial understanding. She is caught in an ideological double bind: when she speaks in the voice of the Englishman (or woman) she is accused of racist, imperialist attitudes; when she speaks in the voice of the Indian, she is accused of misunderstanding Indian culture or of colonizing the other. The question is not really "Is Steel imperialistic or racist?," for even the Victorians most able to think outside of accepted constructs often betrayed their own racist ideology (from condescending assumptions about the "noble savage" to advocacy of racial eugenics). The more productive question is how Steel orchestrates the multiple perspectives she attempts to represent in her novel, eschewing a single, race-specific perspective.

Steel's position as a woman, whose early childhood experiences made her aware of the iniquities of strict gender roles, likely made her more receptive to the iniquities of oppressive racial categories. Nonetheless, she remains a product of her culture and, like Haggard and Kipling, displays unconscious racism in her fiction. Less reductive than her male counterparts, however, Steel's negative characterizations are countered by images of Indians who are true to their beliefs, brave, compassionate, and intent on doing their duty. Like the British characters, they have flaws, hold prejudiced attitudes, and make mistakes in judgment. Neither race is wholly "good" nor wholly "bad."

In *The Story of an African Farm*, Schreiner presents African characters as negative stereotypes. Nonetheless, her novel expresses a sense of equivalence between the Africans and the colonists. Looking at cave paintings causes Waldo to see himself in conjunction with an unknown African artist. Like Waldo, this artist "was different from the rest" (16) because of his need to express himself. Waldo also expresses cultural relativism rather than Western superiority: "To us they are only strange things, that make us laugh; but to him they were very beautiful" (16). Steel's belief in British superiority, too, is mitigated—in her case by her respect for Indian culture and by her certainty that some aspects of Indian culture are indeed superior. In an 1897 interview, Steel expressed her ambivalence about British missionary influence in India, declaring, "I do not honestly think we have much right to thrust our nineteenth-century religion, with the civilization which it has called into existence, down the throats of a nation which in many ways seems to me more moral than we are" ("An Anglo-Indian Novelist" 348–49).

In the very first pages of the novel, Steel makes clear that both Indian and British perspectives will be represented. She opens the novel with an event that was, for her, the first step on the road to mutiny: the British annexation of Oude. Indians and Englishmen observe the auction of the deposed King of Oude's household goods; the British are smug and the Indians embittered. The English bystanders believe, in their insular fashion, that

> The King, for some reason satisfactory to the authorities, had been ex-iled, majesty being thus vested in the representatives of the annexing race: thus, in themselves. A position which comes naturally to most Englishmen. (2–3)

The situation "was simple also" to the Indians observing the auction:

> The King, for some unsatisfactory reason, had been ousted from his own. His goods and chattels were being sold. The valuable ones had been knocked down, for a mere song—just to keep up the farce of a sale—to the Huzoors. The rubbish—lame elephants and such like—was being sold to them. (3)

Steel makes it clear that the Indians, far from being grateful for British rule, feel that they are being sold a bill of goods—or, more accurately, a pile of rubbish.

Moreover, Steel represents misunderstandings between British and Indian characters in a way that shows not that one is right and one is wrong, but that each has different reasons for thinking the ways she does. For instance, when the fighting in Delhi escalates, Kate wonders at Tara's calm: "Did she not know that *brave men on both sides* were going to their deaths?" (312). For her part, Tara wonders that Kate, because she has given birth and seen life enter the world, should be so anxious about the possibility of death: "Did not the Great Wheel spin unceasingly? Let brave men, then, die bravely" (213). Even if this is a somewhat reductive version of "Eastern" and "Western" philoso-phies, it is nonetheless a recognition that each party has a comprehensible belief system, and it represents a refusal to demonize or infantilize non-Brit-ish modes of thought.

Indeed, in *On the Face of the Waters*, learning Indian ways is more than a technique of appropriation necessary to survival in dangerous times (as it is with Kim's knowledge of foreign ways and talent with disguises). Allen J. Greenberger, in *The British Image of India* (1969), writes that "The Brit-ish in this period . . . imagined that they had to reject everything Indian in order to retain their own individual identity and to succeed in what ever their endeavors might be" (19), and adventure novelists generally conform to this program. Steel, however, makes native knowledge systems a means of better understanding the self, the world, and others. During the siege of Delhi, Kate finds refuge in the garden of the Swami Sri Anunda. Mired in Western ways, Kate cannot imagine what she will do with herself, disguised as a Hindu wife meditating there under a vow of silence. Kate is agitated at the news of increased military action, and she is initially aware only of the material world, herself, and her troubles. But she finds that "Time slipped by with incredible swiftness. . . . And what a strange peace and contentment the life brought!" (403). After Kate spends two weeks in silent meditation, Sri Anunda himself comes to her to say, "The lesson is learned, sister" (413), for Kate has learned to lose "her grip on this world without gaining, without even desiring, a hold on the next. She was learning a strange new fellowship with the dream of which she was a part" (412). At the end of her fifteen days of meditation, Kate's outlook is so transformed that she says, "I feel as if I had just been born" (419). Although this gloss on Eastern philosophy is superficial, it contrasts starkly with the soldierly concerns and standard prejudices of a man like Major Erlton.

Most adventure novels valorize men like Erlton, men with physical prowess but without learning or gifts of expression. Allan Quartermain is always half apologizing for his "blunt way of writing" because he is "more accustomed to handle a rifle than a pen" (Haggard, *King Solomon's Mines* 6). Schreiner overturns this model with her antagonist Bonaparte Blenkins, who lays claim to adventures out of an H. Rider Haggard novel (fighting wild animals, surviving against probability, overcoming dire adversity). Although he is eventually proven a liar, his idealization of these qualities and actions registers in his unthinkingly suspicious nature, his unscrupulous dealings, and his masochistic tendencies. Steel, too, shows how automatic recourse to the rifle leads to misjudgments, then to violence and massacre. When British troops make the "mistake" of firing on and killing twenty friendly Indian civilians—their own servants, including a woman—the Colonel says, "There have been too many mistakes of that sort. . . . I wish to God some of us would think a bit" (326).

Yet Major Erlton is an exemplary soldier, "up for the Victoria Cross" (426), and he does not want to dwell on complexities, "for he hated thought" (386) and "the complexity of his emotions irritated him" (386). Like the British military as a whole, he fails to understand India; an enormous country with a complex social and religious organization, comprehending it requires concerted effort and concentrated thought. But when Erlton surveys the Indian landscape, he sees only the besieged city of Delhi and the "enemies" he imagines reside within: "That, to him, was India" (327). Steel highlights the limitations of his vision with a reminder that "millions" of Indians in rural areas are thinking only of the harvest; to them the British are merely "the claimer of revenue" (327), not necessarily enemies to attack. But this complex picture is beyond Erlton's scope. Never "good at formulating his feelings into definite thoughts" (370), Erlton cedes responsibility for thinking to others. As he says to Kate, "You were always a oner [*sic*] at thinking. So—so you had better do it for both of us" (424).[11]

Erlton's willingness to let others think for him and to follow their directives links him with the stereotypical Indian native; comparing him with the Indian soldiers, Steel explodes many of these stereotypes. Although Erlton is not able to say why, he is "vaguely" glad that Colonel John Nicholson comes to head the siege of Delhi. Noting that Nicholson "was the sort of man a fellow would be glad to follow" (370) is the best formulation Erlton can produce. If Indians are "natural" followers, as nineteenth-century racial characterizations had it, they are no more so than the typical British army officer, who shows a comparable eagerness to follow a strong leader. Erlton is Steel's primary example of British soldiery; his Indian counterpart is Tara's brother Soma (who, as a sepoy, is not an officer). The Rajput soldier's thoughtfulness and his ability to analyze his position between divided loyalties shows the complexity of British/Indian interactions as well as Steel's belief that many aspects of Indian culture were superior to British civilization.

Soma's trouble is that entertaining complex thought makes it difficult for a soldier to know where duty lies. He appreciates his complex emotions and cannot be satisfied with having someone else think for him. So he is torn. He is from a long line of soldiers, for whom loyalty to one's officers and confidence in the line of command is as highly valued as martial prowess. But he is also loyal to the Bengal Army and his comrades there (including the ones who are court-martialed for refusing to use new cartridges rumored to contain pork and beef tallow) because the Bengal Army "was not—as a European army is—a mere chance collection of men . . . but, to a great extent, a guild, following the profession of arms by hereditary custom from the cradle to the grave" (167). Before he witnessed the unjust and humiliating court-martial of eighty-five of his comrades, military law seemed just. After, the British officers seemed profoundly unjust. At play also is his respect for his commanding officer, Captain Craigie, whom Soma knows to be honorable, brave, trustworthy, and an able leader. But Craigie is a captain who too must obey his commanding officer—the officer responsible for jailing Soma's comrades.

On the Face of the Waters as an Anti-Adventure Novel

Despite "the sweep and swing of [Steel's] tale" and "the amplitude of its military march" ("The Novel of the Mutiny" 81), Steel often voices an antiadventure aesthetic in *On the Face of the Waters*. Rebecca Saunders claims that "Steel wrote what may be thought of as a woman's adventure novel, inverting the elements of adventure so that her work remains that of a woman who could not glory outright in the emotions of adventure" (321). Steel's narrative is a critique of the adventure genre and its concomitant glorification of killing and oppression.[12] It is not merely that Steel cannot "glory outright" but that she questions the very "emotions of adventure" that cause unthinking violence. A detailed analysis of a key passage in the novel will demonstrate how Steel constructs typical adventure scenarios only to deflate their bellicose rhetoric of superiority and survivalism.

In a chapter of rising tension, Kate is worried about Jim's long absence. He has been ill and still has not entirely recovered his strength. In a besieged city, traveling under disguise as an Afghan horse trader, he faces great peril, especially since his fatigue may cause lapses in his behavior, mastery of argot, and demeanor. As any adventure novelist would, Steel reminds the reader of all the dangers facing Jim, represents the anxiety of those waiting for him, and heightens the tension with presentiments of impending peril. During her anxious vigil, Kate is alone on the rooftop, still disguised as an Afghani horse trader's secluded wife. Because of her worry about Jim, when she hears footsteps on the stairs she incautiously opens the door wide. Out hisses an unfamiliar voice that identifies Kate as a white woman: "Salaam! Mem-sahib" (347). Is she discovered? Will she be killed? She pulls back, but the figure slips past her and Kate is trapped. It is not danger, we learn; it is Alice's Mai, who according to Alice's last wish has been sheltering Sonny Seymour, the son of a British official.

The Mai had detected Kate's hiding place within the besieged city (where discovery by native troops means certain death) by a process of deduction far beyond Kate's safeguards. The market seller noticed that the Mai bought enough chickens to make broth and remarked to her that "there was more *chikken-brât* . . . being made in the quarter. . . . A sweeper woman, he said, bought 'halflings' for an Afghan's bibi" (349). The Mai, who has knowledge of both British and Indian ways, is thus able to discover Kate's hideaway. The Mai scoffs at the idea that "an Afghani would use three halflings in one day!" because "No one but a mem making *chikken-brât* would do that. So I watched and made sure, against this day" (349). Despite the display of superior Indian reasoning, the threat of danger dissipates and Kate is happy that "The house would be a home indeed with [Sonny's] sweet 'Mifis Erlton' echoing through it" (350).

But even this happy thought brings with it presentiments of harm. Kate realizes that "[t]here would be danger in English prattle" (350) and, indeed, Sonny calls out to her in English and only calls more loudly when she desperately tries to quiet him: "Steps on the stair, and Sonny prattling on in his high, clear lisp!" (351). The tension again mounts when Kate realizes that there are two people on the stairway in a scuffle. Sonny is screaming in English; they are certain to be discovered. Even worse, Jim frantically shouts for Kate to open the door.

More adventure ensues when two men burst over the threshold, each fighting for supremacy. Jim, with "his knees to the ribs below them," calls for a knife or a revolver because "I can't hold——the brute long" (351). He "loosened one hand cautiously from the throat and held it out, trembling, eager" (352). But Kate thwarts the expectations associated with this plot strand when she refuses to hand over a knife, saying "No! . . . you shall not. It is not worth it" (352). She refuses to enable the adventure narrative, to valorize survival if it means brutality, to associate honor with killing, to let the plot climax with violence and death.

The man turns out to be Tiddu, the old Baharupa who taught Jim the art of disguise. Tiddu had seen Jim in the market, in obvious difficulties from his recent illness, and insisted on seeing him safely home. Jim acknowledges that "but for Kate, he would have knifed the old man remorselessly. Even now he felt doubtful" (352). The conventional adventure plot would reinforce Jim's suspicions, would license killing the intruder to protect the heroine. But here, Tiddu becomes the nobler figure when he points out that Jim need not fear for Kate on his account. He will remember that Kate saved his life and will act accordingly. Unlike Jim, Tiddu and his tribe "know gratitude" (352); unlike Jim, Tiddu is too noble to attack someone who has aided and protected him.

Jim's desire to lash out and thereby prove himself a man stems from his being cast in the feminized role. Women writers who take on the adventure mode often modify what they value in men and therefore rework the range of acceptable masculine roles. In *The Story of an African Farm*, Schreiner mocks Gregory Rose when he attempts to play the conventional hero's role—he is ridiculous and clearly unfit for stereotypically masculine pursuits. Gregory becomes truly heroic, though, when he casts himself as a woman and nurse to care for the dying Lyndall. The adventure hero's typical role is the strong protector of innocent weakness; adventure ideology—and the ideals of British masculinity that inform it—dictate that men not be weak or vulnerable (as Gregory is in his woman's attire, or as Jim is after his illness). That is woman's role. So when Kate is missing from the rooftop, Jim cannot imagine that she will survive on her own. Jim's vision of male-female roles prompts him to claim that the "whole duty of man" is to "find and save Kate, or—*kill somebody*" (395). His first idea is to protect the innocent woman. But if he cannot, then killing an Indian—whether guilty of harming Kate or not—will do. To *kill somebody* is an appalling manifestation of the "whole duty of man," and Steel reveals the inadequacy of this vision by entirely deflating Jim's martial rhetoric.[13] The paragraph that follows Jim's declaration of intent underscores this: "Kate, however, had already been found, or rather she had never been lost" (395). Kate, we find, is fully able to take care of herself, and Jim's idea of man's "whole duty" is entirely irrelevant.[14]

On the Face of the Waters as New Woman Novel

It is in the character of Kate that the New Woman enters *On the Face of the Waters*.[15] Because the novel is set in 1857, Kate has no recourse to an established women's movement, discussions of the marriage question, or work for suffrage. Her intelligence, her reactions to events, her decisive action, and her dissatisfaction with her current state, however, reflect the cultural climate of the novel's 1896 composition. As the novel opens, Kate is a New Woman in thought but an "old" one in deed. Her husband is thoroughly disreputable: he is openly having an affair, he gambles, and he cheats at cards. Kate admits that "I do not love him" (21) but like many other New Women, she feels trapped because all her options are equally disagreeable. She could leave her husband, or have him dismissed from the army for improper conduct, but that would harm the son she sent to England in order "to keep him from growing up in the least like his father. And she had stayed with that father simply to keep him within the pale of respectability for the boy's sake" (14).

At this point in the novel, Kate is entirely mired in conventional English ways. Even though these domestic conventions are what doom a divorced mother's son and license the sexual double standard, English domestic ideals are represented as her only comfort during what she regards as cruel exile from home and child. Initially, she plays the role of the "mem," living in a house with an English garden, desperately trying to grow English plants in the Indian climate. She does not mix with Indian society, because she does not know the language or understand the culture. And "what she did not understand" is what she "did not like" (10). She can imagine only that Indians are "uncivilized, heathen . . . tied to hateful, horrible beliefs and customs" (10). Kate's growth as an autonomous woman is enabled and measured by her increasing respect for, understanding of, and participation in Indian culture.

Circumstances make Kate change her attitudes and her actions. The rising in Meerut coincides with Erlton's letter that he is divorcing her because Alice is pregnant by him. Ironically, concern for English morality dictates and explains his career-ruining decision to divorce: he writes to Kate that he knows that she will be upset only so far as his decision affects their son. He respects this, but he has a more pressing concern: "it isn't as if he were a girl, *and the other may be*" (182). So Kate is left to fend—and, most important, to think—for herself. She "was trying to understand what it all meant; really—deprived of her conventional thoughts about such things" (222). Kate initially sees Alice only as "the woman at whom other women held up pious hands of horror" (223). But then she realizes that it is only by conventional standards that she has any cause to blame Alice.[16] Kate does not love Erlton and is not physically attracted to him. Alice has, in essence, picked up something that Kate did not want. Viewing the situation against the grain of convention, Kate muses: "What wrong had [Alice] done to one who refused to admit the claims or rights of passion? What had she stolen, this woman who had not cared at all?" (234). All Alice had "stolen" was "motherhood; and that was given to saint and sinner alike" (234).

Steel hereby rejects the assigned role of women in the colonial project: bearing the sons of empire. As Rosemary George notes, women's only *national* role before achieving the franchise was motherhood; women's imperial role is the same, for in the colonies women also cannot vote, work for the government, or join the army. John MacKenzie explains how the eugenics and motherhood movements of the late-Victorian and Edwardian eras were inextricably linked to imperial ideology. Disturbed by falling birth rate and the revelation during the Boer War of the physical inadequacy of a third of all recruits, "The majority of Fabians, together with the leading Liberal imperialists, supported a programme to keep mothers at home, educate them in motherhood, encourage 'eugenic' marriage, and provide State inducements to procreation, nutrition, and health" (159). The exalted nature of women's maternal role in maintaining the nation's standards becomes a mere biological reality in Steel's rendering. Motherhood as an imperial imperative and a eugenic duty is incompatible with something freely given to "saint and sinner alike." For Steel, motherhood is allied with the sacred—Kate's strongest bond is with her absent child and with Sonny—but not with a woman's political and national duty. In this, Steel is again aligned with Schreiner. As Carolyn Burdett notes, for Schreiner, the mother-trope is "far more dense and contextual" and "far more *contested*" (72) than propaganda for imperial discourse or eugenics.

Kate's emergence as a heroine coincides with her falling away from British domestic ideology. In her role as memsahib, Kate was superior to all things Indian, but trapped by circumstance and circumscribed by convention. This changes when she is left on her own to escape from the cantonment in Delhi, which is overrun with insurgent sepoys. She is safely hidden in a dark niche near the gate, but tempted to leave her haven for the mercy of a quick and certain death. The idea of having a chance to change, to survive, to prosper, however, spurs her to save herself: "Chance! There was a spell in the very word" (256). Kate takes her chance, ventures out, and wraps herself "in ayah's fashion" with skirt and veil (268): "So, boldly, she slipped out of the corner, and made for the gate, remembering to her comfort that it was not England where a lonely woman might be challenged all the more for her loneliness" (268). This is the first time she realizes the advantage of being a woman in India, the place she previously disregarded as merely "heathen" and in all ways inferior to England.

Kate next stumbles upon Jim, who saves her with a daring ride through throngs of fighting men. Steel once again engages the adventure genre, complete with wild war whoops and derring-do. But when Jim stops to contemplate how best to keep Kate safe, we again see the folly of his idea of "the whole duty of man." Jim decides that he and Kate cannot continue moving from place to place without a set plan of action:

To begin with, Kate's nerves could not stand it. She was brave enough, but she had an imagination, and what woman with that could stand being left alone in the dark for twelve hours at a time, never knowing if the slow starvation, which would be her fate if anything untoward happened to him, had not already begun? He could not expect her to stand it, when three days of something far less difficult had left him haggard, his nerves unstrung. (280)

His concern for the state of Kate's nerves (which ironically reveals the delicacy of his own) is gallant, but unnecessary. The woman for whom mere "chance" is a call to action will not sit still waiting for "slow starvation." Indeed, during Jim's subsequent illness, the formerly helpless Kate learns enough of Indian language and customs to take care of herself. This, however, is a source of discomfort to Jim, who finds he is no longer needed in the protector's role:

You've learned everything, my dear lady, necessary to salvation. That's the worst of it! You chatter to Tara—I hear you when you think I'm asleep. You draw your veil over your face when the water-carrier comes to fill the pots as if you had been born on a housetop. You—Mrs. Erlton! If I were not a helpless idiot I could pass you out of the city to-morrow, I believe. It isn't your fault any longer. It's mine. . . . It gets on my nerves—my nerves! (331)

He is in the position Kate had been in, waiting for care, unsure of what is happening around him, and unable to effect any change in the outcome. But Jim lashes out irritably, unable to bear the strain the way Kate does.

Kate's placidity is not due to feminine passivity, as Jim suspects; she is merely too strong to waste her energies fretting and complaining. Like Schreiner's Lyndall, who "waited . . . watched . . . collected clothes . . . wrote" (184) for the time "when all was ready" (184) for her to make her way into the wider world, Kate learns Hindi, studies Indian culture, and prepares for the time when she may be able to take her chance. When Kate claims that the presages of military actions they have heard are not fearful to her but "a great relief," Jim is offended, stressing how much more relieved he, as a man, must be. He claims that "women can scarcely understand what inaction means to a man" (299). Jim's statement reveals how little he understands women's need for agency, and to what degree his culture invents women's supposed desire to be guarded and guided by a strong man. Kate's personal experience with "long weary hours of waiting" (299) tells her different.

The opportunity to think and act for herself prompts Kate to be "interested in her own adventures, now that she had, as it were, the control over them" (400). Control over her life and actions brings her alive. Ironically, she achieves this control by joining a community of women.[17] Unlike Jim, who wants to *kill somebody*, Kate finds her course of action in appealing to the common humanity—the common womanhood—of those around her. Unable to regain the rooftop from which she escapes, Kate decides to "throw herself on the mercy" (377) of Newâsi, an Indian widow princess. "I am . . . a woman like yourself" (378), Kate exclaims, and it is not just that both are women. Both are spirited, independent, strong-minded women. The narrator points out that "Abool-Bukr had been right when he said that Kate Erlton reminded him of the Princess Farkhoonda da Zamâni [Newâsi]. Standing so, they showed strangely alike indeed, not in feature, but in type; in the soul which looked out of the soft dark, and the clear gray eyes" (378). Instead of killing the other in order to find action and affirm one's own right to act (as Jim would do), Kate sees the womanhood, the humanity, of the other and finds herself affirmed. The New Woman's adventure is to find empowerment not by stepping on but by walking with the other.

The result of Steel re-viewing colonial romance through feminist eyes is a New Woman's adventure novel. This scene is reminiscent of Ella Hepworth Dixon's *Story of a Modern Woman* (1894), which climaxes with Mary Erle's decision that "I can't, I won't, deliberately injure another woman. Think how she would suffer! Oh, the torture of women's lives—the helplessness, the impotence, the emptiness! . . . All we modern women mean to help each other now. We have a bad enough time as it is . . . surely we needn't make it worse by our own deliberate acts!" (255). Mona Caird, in *The Daughters of Danaus*, similarly focusing on strength in numbers, draws an analogy between opportunities for resistance by oppressed peoples and by women. Algitha Fullerton says to her sister Hadria, "A conquering race, if it is wise, governs its subjects largely through their internecine squabbles and jealousies. *But what if they combine——?*" (473). By extending the ideology of feminism to the empire, Steel suggests, a community of women can join together to re-imagine colonial relations and to redistribute power.

Inasmuch as Kate proves to be thoroughly independent and capable, Jim's proclamations about women are clearly wrongheaded. Indeed, he is fallible, flawed, and often mistaken. Far from the perfect hero, Jim lacks adequate understanding, and his responses are often irrational. When impatient or angry, his "sheer animal hatred" (294) and his "arrogance and imperious temper" (294) cause him to lash out and make sweeping statements like "women were trivial creatures" (294). In calmer moments, as when he is reasonably discussing policy, he says the opposite. The conventional adventure hero, by contrast, is always strong (even in weakness: *Ayesha* has Holly and Leo recovering from exhaustion, while the narrator stresses that any other men would have been killed by their experience), always incisive in his analysis of the situation, always successful in achieving his goal. Jim's success instead comes in changing his goal. He does not find and save Kate, nor does he *kill somebody*. Kate convinces him to understand success differently: success is not global domination, but local victory.

Kate moves from extreme stereotypes of Indian people and their culture (based on ignorance and prejudice, not on experience) to an epiphany akin to Everard Barfoot's realization that a woman can be strong, intelligent, *and* attractive. Instead of investing difference with the power to make herself superior, she gains individual power by consolidating her efforts with others. Whereas Barfoot begins in a position of power, which he will retain with or without Rhoda Nunn, Kate's position is much more tenuously held. Her status stems merely from her skin color, and when the sepoy troops mutiny against their British commanders, she learns how arbitrary her power is. Her whiteness, which had once protected her from insult or injury, becomes a danger to her. She also intimately understands what it means to be dominated, ruled by forces outside her control. Because of her experience as a woman trapped in an unhappy marriage, prevented by social codes from either exposing her husband or extricating herself from the relationship, she cannot be a typical adventure hero. Instead, she must find a new solution that avoids stereotype and the ill-gained mastery that stems from it.

The New Woman adventure novel aims to fulfill the ideal of social understanding and reveal the shortcomings of sexual and political imperialism. A woman who discovers her own powers and self-reliance through an "adventure" situation goes outside her known world for help coping with and finding answers to this situation. She eschews violence and killing, and instead of defining her self in opposition to a racial other sees herself in solidarity with the other. As Hafzan, a maid of the Mogul court at Delhi, says, "God save all women, black or white, say I!" (279). Conventional adventure novels feature supposedly knowing men, who describe events in terms of race. Wise women in New Woman adventure novels try to look beyond race. *On the Face of the Waters*, like *The Story of an African Farm* before it, creates new possibilities for women of all colors, in constant dialog with the adventure genre it often mimics but more often critiques.

"Unhand her!"

Possession and Property

Issues of property and possession pervade colonial adventure and New Woman novels. The possessive, patriarchal attitudes New Woman writers expose are mirrored in adventure novels, embodied in the white man's relationships with both women and native men. While all nineteenth-century fiction is informed by the ideology of property, the Married Women's Property Acts of 1870 and 1882 and the Scramble for Africa in 1885 brought questions of property and its relation to self-possession into the cultural mainstream. In the nation's political life as well as its fiction, property came to the fore in discussions of identity, opportunity, and autonomy, which in turn informed debates over abolition, colonization, and women's rights.

New Woman novels and colonial adventure novels come at questions of possession and equal rights from opposite sides of the debate. Adventure novels are, of course, essentially conservative; they intend to preserve the rights and privileges and assumed characteristics of the Western world—most specifically, the male world. The New Woman novel, by contrast, concerns itself with denaturalizing sexual relations as they have existed; redefining femininity, womanhood, and purity; contesting women's subordinate status; and destabilizing women's presumed role as mother and wife. Analyzed in conjunction, however, as part of a larger cultural discourse, these subgenres illuminate the discursive production of power relations that Michel Foucault describes: "we must not imagine a world of discourse divided between accepted discourse and excluded discourse, or between the dominant discourse and the dominated one; but as a multiplicity of discursive elements that can come into play in various strategies" (*History of Sexuality* 100).

A fundamental connection between freedom and possession is inscribed in what C. B. Macpherson, drawing on seventeenth-century political theorists, calls "possessive individualism," which describes an individual as "free inasmuch as he is proprietor of his person and capacities" (3). Freedom then becomes, in John Locke's words, an individual's "*Liberty* to dispose, and order, as he lists, his Person, Actions, Possessions, and his whole Property . . . and therein not to be subject to the arbitrary Will of another, but freely follow his own" (306). Nineteenth-century feminists want "self-possession" both politically and metaphorically: they want the ownership of self that signifies both freedom and self-management. Typically characterized as sentimental beings, prone to hysteria, not fully in command of their faculties, women increasingly sought to wrest their public as well as their psychic identities from male control. The struggle for individual and political rights in the nineteenth century became a struggle for self-possession informed by and informing the discourses of property, ownership, enslavement, and abolition.

Throughout the nineteenth century "master-slave" and "male-female" were analogous dyads. As I have already noted, Victorian writers, politicians, scientists, and activists repeatedly connected women and "inferior" races. William Thompson and Anna Wheeler make explicit the terms of this association in their *Appeal of One Half the Human Race* (1825): "To be a woman is to be an inferior animal; an inferiority by no talents, by no virtues, to be surmounted; indelible like the skin of the Black" (164). Because these discussions represent another stage on which the convergence of New Woman and adventure fiction played out, I want briefly to discuss the larger social and political context of these analogies before returning to the fiction that represents them.

Racial Equality and Women's Rights

The "Declaration of Sentiments" presented by the suffragists at Seneca Falls, New York, in 1848 is often considered the foundational document in the history of women's suffrage. Significantly, the manifesto's opening paragraph, which closely follows the wording of the Declaration of Independence, links the cause of women to all oppressed peoples:

> When, in the course of human events, it becomes necessary for one portion of the family of man to assume among the people of the earth a position different from that which they have hitherto occupied, but one to which the laws of nature and of nature's God entitle them, a decent respect to the opinions of mankind requires that they should declare the causes that impel them to such a course. (77)

This is intentionally unspecific: "one portion" of the population must assume "a different position" because the "laws of nature" require it. The opening of the most famous document on women's rights omits explicit reference to women, and thus identifies the struggle of women with all oppressed groups, including African American slaves and American Indians.

This was a strategic identification. Nineteenth-century scientific discourse consistently identified women with racial others. The same "scientific" methods used to sanction racism were marshaled as "proof" that women were lower on the evolutionary scale than men. In *The Descent of Man* (1871), Charles Darwin posits that supposedly feminine traits of intuition and perception are "characteristics of the lower races, and therefore of a past and lower state of civilization" (2: 326–27). Like racial "science," the science that diagnoses female inferiority is infinitely adaptable, always changing to meet new needs and adjusting to new data. Early in the nineteenth century, physicians asserted that women's frontal lobes were less developed than men's (the frontal lobes were considered the locus of intellectual ability). However, as Ann Oakley notes, "At the turn of the century, when the parietal lobes replaced the frontal lobes as the seat of intellect, it was discovered that women's frontal lobes were actually more developed than men's—but were not a sign of intelligence after all" (122). Scientific racism and scientific paternalism alike created boundaries and definitions for their subjects, which limited and circumscribed the realms of possibility those subjects inhabit.

The so-called scientific facts about women and "lower" races required that they be debarred from the privileges of property. Harriet Martineau, in *Society in America*, quotes Thomas Jefferson in order to refute him. He claims that, even in pure democracy, three groups need to be excluded: infants until of age; "Women, who, to prevent depravation of morals, and ambiguity of issue, could not mix promiscuously in the public meetings of men"; and "Slaves, from whom the unfortunate state of things with us takes away the rights of will and property" (qtd. in Martineau 72). Martineau counters that Jefferson's reason for the slaves' nonparticipation in public life—their exclusion from "the rights of will and property"—is also the reason women are disenfranchised from American political life. The "unfortunate state of things," Martineau writes, is actually the institutionalized slavery of both Africans and women.

The science that deems women and people of color unable to possess property or themselves presents its findings as laws of nature, not of the state. As John Stuart Mill noted in "The Subjection of Women" (1869), male superiority is a form of the law of the strongest, based on custom and disguised as nature. Frances Power Cobbe, in "What Shall We Do with Our Old Maids?" (1862), also notes how often custom is deemed "nature" in regard to the mental and moral faculties of women and slaves. Indeed, women and slaves are similarly constrained by their social roles and expectations: "To cramp every faculty and cut off all large interest, and then complain that a human being so treated is narrow-minded and scandal-loving, is precisely an injustice parallel to that of some Southern Americans whom we have heard detail those vices of the negroes which slavery had produced, as the reason why they were justified in keeping so degraded a race in such a condition" (255). Because of women's slavelike status under British law, critics like Cobbe and Mill describe marriage as a contract that degrades women, strips them of power and property, and puts them into service of a legal master. This is a concept taken up by the New Woman writers, as when Mona Caird equates slavery and marriage: "To work without pay—what is it but to be a slave?" ("The Morality of Marriage" 631).

Locke is careful to distinguish a man's power in domestic relationships from political authority, writing in the *Second Treatise on Government* that "the Power of a *Magistrate* over a Subject, may be distinguished from that of a *Father* over his children, a *Master* over his Servant, a *Husband* over his Wife, and a *Lord* over his Slave" (268). Because a man's power over his children, his servants, and his wife does not include the power to take their lives, he does not have governmental power over any person's property in himself. Although "every Man has a *Property* in his own *Person*" which "no body has any Right to but himself" (287), it is nonetheless natural that the man "as the abler and the stronger" (321) should have "the Rule" (321) in a marriage relationship. Locke stresses that this does not create a master/slave relationship, nor any sort of absolute rule, for a marriage "leaves the Wife in the full and free possession of what by Contract is her peculiar Right, and gives the Husband no more power over her Life, than she has over his" (321). Indeed, Locke asserts, "The *Power of the Husband* being so far from that of an absolute Monarch, that the *Wife* has, in many cases, a Liberty to *separate* from him" where "their Contract allows it" (321). This declaration of equality includes two vital qualifications: the wife has the power to leave a husband only "in many cases," and only where "their Contract allows it." Natural laws and rights are no longer in play in this relationship: the real power is determined by individual variances and "their Contract." This is exactly the point that fin de siècle feminists were making: no matter what natural law deems a just relationship between husbands and wives, social contract and legislation debar women from property in their selves and the rights that stem from self-possession.

William Thompson and Anna Wheeler, writing in 1825, note that females in England are *not* in a state of perpetual servitude. Rather, the law considers unmarried adult women masters of themselves; it is only when women marry that they lose self-possession: "From the time of adolescence up to the time of marriage, the law of England supposes a perfect capacity on the part of the adult woman as well as of the adult man. . . . But as soon as adult daughters become wives, their civil rights disappear" (58–59). Once again the figure of the slave best describes the position of women: when women marry, write Thompson and Wheeler, "they fall back again, and remain all their lives— should their owners and directors live so long—into the state of children or idiots, the passive property of their owners; protected by the law in some few respects only, like other slaves, from the excessive abuse of despotic power" (59).

By the 1890s, the conception of a married woman's position as "involuntary breeding machine and household slave" (Thompson and Wheeler 63) was both widely recognized and increasingly debated. As historian Lucy Bland has noted, the 1890s were a time of an "increasingly voiced demand for a woman's right over her own person" (141). In this period, after women's agitation for the abolition of slavery and before the largest demonstrations for women's suffrage, feminists focused on reforming laws as well as attitudes regarding the position of married women. Legal possession became the focus of contention, because "Once married, a woman became effectively her husband's property, including his sexual property, given his irrevocable sexual rights over her" (Bland 146–47). The primary claim of fin de siècle feminists was that marriage was profoundly immoral "because sex was frequently nonconsensual, as too was the consequent endless childbearing" (146).

Like Martineau, late-century feminists found the primary solution to the marriage problem in releasing women from legal ownership by their husbands. Mona Caird's groundbreaking essay "Marriage" (1888) in the *Westminster Review* argues that marriage as a legal institution is "a vexatious failure."[1] What is needful in marriage is "a full understanding and acknowledgment of the obvious right of the woman to *possess herself* body or soul, to give or withhold herself . . . exactly as she will" (198; italics in original). This needed to be said precisely because a woman in nineteenth-century England was her husband's property, even after the Married Women's Property Acts gave her limited rights of possession. And, according to Sandra Gilbert and Susan Gubar, women's dispossession was highly reassuring to many: "Clearly many men reacted with dread to the legal and social reforms that provided women a modicum of property and custodial rights at the beginning of the modernist period. The *Times*, for example, deplored the 1891 decision of *Queen v. Jackson* (which declared that a man could no longer imprison his wife in his house so as to enforce conjugal rights)" (49). Eliza Lynn Linton, commenting on the *Queen v. Jackson* decision, wrote that "marriage, as hitherto understood in England, was suddenly abolished one fine morning last month!" (qtd. in Rubinstein 47).

Marriage, of course, was not abolished, but the pivotal role of women in the abolition movement that freed both British colonial and American slaves caused many men to worry about women's relatively new political power. As Louis and Rosamund Billington point out, women's participation in the antislavery movement was sanctioned by its association with already-prescribed Christian moral duties; it was thus less threatening than the New Woman's later, largely secular excursions into masculine territory. Women's outreach to those in need "fitted easily into the dominant evangelical model for the gender-based division of moral labor" (85), even when it extended women's reach to the public and political sphere. As Elizabeth Helsinger, William Veeder, and Robin Lauterbach Sheets note, "Although the actual campaign for female suffrage did not get under way until the 1848 Seneca Falls Convention, women abolitionists were asserting their right to engage in political activity by speaking in public and by participating in anti-slavery activities" (1: 4). Involvement in antislavery agitation gave women an "ideology of injustice" (Billington 82), which was invaluable in the campaign for women's rights. By the late 1850s this ideology of injustice, which linked racial and gender discrimination, was prevalent among progressive women. The early feminist Barbara Bodichon "absorbed the view that anti-slavery and women's rights were interrelated" (Billington 106), writing that "Slavery is a greater injustice, but it is allied to the injustice to women so closely that I cannot see one without thinking of the other and feeling how soon slavery would be destroyed if right opinions were entertained upon the other question" (qtd. in Billington 106).

Self-Possession in Pre–New Woman Fiction

The struggle over possession occurred throughout the Victorian era; what is "new" in the works of New Woman writers is their explicit critique of the ideological and legal conditions that make ownership of women possible. Charlotte Brontë's *Jane Eyre* (1847), for example, addresses the right of a woman to "own" herself. Jane's life story is a series of struggles for self-possession in the face of male domination. This is why it is so important to her later marriage with Rochester that she be "independent . . . as well as rich" (388). If she is her "own mistress" (388) then not even her husband can own her.

These concerns were pervasive in nineteenth-century fiction, present in novels by men as well as women. Although Brontë's feminism extends beyond the sympathy Charles Dickens displays for oppressed wives in *Dombey and Son* (1848), *Jane Eyre* shares with *Dombey* a concern over the dependence and subservience of married women. Dickens metaphorically extends the idea of prostitution to include women "bought" on the "marriage market," thus making explicit the connection between "white slavery" and the dispossessed state of married women generally that informed the work of Millicent Fawcett, Emmeline Pankhurst, and Josephine Butler. Edith Dombey perceives herself as a prostitute, bought and paid for by Mr. Dombey, and Dickens figuratively associates her with the literal prostitute Alice. The novel thus characterizes the upper-class marriage market as a legalized form of prostitution.[2]

This theme of woman's self-possession and her struggle to be free of male ownership becomes increasingly explicit as the century progresses and fully enmeshed in the New Woman and colonial adventure fiction of the late century. George Eliot's *Daniel Deronda* (1876) illustrates how the issue of woman as property rises to political consciousness and how issues of masculine and national power infuse this consciousness. The first modern critical monographs on New Woman novels—Patricia Stubbs's *Women and Fiction* (1979), Gail Cunningham's *The New Woman and the Victorian Novel* (1978), and Lloyd Fernando's *"New Women" in the Late Victorian Novel* (1977)—classify Eliot's novels as New Woman fiction.[3] Although *Daniel Deronda* examines and disparages *the effects* of woman's status as property, it incorporates elements of paternalism and masculine power in ways that align it with adventure fiction, creating a hybrid more similar to *She* and *Dracula* than to "purer" examples of New Woman fiction like Sarah Grand's *The Heavenly Twins* or Mona Caird's *Daughters of Danaus.*

Although the classification is misleading, the reasons for grouping *Daniel Deronda* with New Woman fiction are clear. Daniel's mother, although she appears for only a few chapters, is a prototype of the New Woman: she has artistic talent; she feels acutely the "slavery of being a girl" (588) and thus being subject to the direction of others; and she wants nothing more than to be free to carry out her own designs. Marriage is her way to "seek my freedom from a bondage that I hated" (617)—her subjection to her father's iron rule.[4] She is a model New Woman when she exclaims, "Had I not a rightful claim to be something more than a mere daughter and mother? . . . Whatever else was wrong, acknowledge that I had a right to be an artist" (619). But Alcharisi is, at the same time, an unlikely foremother of the New Woman: she is explicitly colonized by the forces of masculine inheritance and national duty, and ultimately, George Eliot's depiction of Deronda's nation-building project assumes primacy over Alcharisi's protofeminist resistance.

Deronda's peaceful crusade for a Jewish state bears little obvious resemblance to the colonial conquests of late-Victorian adventure fiction. The novel's theme of nationalism and of nation-building, however, has direct links to the Victorian sense of national identity and the British imperial mission. For Deronda as well as for the young men of Britain generally, laying the foundation of a new nation provides a sense of purpose for otherwise idle, dandified young men. Deronda is a man of intelligence and abilities, but little direction; his discovery of a Jewish heritage gives him a sense of mission and duty, inspired by racial pride.

The antifeminism implicit in this mission, and imperial ideology generally, is evident when Daniel snubs his mother in order to take on the mantle of his grandfather.[5] Alcharisi's father "never thought of his daughter, except as an instrument" (617) that would give him a grandson. Her involvement in the affairs of state is purely domestic: she will be a mother of the sons of empire. Her father proclaims, "I desire a grandson who shall have a true Jewish heart. Every Jew should rear his family as if he hoped that a Deliverer might spring from it" (617). When Alcharisi betrays her racial heritage and duty by concealing Daniel's Jewish heritage, Eliot shows that she is misguided, and Daniel condemns her. Daniel represents his mother's ultimate failure to forestall his Jewish destiny as "the expression of something stronger, with deeper, farther-spreading roots, knitted into the foundations of sacredness for all men" (618). Alcharisi is alienated from the sacredness felt *by men*, for national duty is stronger than mere familial ties. Moreover, the woman's attempt to interfere with nation-building, and the son's subsequent return to masculine power structures, have only made him a more committed nation-builder: "that stronger Something has determined that I shall be all the more the grandson whom also you wished to annihilate" (618). By denying him his racial heritage and duty, Daniel suggests, Alcharisi has denied him his life, has attempted to "annihilate" his self. When the nation is identified as a domestic genealogy (McClintock 157), Deronda's identification with his grandfather becomes inseparable from his sense of a national mission.

Indeed, *Daniel Deronda* rather surprisingly anticipates many characteristics of H. Rider Haggard's *She* (1887). In it, Leo Vincey is driven by family history and a consequent sense of duty to fulfill a family quest. Like Deronda, Leo is not raised by his family; like Deronda, the secrets of his heritage are revealed in ancient papers contained in a family chest; like Deronda, he is specially trained in college for the duties he will need to undertake later. Most important, however, are the vitality of the past, the living force of family history and heritage, and the sense of duty that impels each man to abandon his life in England and pursue a larger purpose in foreign lands. This narrative structure easily accommodates varied ideological attitudes in both popular and elite literature.

The Politics of Self-Possession in the New Woman Novel

Coming into property changes women's lives, as well as their self-conceptions. Jane Eyre learns what money can do, but in 1847, when *Jane Eyre* was published, Jane needed to be independently wealthy and Rochester needed to be maimed and partially blinded for them to be equals. At the end of the century, when women submit to being owned because they or their families need money, a tragedy familiar from earlier novels results. (Tess Durbeyfield and Gwendolyn Harleth, like Edith Dombey and Maggie Tulliver before them, suffer because their families superintend their affective lives.) It is, as Frances Power Cobbe writes, "The notion that a man's wife is his PROPERTY, in the sense in which a horse is his property" that "is the fatal root of incalculable evil and misery" ("Wife Torture in England" 299). But new legislation and changing attitudes meant, for women, that coming into property held the promise of entering a new world. Marion Yule in George Gissing's

New Grub Street (1891) steps into this world. An impoverished, unhappy amanuensis, she unexpectedly becomes an heiress and learns that "Money is a great fortifier of self-respect. Since she had become really conscious of her position as the owner of five thousand pounds, Marian spoke with a steadier voice, walked with a firmer step; mentally she felt herself altogether a less dependent being. . . . The smile which accompanied the words was also new; it signified deliverance from pupilage" (314). Marion's friend and sometime-suitor Jasper Milvain notices this too: "She spoke with quite unaccustomed decision; indeed, he had noticed from her entrance that there was something unfamiliar in her way of conversing. She was so much more self-possessed than of wont, and did not seem to treat him with the same deference, the same subdual of her own personality" (325). This makes her far less attractive to Jasper; he decidedly does not like "the tone of independence" she unconsciously acquires (326).

The first New Woman novel, Olive Schreiner' *Story of an African Farm* (1883), cultivates and commends women's "tone of independence." Lyndall refuses to marry her lover because "if once you have me you will hold me fast. I shall never be free again" (203). But she sometimes wears his engagement ring, sometimes puts it off, desiring *both* love and freedom (what Schreiner's "Life's Gifts" [1890] had deemed impossible). Love and freedom, however, cannot coexist within the confines of legally sanctioned marriage, and her conflicting impulses reflect marriage's irresolvable tensions. Leslie Rabine, in *Reading the Romantic Heroine*, writes that romantic love "provides one of the few accepted outlets through which women can express their anger and revolt against their situation in a patriarchal order." But at the same time, it "idealizes and eroticizes women's powerlessness and lack of freedom." This contradiction is what has made the romantic love narrative "so resilient as a literary form and so potent as a cultural myth" (viii). Thus, Lyndall angrily tells the man she loves, "You resolved to have me because I seemed unattainable. That is all your love means" (205). She fears being owned, and thus begins the New Woman's refusal of traditional marriage (a theme taken up most famously in Grant Allen's *The Woman Who Did*) as an egregious form of patriarchal possession and political dispossession of women.

Literary attention to possession—and dispossession—grows as the century progresses because political power, traditionally based in masculine property rights, is increasingly encroached upon by property-owning women. The first major women's suffrage petition, presented to the House of Commons by John Stuart Mill on 7 June 1866, was largely based on property ownership. Helen Taylor limits her support to the enfranchisement of single, property-owning women—a strategy meant to garner as much support as possible (because espousing universal suffrage was too radical at that time). She draws on ancient and revered British law to support women's voting rights: "the possession of property in this country carries with it the right to vote in the election of representatives in Parliament" (464) and women are the only anomaly to this rule. Enid Stacy, writing in 1897, called the 1882 Married Women's Property Act the "Magna Charta of British Married Women" (93), because she too recognized that legal rights in Britain were based on ownership.

But women often opposed the legislative reforms of the 1880s and 1890s in terms that linked women's possession to the fate of overseas possessions. The conservative journalist Eliza Lynn Linton, for one, denied that women need economic and political independence. In "Nearing the Rapids" (1894), she resurrects the traditional argument that women have domestic strength and thus do not need political power. Asserting that women in politics are "a national danger and a national disgrace" (378), Linton claims that women already have "an overwhelming influence over men" (378) as mothers, as wives, and as moral arbiters. She is not concerned about equal representation or political justice; she is worried that prostitutes will be able to vote. Further humiliation (as Linton describes it) awaits Britain should women gain the franchise because of the "voting power of that large class of futile spinsters and widows.... These women, and the still lower stratum of rent-paying village shopkeepers and charwomen, will have votes whereby the maintenance of our naval power, or the destruction of our Imperial prestige, will be determined" (379). Contrary to the prevailing ideology of possessive individualism, Linton wants to disassociate property-holding from political power. She pulls out all the stops in her organ of cultural panic, and links the harmony of empire to the question of women's suffrage: "the safety and the dignity of the empire are balanced against private fads and ineffectual voters" (380).

Grant Allen restates Linton's concerns by emphasizing a first-order inference from it: if women's power endangers empire, then empire requires the subjection of women. Allen's essay "The Monopolist Instinct" associates patriarchal ideology with imperialist precepts, for both view power in terms of possession. Allen writes that, although race-slavery had been abolished in Britain, slavery still exists as regards women: "There you have in all its natural ugliness another Monopolist Instinct—the deepest-seated of all, the vilest, the most barbaric. She is not yours: she is her own: unhand her!" (84). He sees the "instinct" to monopoly not only in attitudes toward women but also in patriotism, capitalism, property rights, and slavery. All of these are part and parcel of an atavistic need to own, to control, to show one's power by any means necessary, even if it means impoverishing others (in the case of the capitalist who accumulates far beyond his needs) or usurping lives (in the case of both the slave owner and husband).

Although patriotism might seem unconnected with these impulses, Allen stresses that it is the definitive monopolist instinct. Moreover, it is the most dangerous because it masquerades as a virtue. When one demystifies the seeming probity of national pride, he writes, one sees that it is nothing more than a wider form of selfishness, or pure jingoism: "It means, 'My country against other countries! My army and navy against other fighters! My right to annex unoccupied territory over the equal right of all other people! My power to oppress all weaker nationalities, all inferior races!'" (81).

Note, however, that despite his understanding of "The Monopolist Instinct," Allen assumes the weakness and inferiority of other races and nationalities. Similarly, in his "Plain Words on the Woman Question," he asserts women's need to enter into free unions, to get a sound education—but only so that they can fulfill their function as mothers. Mentally weaker than men and therefore unfit for masculine professions, but affectively stronger and naturally fit for domestic care, women should be "educated to suckle strong and intelligent children" (453). The present system of university education for women is flawed, because "the mistake was made of educating them like men—giving a like training for totally unlike functions" (453).

This replication of the separate spheres ideology works against much that 1890s feminists were working toward, but Allen declares himself the very model of an ardent feminist: "I am an enthusiast on the Woman Question. Indeed, so far am I from wishing to keep her in subjection to man, that I should like to see her a great deal more emancipated than she herself as yet at all desires. Only, her emancipation must not be of a sort that interferes in any way with this prime natural necessity" (450)—that of bearing children. In an argument revealing its sources in Jean-Jacques Rousseau, Allen asserts that biology is indeed destiny. Because women bear children they should find fulfillment in so doing. It is only an unnatural woman, succumbing to anti-motherhood sentiment, who would want anything else: "A woman ought to be ashamed to say she has no desire to become a wife and mother" (452); such a woman is "really a functional aberration" (452). In fact, Allen has the monopolist instinct himself; he wants to own all knowledge about women. He "feel[s] sure" that "while women are crying for emancipation they really want to be left in slavery; and that it is only a few exceptional men, here and there in the world, who wish to see them fully and wholly enfranchised" (452). Allen sees himself as possessor of the one true knowledge about both women and other races, as the one rational being in a society filled with illogical ideas and practices.

Patriarchal ownership of women so constitutes the way Allen thinks of women that he unwittingly reproduces these institutionalized structures of feeling—even as he critiques them. In *The British Barbarians: A Hill-Top Novel*,[6] Allen's hero, an evolved man from the twenty-fifth century named Bertram Ingledew, dispenses moral wisdom and debunks what he calls the "fetich-taboos" of British society. In thus naming accepted British practices and customs, Ingledew draws a parallel between savage belief in supernatural powers and civilized obeisance to social norms. British citizens bow to respectability and custom en masse, which makes them do illogical things: go into mourning even if they never cared for the departed, deem a game of tennis which is perfectly acceptable on Saturday a sin if played on Sunday, believe that one man has the right to forbid another to walk across his undeveloped fields or to shoot the animals that roam there.

Ingledew's list of unreasonable taboos includes most of those concerning the relations between the sexes—or more accurately, the regulation of women.[7] Ingledew finds in Frida a soul mate, one with a spirit large enough to cast off British taboos and understand his teachings. She is married to Monteith, a man as small-minded as she is large-souled, whom she has never loved. (It was a "good match" because he is wealthy.) Frida comes to agree that her husband cannot make her "taboo" to Ingledew the way an African tribal chief can make certain foods taboo to his people, but she still believes that "he's my husband, and of course I must obey him" (157). Ingledew answers: "there must be no more silly talk of farewells between us. I won't allow it. You're mine now—a thousand times more truly mine than ever you were Monteith's; and I can't do without you" (157). Ingledew is "here to help you, to guide you, to lead you on by degrees to higher and truer life" (158). Moreover, he tells Frida, "now you belong to me. I sealed you with that kiss" (161). So Allen reproduces the monopolist instinct in both Monteith, who follows with a gun when Frida leaves with Ingledew, and in Ingledew himself. Yet he approves of this instinct in the enlightened man and disparages it as savagery in the dull man. Frida has traded one keeper for another—though admittedly a more pleasant one. Once again, Allen's professed devotion to feminist issues—as well as Ingledew's professed desire to "liberate" Frida—is belied by his writings. The "instinct" to monopoly proves impossible for Allen to overcome.

Because of the imperial desire to possess, even on the part of a self-described "enthusiast on the Woman Question," is it unsurprising that a keynote of New Woman novels and of late-century feminist thought is women's independence from, among other things, male possessiveness. But it is not merely masculine possession that troubles late-century feminists. The language of ownership intertwined with the language of passion so that authors like Charlotte Mew represent how women and men both associate love with "belonging" to another. In Mew's short story "An Open Door," Laurie changes her mind about marrying Tony in light of her new decision to become a missionary. Tony, to convince her to stay and marry him, says, "I can't offer you anything more, anything less than love." She replies: "I would keep that. . . . Only to you it means simply possession, satisfaction." But he reminds her that this is precisely what love used to mean to her: "To 'have and to hold,' and all the rest. It means the same to everyone. Why, Laurie, I remember you used almost the same words. . . . 'Yes, I am yours to care for and to keep.' Don't *you* remember? And now you speak as if it were some paltry version of my own. It once was yours" (131). She cannot dispute it, for the notion of "to care for and to keep" has colonized women's as well as men's view of human relations.

Mona Caird's *The Daughters of Danaus* illustrates the dual sense of "to care for and to keep"; not only do loved ones nurture and provide for women, they worry over and restrain them as well. Love in this novel becomes a metaphor for tyrannical control: a woman is surrounded by monsters of affection, caring guides who in reality domineer. But this control is hegemonic in that it is principally exercised with the consent of the controlled. Love requires certain sacrifices in deference to the wishes of the loved ones, just as it inspires willing sacrifice for the loved ones. This ideal of sacrificial love becomes problematic when women alone make the sacrifices, when women alone are taught that to be loving is to be submissive, obedient, and self-sacrificing.

Sacrificial love is a constitutive part of the ideal of romantic love, which in turn is based on the chivalric code that celebrates a knight's selfless devotion to a woman's needs. Jan Cohn argues that the rising middle class corrupted the chivalric code into a new version of romantic love that better met its needs and served its values: "It is perhaps the most extravagant irony in the history of women that romantic love, with its source in the celebration of woman in chivalric romance, should have become a means for exacerbating the powerlessness of women. To that end, much in the tradition of courtly love was inverted, most significantly the power relations between lovers" (129).[8] The language of love is often deployed (as it is in *The Daughters of Danaus*) to the detriment of women—and, as we shall see in the next section, colonized people. As Cohn argues, patriarchal restrictions against women seeking their own economic success "worked together to consolidate male power by enlisting romantic love itself as an ideology of the patriarchy" (131). Indeed, in both of these late-century subgenres, "love" is typically invoked to engender a woman's compliance with gender norms or a native's adherence to British rule.

Even when women escaped the mind-forged manacles of patriarchal thought, when late century feminists (both male and female) worked to change the legal status of women, when economic restriction lessened and legal reforms ameliorated prejudices, women still were not free. Caird's novel demonstrates that the power of *love*, of ties to family and children, is much more constraining than governmental statutes. When a woman like Hadria feels empowered to pursue her career as a composer because of her emancipation from repressive ideas about women, she still is not emancipated from her sense of duty, obligation, and love. It is important to note that Hadria's brothers, both good sons and fine men, do not share Hadria's sense of responsibility for their parents' happiness. In a society that views women primarily as domestic beings, social expectations and the needs of family are "supposed" to be more important to women because of their "natural" affection. Domestic ideology *owns* women by defining what is possible and what is acceptable in wife, mother, and daughter.

The Daughters of Danaus directly addresses the issue of "possession" of women by men in the character of Mrs. Gordon, who is a constant concern to young Hadria Fullerton. Mrs. Gordon had been "given over" to Mr. Gordon when she was young, unschooled, and without thoughts and opinions truly her own. That Mrs. Gordon is never given a name of her own indicates how subsumed she is in her identity as wife and married woman and how little individual subjectivity she possesses. Hadria, appalled at the actions of a family that would not only allow but also encourage this to happen, says, "From ferocious enemies a girl might defend herself, but what is she to do against the united efforts of devoted friends?" (26). When Hadria's sister Algitha doubts that Mrs. Gordon feels ill-used, Hadria replies: "Another gruesome circumstance . . . for that only proves that her life has dulled her self-respect, and destroyed her pride" (26).

As John Stuart Mill and Frantz Fanon have both written, the goal of the dominator is to make the subject believe in her or his subjection, and thus both identically identify the imperialist's and the patriarch's goal: colonizing the mind of the subject people. In *The Subjection of Women*, Mill writes that men "have therefore put everything in practice to enslave [women's] minds. . . . The masters of women wanted more than simple obedience, and they turned the whole force of education to effect their purpose" (144). Fanon similarly observes: "Colonialism is not satisfied merely with holding a people in its grip and emptying the native's brain of all form and content. By a perverted logic, it turns to the past of the oppressed people and distorts, disfigures, and destroys it. . . . [T]he total result looked for . . . was indeed to convince the natives that colonization came to lighten their darkness" (37). Likewise, Caird's Hadria considers woman's possession in marriage to be truly savage because the woman's own sense of honor is enlisted to safeguard the marriage rite: "That enlistment is a masterpiece of policy. To make a prisoner his own warder is surely no light stroke of genius" (345).

Hadria does in fact marry, despite her reaction against Mrs. Gordon's sacrifice on the altar of marriage, because she sees marriage as "the hope of escape" (165) from her parents' home. Mary Wollstonecraft's depiction of parental tyranny in *A Vindication of the Rights of Women* (1792) prefigures Hadria's dissatisfaction with a parent's control over adult children: "To subjugate a rational being to the mere will of another, after he is of age to answer to society for his own conduct, is a most cruel and undue stretch of power; and, perhaps, as injurious to morality as those religious systems which do not allow right and wrong to have any existence, but in the Divine will" (153). As Wollstonecraft understands, a daughter has no recourse to an authority beyond paternal authority. When Hadria's parents claim "Divine will" in the form of social custom, Hadria sees no other solution to her dilemma outside of marriage, the one socially sanctioned way of moving from her parents' home.

Hadria's elder sister Algitha moves from home unmarried to pursue charity work in London. While she recognizes that "the truly nice and womanly thing to do, is to remain at home, waiting to be married," she has "elected to be *un*womanly" (31). Algitha's decision has a positive effect on her: "The change in Algitha since her departure from home was striking. She was gentler, more affectionate to her parents, than of yore. The tendency to grow hard and fretful had entirely disappeared" (132). But it is to the detriment of Hadria, who now has to assume all the filial duties that she and Algitha used to share, as well as comfort her parents for the loss of a daughter who chose to be "*un*womanly." In the words of her brother Ernest: "I believe Hadria married because she was sick of being the family consolation" (165). Like Alcharisi, Hadria wants to be an artist, to be more than a dutiful daughter. And like Alcharisi, Hadria marries to escape a daughter's duties.[9]

Hadria's views of marriage are not sanguine, for she recognizes that for a woman to be married is to be owned. She says to her future sister-in-law: "If *that* is what love means—the craving to possess and restrain and demand and hamper and absorb, and generally make mince-meat of the beloved object, then preserve me from the master-passion. . . . Do you suppose I could ever love a man who had the paltry, ungenerous instinct to enchain me?" (130–31). Marriage thus becomes a "savage rite of sacrifice" (249)—girls who belong mainly to themselves are absorbed and enslaved by their husbands in this ceremony full of artifice and hypocrisy. As chapter 2 of this study has demonstrated, the marriage ceremony is an example of "sly civility": a ritual of suppression masked as a benefit to the suppressed.

The choice between losing one's individuality in a restrictive marriage or losing one's emotional, financial, and familial support creates the most tragic situations in the novel. Caird displays a strange mixture of resentment and pity for Hadria's mother, Mrs. Fullerton, because every mother is one more link in a long chain binding women to renunciation and sacrifice. Like Hadria's mother, every mother demands vicarious restitution. Stifled as a girl, discouraged from pursuing "unfeminine" interests, disallowed from realizing her full potential, Mrs. Fullerton expects and feels justified in wanting the same type of sacrifice from her own daughter. And, again because of filial bonds, the daughter *wants* to obey. Love both inspires generous obedience and *demands* it. The tragedy is that the one woman who should most completely understand Hadria's struggles against repressive roles and corrosive conventions is the one woman who is consumed instead by the recollection of her own sacrifices, renunciations, and resignations in the name of love: "The memory of her own youth taught her no sympathy" (33). In order to feel loved in return, she must have the same self-sacrifice performed on her altar.

And this is the special lot of the daughter. Her brothers, who laugh at her inability to compose music because she has the duties of the household to take care of and the responsibilities of a daughter to fulfill, do not understand what it means for Hadria that "Instead of *doing* a thing, she had to be perpetually struggling for the chance to do it" (29). To their cajoling insistence that social obligations wouldn't hamper their intellectual or artistic pursuits, Hadria replies: "I wish *you* would go to eternal tennis-parties, and pay calls, and bills, and write notes, and do little useless necessary things, more or less all day" (30).[10] Then she gets to the heart of a woman's situation. Her future holds only three possibilities—all of which are untenable, as she tells her brothers: "I wish *you* had before you the choice between that existence [paying calls and bills in the parental home] and the career of Mrs. Gordon, with the sole chance of escape from either fate, in ruthlessly trampling upon the bleeding hearts of two beloved parents!" (30). Hadria is possessed by her love for her parents—and they possess her too. It is necessary for them to restrict her, to restrain her, because they cannot abide her rebellion, cannot sanction unorthodox behavior, must bring her in line with their wishes. And they convince themselves that their actions are ultimately for their daughter's own good.[11]

In this novel, every man in some way wishes—or believes himself *obliged*—to dominate women. Even Hadria's composition teacher M. Jouffroy, while encouraging her talents, supporting her unconventional decisions, and advising her in ways that seem attuned to Hadria's best interests, dominates and bullies her when she "disobeys." He makes certain decisions for her, without her knowledge or consent, as when he chooses to send away the messenger from home who brings Mrs. Fullerton's request for Hadria's return. He goes on a "tirade—about her art, and her country, and her genius, and his despair; and finally his resolve that she should not belong to the accursed list of women who gave up their art for '*la famille.*' . . . She had a great talent that she had no right to sacrifice to any circumstances whatever" (333–34). But Hadria decides she must return to her husband and her parents. *Love* requires that she give up her career as a composer, that she bid farewell to her opportunity to be remembered as the greatest composer of her age, the one "who could give such a sublime gift to her century" (334). When in the midst of composing, Hadria is possessed by her artistic genius. She finds, however, that she is even more relentlessly possessed by other considerations.

Parental tutelage mirrors the imperial logic of British superiority, in which taking away autonomy from darker-skinned people constitutes the first step toward civilizing them. This inversion of meaning (oppression as a means of emancipation) justifies colonial rule even when it involves cruelty and oppression. The myth of the Dark Continent, inscribing the idea that Africa needed colonizing on moral, religious, and economic grounds, can justify and make heroic actions that, in a different context, would be merely brutal, criminal, condescending, or deceitful. Likewise, the logic of familial duty and patriarchal care determines that daughters and wives be guided and restrained for their own good. Caird develops the connection between patriarchal and imperial logic, perceiving that parents of rebellious daughters experience real grief that is situated in their best understanding of their parental duty and their desire to help and guide their progeny. Nonetheless, like an anti-imperialist railing against the follies of imposing British customs on Africans or Indians, Caird also presents these parents as thoroughly misguided.

Caird gets to the heart of the connection between patriarchal attitudes and imperialist ideology when her narrator explicitly compares women to "*other subject races*" (287; italics mine). Men have an "instinct" (131) to dominate others different from them, whether different in terms of gender or of race. Professor Theobald, who seems like a kind, intelligent, gentle man, turns out to be exactly what Hadria fears in men. His true nature is not kind and gentle; it is egoistic and characterized by a desire for mastery. He begins his relationship with Hadria as a friend and comforter, but as he grows to love her, "He felt the savage in him awake, the desire of mere conquest" (431). Hadria's admission of love for him "would be the climax of his victory" (432).

Possession of Self and Others in Colonial Adventure Fiction

Colonial adventure and New Woman novels converge around the question of possession. One might imagine that the possession of *land* would be central in a novel of colonization; nonetheless, colonial adventure plots also hinge on the possession of *people*. Patriarchal possession finds its analog in imperial possession, although, in positing it as the province of savages, the imperialist works to deny any associations with possessive treatment of women. Indeed, native women are often contrasted with the white women of England in a move that both fictionalizes British gender relations and elevates white women above their actual legal position. But where men of color are concerned, British men adopt the patriarch's attitudes and actions.

When white women are present in a colonial adventure novel, for instance, the relations between men and women mirror those that exist at "home."[12] In *Allan Quartermain*, a trio of British men—Allan Quartermain, Sir Henry, and Captain Good—discover a lost African tribe *"nearly as white as ourselves"* (148; italics in original).[13] Nyleptha falls in love with Sir Henry, saying to him: "now hearken unto me, oh man, who hath wandered here from afar to steal my heart and make me all thine own. I put my hand upon thy hand thus, and thus I, whose lips have never kissed before, do kiss thee. . . . And I swear that I will love thee and thee only till death, ay, and beyond, if as thou sayest there be a beyond, and that thy will shall be my will, and thy ways my ways" (222). Nyleptha is the fantasy projection of British domestic life: a virginal woman who wants only to become her husband's property, to make her husband's law her law. She is a pure woman who knows what a man wants. Nyleptha belittles herself in comparison with Sir Henry: "I be as nothing in the eyes of my lord . . . who come from among a wonderful people, to whom my people are but children" (220), elevating both the ego and the national pride of the British conqueror. Then she talks of savage marriage rites: "ever since I was a woman the great lords of my kingdom have made quarrel concerning me as though . . . I were a deer to be pulled down by the hungriest wolf, or a horse to be sold to the highest bidder" (220).

But H. Rider Haggard disavows any likeness between Nyleptha's experience on the African marriage market and the state of affairs in England. Unlike Hadria, Nyleptha sees in British culture an alternative to savage bartering for brides. Nyleptha (and other woman characters in colonial adventure novels) functions to justify conventional British gender relations; she achieves this end, however, by projecting the colonizer's "savage" domestic relations onto those of the colonized. The contradiction between representations of a colonial world that mimics "home" and a colonial world that disavows home practices is characteristic of colonial discourse. The dominant discourse believes that the native is inferior and deserves to be dominated; at the same time it disavows a connection with slavery and oppression. In patriarchal discourse the same is true. Grant Allen's *The British Barbarians* suggests that women "want" to be ruled, just as the countryside in Africa "only wants the hand of civilized man to make it a most productive one" (Haggard, *Allan Quartermain* 72). This slippage between the two senses of "want"—meaning to lack and to desire—is again characteristic of the slippage between a discourse that draws the other in as it pushes the other away.

To dissolve the connection between Africa and Britain, Haggard projects the male impulse to regard women as property onto the African body. When Quartermain, Good, and Henry rescue a woman from drowning, they find she soon gets over her fear of the strangers "and was by no means anxious to return in such a hurry to her lawful owners" (159). Similarly, Quartermain's unsentimental sentiments in response to Nyleptha's confession of love for Sir Henry ("I really do not know what happened [next], for I could stand it no longer" [222]) are transferred to his African guide Umslopogaas: "I suppose it is because I am getting old, but I don't think that I shall ever learn to understand the ways of you white people. . . . He wants a wife, and she wants a husband, then why does he not pay his cows down like a man and have done with it?" (222). Quartermain, given his age and his cynicism, would likely say much the same. But part of the colonial process is a *disavowal* of likeness to the colonized, including avoiding any acknowledgment of similarity between African dowry rites and the British idea that a woman (like Grant Allen's Frida) is well married if her husband is wealthy.

Relations with white women, however, are relegated to the background in most colonial adventure novels. Although this background is foundational, the world of colonial adventure novels is largely male. When we consider passages in which white women are not present, we need to analyze, in terms of the late Victorian gender system, the relationship between the dynamics of the private sphere and the colonial sphere. Jeff Nunokawa's *The Afterlife of Property* claims that male Victorians sought a transcendent space of ownership; the permanence of home, as an arena of "pure possession," was comforting in regard to the insecurity of public/material goods. All could be lost in the marketplace, but a man's home was secure. In the colonies, "home" is not a particular place but a complex ideological place-holder. Home is an "ideological determinant of the subject" (George 2), so that one's self cannot be separated from one's concept of home. To the British colonizers in Africa, "home" is England, where permanence and security reside. Africa, where the very fact of British colonization proves that possession is always contested, is then a public sphere. But here again a space of "pure possession" is psychically necessary to secure rule. Within the public sphere that is Africa, relations between white men and natives re-create the domestic realm.

This is especially true in regard to the relationship between missionaries and natives. Christian discourse mediates between women and Africans to similar effect: traditional doctrine that emphasizes women's properly deferential role in relation to men is mirrored by missionary work that stresses the African's submission to both British rule and religion. In *Allan Quatermain*, the patriarchal tone is set in the Reverend Mr. Mackenzie's inspiring speech to the twenty-five native subjects who live on the mission with him, to go out to fight the two hundred-fifty Masai warriors who have captured his daughter. He couches his plea in terms like those that Hadria's family used to garner her obedience: "for years I have been a good friend to you, protecting you, teaching you, guarding you and yours from harm, and ye have prospered with me . . . ye will strive your best to save her, and to save me and her mother from broken hearts" (86). (Hadria's statement might appropriately be paraphrased here: From ferocious enemies an African might defend himself, but what is he to do against the united efforts of devoted friends?) As Mackenzie's statement, "ye will strive your best to save her," indicates, this is not so much a request as an order. They answer, in another instance of white male fantasy: "Say no more, my father . . . we swear it. Me, we, and ours die the death of dogs, and our bones be thrown to the jackals and the kites if we break the oath! It is a fearful thing to do, my father, so few to strike at so many, yet will we do it or die in the doing. We swear!" (87). Like Hadria's parents, Mackenzie wants—and eventually gets—complete compliance with his wishes. Mackenzie's natives (as they are called in the novel) feel compelled to act according to his commands, even though their life choices mimic Hadria's: either face self-annihilation in the face of Masai warriors, or break the heart of their nominal owner.

The patriarchal tone set by Mackenzie is adopted by Quatermain in relation to Umslopogaas, who addresses him as "My father" (35 and passim). Haggard likely formed his ideas about proper British relations to Africans during his years of service in the colonies under Lieutenant Governor of Natal Sir Theophilus Shepstone, whom the Zulu king Cetywayo called "father." This experience forms the basis of Haggard's analysis of the British government's South Africa policy, *Cetywayo and His White Neighbors*. The Transvaal is in a state of upheaval, writes Haggard, because the British have been too lax, too soft. South Africa needs "Firm, considered, and consistent policy" (ix) because "It is our wavering and uncertain policy, as applied to peoples, who look upon every hesitating step as a sign of fear and failing domination, that ... has really caused our troubles" (ix). Boers and black Africans do not understand "political necessities," so they cannot see "why their true interests should be sacrificed in order to minister to those necessities" (ix). This means that the British need to be forceful, strong, domineering. Moreover, this is what the natives most want from the British: "if the Government intends to do its duty and rule Zululand as it ought to be ruled . . . it would be welcomed by the large majority of both Zulus and Colonists" (45).

Quartermain, similarly, reminds Umslopogaas that the native needs a white man's help, advice, and leadership. Quartermain had left Umslopogaas a prosperous, powerful man. When Quartermain returns to Africa years later, he finds Umslopogaas without home or possessions—all because Umslopogaas did not have the benefit of the white man's sage and sound advice: "Years ago, when thou wouldst have plotted against Cetywayo, son of Panda, I warned thee, and thou didst listen. But now, when I was not by thee to stay thy hand, thou hast dug a pit for thine own feet to fall in" (37). By re-attaching himself to the white man's party, however, Umslopogaas regains his former stature. Like Hadria, who is prey to feminine follies without a parental hand to guide her, Umslopogaas just *wanted* a white man's hand to direct him.

Hadria's sentiment is typical of the New Woman novel's view of love: "Love. . . . We call the disposition to usurp and absorb another person by that name, but woe betide him or her who is the object of such a sentiment" (268). Rhoda Nunn in George Gissing's *The Odd Women* has a similar view of love, as does Marian Erle in Ella Hepworth Dixon's *The Story of a Modern Woman*, and Hester Gresley in Mary Cholmondeley's *Red Pottage*. Haggard represents the other side of the coin; he sees it as a man's duty to rule, to define, to set the standard. "[I]t is the undoubted duty of us English, who absorb peoples and territories in the high name of civilization, to be true to our principles and our aim, and aid the great destroyer [Time] by any and every safe and justifiable means" (*Cetywayo* 293–94). In Victorian Britain the conquest and possession of disempowered people becomes a central means of understanding and contesting relationships between men and women as well as colonizers and colonized.

Conclusion

The Territory Ahead: Wilde, Wells, Woolf

"Look within and life, it seems, is very far from being 'like this.'"
Virginia Woolf, "Modern Fiction"

By exploring the dialogic relationship of colonial adventure and New Woman fictions, this study has sought to enrich and complicate our understanding of late-nineteenth-century literary and political culture. Considering the subsequent evolution of these subgenres—how each responds to the contingencies of history, ideology, and literary form—is similarly instructive. Thus, this concluding chapter positions New Woman novels and colonial adventure fiction in relation to a wider array of fiction, beginning with the decadent movement of the fin de siècle and then moving on to modernism and science fiction. As previous critics have demonstrated, modernism emerges in part out of the experimental strategies of some New Woman novels, and science fiction is a major legacy of colonial adventure fiction.

To draw out the interrelationships among these movements and forms, this chapter will explore how each represents looking, seeing, and being seen. When Virginia Woolf argued that the strategies of traditional fiction were unfitted to twentieth-century life, she advised readers instead to "look within" (154) to discover how unlike life "realist" novels were. Woolf's mode of "looking within" became closely identified with her individual politics as well as her modernist aesthetic; other responses to looking will similarly register specific aesthetic and political allegiances. This study will conclude as it began—with Virginia Woolf—because not only does Woolf look forward to a new way of "looking" in her narrative mode, she does so while often casting significant backward glances at New Woman and colonial adventure fiction as well. That "ways of seeing" are important to all these genres reveals a continued dialog not only between New Woman and colonial adventure novels but also their literary heirs.[1]

Up to this point I have considered how colonial adventure and New Woman novels provide a medium for examining struggles for autonomy and the technologies of power that advance or suppress them. My focus on sight in this chapter envisions the gaze as a supplement to these other technologies, functioning analogously to discourse, possessiveness, and stereotype in the way it can be turned to varied ends for various purposes. Kimberly Devlin cautions that "the gaze is illusory—a constructed psychic possession or phantasmal projection; as a result, no one can actually 'have' it. But even though the perspectivally limited subject can never attain this site of visual wholeness and omniscience, he can . . . fantasize that he does indeed occupy it" (714). I would extend her note of caution, because critics tend to see only that visual power denies other viewing positions and, therefore, do not focus on the potential for rejection or re-appropriation of visual power. The Panopticon is the exemplary model of visual authority, but rarely can the power to see without being seen be so carefully controlled. As the interactions of New Woman and colonial adventure novels suggest, assertions of power are rarely uncontested and expressions of authority are rarely reduced to a single ideology.

Franz Fanon emphasizes the dual nature of vision in his pun on *scene* and *seen* (which Homi Bhabha reformulates as *site* and *sight*), to demonstrate that location and vision—one's point of view and what one sees—are intimately connected. Indeed, if one's "scene" is sufficiently sheltered, one might avoid being "seen" despite any apparatus of power the gazer possesses. Decadents, New Woman writers, colonial adventure novelists, science fiction writers, and modernists each exploit this trope because the gaze is not only an instrument of power but also a highly mutable and variable one. The economy of the gaze involves negotiation of dynamic variables—as do patriarchal and colonial rhetoric, hybrid forms, and discourses of possession. The economy of the gaze imposes a distance between seer and seen, and in that space, power can shift. Like discourse, the gaze is an instrument of power, and inherently unstable.

For obvious reasons the sovereign gaze is the point of view most often adopted by colonial adventure writers. It is interesting that H. Rider Haggard's works are often in implicit conversation with Oscar Wilde's, echoing many of the latter's ideological intimations. Wilde's aphorisms, felicitous phrasing, and his decadent characters' conversations on the value of doing nothing are far different from Haggard's earnest (and often awkward) rhetoric of action and adventure. Although their differences in style and subject are undeniable, they employ similar strategies in their common quest for the regeneration of British culture: male solidarity sustained by denigration of women; male power supported by male secrecy and action; a desire to exclude others through methods of scopic and discursive control.

Wilde's "The Critic as Artist" (1891) and Haggard's "About Fiction" (1887), manifestos on the function of literature at the present time, both valorize mystery, romance, and imagination—and do so in remarkably similar terms. "More and more, as what we call culture spreads, do men and women crave to be taken out of themselves," Haggard writes.

> More and more do they long to be brought face to face with Beauty, and stretch out their arms towards that vision of the Perfect, which we only see in books and dreams.... There are now royal roads to everything... but it is dusty work to follow them, and some may think that our ancestors on the whole found their voyaging a newer and fresher business. However this may be, a weary public calls continually for books, new books to make them forget, to refresh them, to occupy minds jaded with the toil and emptiness and vexation of our competitive existence. (173–74)

Compare Wilde's analysis of the current state of fiction:

> The old roads and dusty highways have been traversed too often. Their charm has been worn away by plodding feet, and they have lost that element of novelty or surprise which is so essential for romance. He who would stir us now by fiction must either give us an entirely new background, or reveal to us the soul of man in its innermost workings. The first is for the moment being done for us by Mr. Rudyard Kipling. ... As for the second condition, we have had Browning, and Meredith is with us. But there is still much to be done in the sphere of introspection. (402)

The goals are identical: to refresh the medium of the novel, reclaim the aesthetic, and regenerate British culture. Wilde does this by traveling the road of psychological introspection, Haggard by following the path of exoticism.

At the moments when their ideological agendas converge, both men depend on the power of spectacle to authorize their articulations of cultural solidarity and difference. As Bhabha points out, the danger of the gaze is that it can be returned, making the powerful subject into the object of the gaze. Wilde and Haggard, however, stave off this danger by having their male protagonists stage and participate in spectacle. By a conscious and conspicuous self-display, their heroes require that others look at them but retain power by prescribing how others perceive them. The hero who creates a spectacle is seen as he displays and defines himself. The legacy of empiricism insures that the spectator does not question the truth of what he sees; seeing is believing.

The Picture of Dorian Gray (1890) is perhaps the most famous example of the power of self-display. The artist Basil Hallward chastises Dorian about his reputation but ultimately reassures him, saying: "I don't believe these rumors at all. At least, I can't believe them when I see you" (161–62). Thus, because of his youthful look of innocence, Dorian continues to dominate London society and be accepted into proper circles despite continuous talk of his debauchery. He is protected from social harm by keeping his vulnerable self hidden away and presenting a spectacle of youth and beauty. Similarly, but to different purposes, the characters in Haggard's *King Solomon's Mines* depend on self-presentation to conquer those who may do them physical harm. When encountering the Kukuanas, a "savage" tribe with no knowledge of the outside world, Captain Good, Sir Henry, and Allan Quartermain are saved by the spectacle Good makes when interrupted in the middle of his toilette. The attacking natives are stopped by the sight of dentures and an eye-piece, of a half-dressed, half-shaved European. By playing upon the natives' incomprehension, Quartermain is able to provoke this response: "I see that ye are spirits. . . . Pardon us, O my lords" (114).

The adventurer and the dandy are united in opposing the familiar paths of literary production, in rejecting the mundane domestic world, and in resisting female power. Creating parallel discursive spaces for regenerating culture and celebrating extremes of masculinity, the adventurous and the effeminate male champion a world devoid of authoritative, autonomous women. The "degenerate" dandy and the imperial "civilizer" each survey the scene of the British novel and discover the same modes of male subjectivity and female subjection.

As I noted in the introduction, however, the decadent is often in accord with the New Woman's aims. Indeed, when we look at the wider scope of Wilde's works, we see that male visual power is less interesting to him than the technology of the gaze itself, no matter who is using it. Wilde puts women's power quite literally on display when he stages *Lady Windermere's Fan* (1892) in such a way that Mrs. Erlynne is seen controlling who sees whom, who sees what, and when. At the end of act 2, she is motionless at the center of the stage, with other actors rushing around her. She sends Windermere out of the room to call her carriage, and she determines not to let him see what she sees: the letter his wife (and her daughter) has written. Cool in a crisis, Mrs. Erlynne controls the action in this pivotal scene, a role she enacts again at the end of act 3. With all the men gathered in Lord Darlington's rooms after Lady Windermere's birthday ball, Mrs. Erlynne puts herself into the center of the action and subjects herself to the men's objectifying gazes in order to distract their attention from Lady Windermere, who slips out the door and out of view. Mrs. Erlynne has heard the men exchange innuendoes about her, and she thus would expose herself to social condemnation if she appears late at night in a single man's rooms. But she makes herself a spectacle to protect another woman, and although she temporarily suffers from the men's knowing smiles of bemusement at having "found her out," they do not gain power over her. Having "explained everything" (63), she realizes her every goal by the end of the play.

Although Haggard's male characters inhabit a predominately masculine world, when female characters appear, they often display visual power. One source of Ayesha's power in *She* is her ability to "see without eyes and hear without ears" (84). Ayesha knows the "secrets of Nature" (152) and can, by looking in a pan of water, see anything "to do with this country and with what I have known or anything that thou, the gazer hast known" (152). She sees the British adventurers approach the Amahaggar and can thus protect them against the tribe's violence, giving the message "White men come; if white men come, slay them not" (74). Her powerful vision—not shared by any of the men—protects them and provides for them.

By the turn of the century, the romance writer needed to find a new field of adventure. H. G. Wells was one of the first writers to annex science to the adventure novel. He is thus, in his own way, an explorer of new territory. Judith Wilt's "The Imperial Mouth: Imperialism, the Gothic, and Science Fiction" suggests that this metaphor of colonial arrogation is especially appropriate for describing the development of science fiction. Wilt argues that imperialism—especially cultural anxiety about its decline—was "a major contributing pressure for the mutation of Gothic into science fiction" (618). Wilt does not specifically draw out the relationship between imperial adventure novels and science fiction, but I would argue that the process she describes was caused by both colonial adventure fiction's registering of imperial angst and the historical process of imperialism. Indeed, Wilt chooses Haggard's *She*, a colonial adventure novel, as an example of the intermediary form of Gothic-science fiction. It is here that Patrick Brantlinger's definition of "imperial Gothic"—"that blend of adventure story with Gothic elements" (*Rule of Darkness* 227)—becomes a useful mediating term in understanding the complex interrelations between these changing fictional forms at the end of the nineteenth century.[2]

Wells's *The War of the Worlds* (1898) is both masterful science fiction and a paranoid parody of the colonial adventure novel: a reverse-colonization fantasy with a helpless hero and a purely accidental victory for the English. The invading Martians are defeated not by British ingenuity or military power but by bacteria, "the humblest things that God, in his wisdom, has put upon this earth" (171). While the bacteria manfully attack the Martians, the humans are in retreat, hiding from the Martians' superior technology and weaponry. In this world, the demise of the imperial adventure novel is signaled by the retreat of visible Western power.

The hero of *The War of the Worlds* prevails not by displaying his power but by hiding himself from the sight of hostile others. When Martians invade, he survives "by crawling, unobserved by these monstrous machines" (47); by having "ducked at once under water" (64), "crawled through dewy nettles and brambles into the broad ditch" (85), "hid in a shed in a garden" (120); and by "lay[ing] all the tenth day in the close darkness, buried among coals and firewood, not daring even to crawl out for the drink for which I craved" (143). When he "fell helplessly, in full sight of the Martians" he "expected nothing but death" (66). Indeed, his guiding philosophy runs entirely counter to that espoused by the likes of Allan Quartermain: "What was needed now was not bravery, but circumspection" (117).

The new ideology of Wells's hero becomes clear when the narrator/hero and an artillery man "crawl under [some] bushes and talk" (154). The artillery man relates his vision of the "state of affairs" (156): he repeats the phrase "We're beat" (154 passim) and declares that "It never was a war [between humans and Martians], any more than there's a war between men and ants" (155). The humans are so thoroughly overpowered, he notes, that they should take their cue from the social insects, re-create their world out of the Martian's sight, and thus find a way to prosper: "You see, how I mean to live is underground. . . . That's how we shall save the race" (160). This seemingly rational plan, however, takes on sinister overtones when the artillery man not only declares that "the useless and cumbersome and mischievous have to die. They ought to die" (160) but then indulges in a flight of power-mad fancy, imagining himself wielding a Martian Heat-Ray and wreaking destruction on all who oppose him. Wells thus suggests the danger of the position of power: the prerogative to use it against anyone who sees things differently than the powerful.

In retrospect, the narrator finds the artillery man's theory outlandish. But he accepts it at the time, and he asks the reader not to judge him harshly, recalling their vastly different points of view: "contrast [your] position, reading steadily with all [your] thoughts about [your] subject, and mine, crouching fearfully in the bushes and listening, distracted by apprehension" (161). The ideology of hiding he embraces influences all his perceptions. This "reassuring sense of hiding" (147) allies him with the lesser creatures of the earth; the shift from possessing the powerful gaze to avoiding the others' sight signals the end of the human reign. He feels an overwhelming "sense of dethronement, a persuasion that I was no longer a master, but an animal among the animals, under the Martian heel. With us it would be as with them, to lurk and watch, to run and hide; the fear and empire of man had passed away" (147).

Even after the Martians are dead, the final scenes the narrator pictures are riddled with doubt and distress. Despite the "Union Jack, flapping cheerfully in the morning breeze" (177) over the site of the Martians' final landing place (which symbolizes the British conquest of Martian territory), the narrator ends with "many debatable questions" (179) and without a sense of solid standing in or understanding of the world. The Martian invasion "has robbed us of that serene confidence in the future" (181) and so humans are required to "keep a sustained watch upon . . . the planet, and to anticipate the arrival of the next attack" (180). His final judgment is that "we can never anticipate the unseen good or evil that may come upon us suddenly" (181); therefore, hiding is a viable strategy of survival when one has "an abiding sense of doubt and insecurity" (182) about one's place in the world.

In other novels, Wells parses hiding quite differently. In *The Invisible Man* invisibility is not represented as passive retreat but as active power. As Griffin—the Invisible Man of the title—asserts to the man he implores for food: "Help me—and I will do great things for you. An invisible man is a man of power" (33). He further asserts his physical power when be becomes a mere "Voice" (38), threatening to use his invisibility to heighten his physical advantage over the Vicar and the Doctor who have invaded his rooms to examine his books. Invisibility, which insures his actions have no immediate consequences, allows him to indulge his bad temper and "set to smiting and overthrowing, for the mere satisfaction of hurting" (42). Indeed, "suppose he wants to rob—who can prevent him? He can trespass, he can burgle, he could walk through a cordon of policemen as easy as me or you could give the slip to a blind man! Easier!" (47). Wells demonstrates the danger that accompanies such unlimited power, though. Exploiting "the mystery, the power, the freedom" (66) of his state, "I was only just beginning to realize the extraordinary advantage my invisibility gave me. My head was already teeming with plans of all the wild and wonderful things I now had impunity to do" (74). But he discovered invisibility could be seriously debilitating: "I had no shelter, no covering,—to get clothing, was to forgo all my advantage, to make of myself a strange and terrible thing. I was fasting; for to eat, to fill myself with unassimilated matter, would be to become grotesquely visible again" (82). But lust for power means that, instead of resuming normal life, the Invisible Man desires an accomplice to help him plan his "Reign of Terror"—judicious killing for monetary benefit. Wells's narrative demonstrates a heightened awareness of what New Woman and colonial adventure fiction had already established: the complex economy of the gaze. The power to see and not be seen is riddled with contradictions, is both empowering and disempowering. A mobile mode of exercising power, it cannot be used to a single predictable end.

In New Woman novels, many of the female heroes want to become objects of public attention, like Hadria in Mona Caird's *Daughters of Danaus*, who brings notice to herself as both an unnatural woman and a famous composer; or Hester Gresley in Mary Cholmondeley's *Red Pottage*, who will be seen as the greatest writer of her age; or Mary Barfoot in George Gissing's *Odd Women*, who makes public speeches. Generally, their relatives—the forces of conservatism—want to hide them and are shamed by them. Feminist New Woman writers respond by representing the threats to highly visible women at the same time they allow women characters to use vision as power. In Olive Schreiner's "The Buddhist Priest's Wife" the feminist protagonist is dead in the narrative's present; the spectacle of her corpse frames her story and offers a ghostly commentary on her fate as a public actor. But this woman also plays with sight and signification when alive: she quite literally disappears before the male narrator's eyes: "he looked round, and she was gone. The door had closed noiselessly" (97). And in Charlotte Mew's "A White Night" (1903), a sacrificed woman enthralls the male narrator with the ritualistic theatricality of her death. The power of masculine vision, however, is ultimately used to feminist effect in both these stories. Both are frame narratives, and both thus foreground the cultural lenses that privilege their masculine narrators.

Schreiner's story opens with an image of a dead woman—"Cover her up!"—who is immediately dehumanized and objectified by the male narrator: "How still *it* lies!" (84; italics mine). Indeed, this woman is never given a name. Although she is an intelligent and independent woman who has gone off alone to India, these qualities are subsumed by the story's title, which identifies her only as the "Buddhist Priest's Wife"—a label that turns out to be a mocking invention imposed by the narrator. Imploring her to marry an Englishman because "a woman like you ought to marry, ought to have children" (89), the narrator jokes that she might at least "Marry some old Buddhist Priest" (86) and partly fulfill his idea of her social duty.[3] Because she does not frame this story, she cannot represent her reasons for going to India, explain what she will do there, or decide what she will be called. In the frame of the story, she is the inanimate object of the narrator's speculations.

The body of the story takes place eight years before the woman's departure for India and narrates the final conversation between the narrator and the woman. Because it is a dialog, readers see both characters' point of view. The scene of farewell is painful not only because it records a failure of genuine communication but also because it emphasizes the man's utter failure to understand the woman. She repeatedly tries to communicate one idea of herself to him; ruled by stereotype, he obstinately sees another. It becomes clear that the woman loves the narrator; she is going to India because staying in England means constant pressure to marry, and, "For a woman, marriage is much more serious than for a man" (90)—especially when the man she loves cannot see her. The man declares his own intent to marry, impelled by the same instinct "that makes a bird build nests at certain times of the year. It's not love; it's something else" (90). He wants "a home . . . a wife and children" (90). When the narrator pictures the wife that would best suit him, and when the woman adds her opinion about the ideal woman for him, it is only the man who fails to see that both are describing the "Buddhist Priest's Wife." Her response to his inability to see her is to remove *herself*; her reaction to his single-minded vision of her life's duty (to marry) is to go to "the East" for "a complex, interesting life" (88).

The narrator of "A White Night" is named Cameron, indicating his function as a recording eye. As the narrative progresses, however, we come to see that viewing himself as a mere spectator, with only the power to record and not to intervene, distances him from moral responsibility for what he sees. The story records an incident that Cameron, along with his sister Ella and her new husband King, witnesses during a turn through the picturesque villages of rural Spain. It is also a colonial encounter of the civilized metropole, represented by the British visitors, with the periphery of "the lawless state of those outlying regions" (120) and the "affable barbarians" (119) who inhabit them. Cameron deplores the inertia and the lack of progress of these Spanish towns whose civilization is a record of previous colonizations—"a Roman gateway . . . Moorish arches . . . A strong illusion of the Orient" (120)—but appreciates "its aesthetic value" (121). Cameron embraces visual pleasure, but Ella has an entirely different point of view. She sees the ugly reality of poverty in the cart driver's abuse of his donkey and the rationalization of male power in her brother's aestheticization of women. In this way, Mew causes her readers to question the "aesthetic pleasure on one hand, information and authority on the other" (Spurr 15) that accompanies expressions of visual power.

While exploring the aesthetic merits of an ancient church and convent, the three are accidentally locked in for the night. Here they observe "something singular" (126): a procession of monks, accompanied by a young veiled woman in white. The monks' chant is interrupted by "a cry—a scream" (126) from the woman, who, it becomes increasingly clear, is to be buried alive under the stones of the altar. Cameron sees in the woman an indifference to her fate similar to his own disregard for her well-being: "this detachment of her personality from her distress impressed one curiously. She wasn't altogether real, she didn't altogether live, and yet her presence there was the supreme reality of the unreal scene" (127). Cameron's use of the impersonal "one" in place of "my" records the uncoupling of his moral agency from her distress.

When Cameron turns his attention to the monks, they are as undifferentiated and detached as he is. They provide the background to the vision that most excites his interest: they are "an accompaniment—a drone" (128):

And then one lost the sense of their diversity in their resemblance; the similarity persisted and persisted till the row of faces seemed to merge into one face—the face of nothing—human of a system, of a rule. It framed the woman's and one felt the force of it: she wasn't in the hands of men. (129)

Like Cameron, the monks are not individually responsible for what is happening. Indeed, not only are they not individuals—they are not even men. They are merely the embodiment of religious and patriarchal power. In seeing the ritual in this way, Cameron absolves not only the monks but also himself from any responsibility beyond that of an observer of a natural phenomenon.

As the monks lower the woman into the ground, replace the slab of stone, and file out, King awakens Cameron to "the human and inhuman elements in the remarkable affair, which hitherto had missed my mind. . . . I saw what King had all along been looking at, the sheer, unpicturesque barbarity" (135). They go to the British Consul to report the incident, but the consul, like Cameron, sees only that "there was absolutely nothing to be done!" (137). Thus is Cameron allied with institutionalized systems of British power; and thus is British institutional power indicted as an enemy of women and their basic human rights.

Ella's identification with the woman, like the solidarity between Flora Steel's Kate and Newâsi, makes her incapable of enjoying the spectacle of the nun's destruction. Indeed, his sister "refuses to admit that, after all, what one is pleased to call reality is merely the intensity of one's illusion. My illusion was intense" (137). Ella knows that the embrace of spectacle and the equation of reality with illusion are fictions perpetuated to maintain masculine authority. She says to Cameron: "Oh, for you . . . it was a spectacle. The woman didn't really count" (137). He further indicts himself by agreeing with and expanding her reproach: "For me it was a spectacle, but more than that: it was an acquiescence in a rather splendid crime" (137). He admits the barbarity of the scene he witnessed and his immorality in letting it go forward; but it does not directly touch him so he experiences nothing but aesthetic pleasure in the beauty of the act and a thrill from participating in its execution.

The connection between Cameron's visual power and an ideology of feminine submission is made clear in the final paragraphs of the story. The moral Cameron draws from this story is that "the woman didn't really count. She saw herself she didn't. That's precisely what she made me see" (138). Indeed, says Cameron, what counts is the esteem with which she is viewed by "her order . . . her kind . . . her race" (138). She is part of a larger system, as are the monks, and this system has granted her the "honor . . . which bore her honorably through" (138). He concedes that she is horribly dispatched, but insists, in the final words of the narrative, that she is "not lightly, not dishonorably, swept away" (138). This is entirely congruent with ideals of women's domestic self-sacrifice that both acknowledge that women are swept away by forces beyond their control and declare that *good* women accept self-sacrifice for the pleasure of men, for the honor of their family, for the good of their race. Mew thus exploits the trope of visual power to expose the far-reaching ideological consequences of this power.[4]

These late-century mechanisms of visual power constitute the historical and literary background of Virginia Woolf's exhortation to "look inward." Literary criticism tends to view the rise of modernism as a rebellion against either the New Woman proper (as Elyse Blankley sees Gertrude Stein's relationship with her predecessors), or realist narrative forms more generally. The latter view sees Virginia Woolf's stream-of-consciousness narration as an entirely new way of representing feminine subjectivity, in that modernist women writers "found it necessary to break with tradition by shifting their focus from the outer world to the inner, from the confident omniscient narrator to the limited point of view, from plot to patterning, and from action to thinking and dreaming" (Kaplan 1–2). Ann Ardis has modified this view in one important way, arguing that modernism was nourished by and grew out of the literary ground prepared by the New Woman novel. By dismantling the marriage plot and demystifying the category "womanliness," the New Woman engendered a more general questioning of identity and character—one that would lead to the decentering of the self that modernism would leave in its wake. In addition, the omniscient narrator is often absent from New Woman narratives because these writers were trying to represent something not yet in existence—a truly "new" woman. This leads, writes Ardis, to questioning the realist "epistemology of representation" (3), because New Woman writers were no longer imagining that art imitates reality. Indeed, "issues of female identity fueled tremendous experimentation with narrative form in the 1890s" (169)—the kind of experimentation generally associated with modernist literature.[5] Restoring recognition of the New Woman's influence on modernist forms serves as an important reminder of the late-nineteenth-century contexts and conflicts that gave rise to the modernist aesthetic.

The very fact of the characteristically modern "limited point of view," as well as the modern writers' own repudiations of their predecessors, has encouraged some critics to view modernist literature as a withdrawal from social purpose and a rejection of Victorian modes. Indeed, Woolf's women characters are privately introspective, not publicly active, and in some respects, a novel like *Mrs. Dalloway* (1925) does represent a retreat from the New Woman novel's publicly visible characters. But it is not a retreat in the terms Elaine Showalter uses to describe modernist women writers; it is not "another form of self-annihilation from women writers, rather than a way of self-realization" nor a "retreat from the ego, retreat from the physical experience of women, retreat from the material world, retreat into separate rooms and separate cities" (*Literature of Their Own* 240). Rather, *Mrs. Dalloway* represents a withdrawal from and a critique of visual power—a move that in some ways echoes Wells's focus on *in*visibility and *not* seeing. In addition to the cautionary examples of New Woman and colonial adventure fiction, the culture of World War One propaganda may well have caused modern writers to rethink the perspective of the powerful. As Trudi Tate notes, when "narrative, along with other forms of representation, is enlisted to prolong and justify mass slaughter" (5), narrative point of view becomes more than a stylistic issue.

In "Women Novelists" Woolf claims that gender unmistakably marks perspective and thus authorship: "There is the obvious and enormous difference of experience in the first place. . . . And finally . . . there rises for consideration the very difficult question of the difference between the man's and the woman's view of what constitutes the importance of any subject" (qtd. in Abel 162). Woolf's insistence that men and women see things differently, that they value subjects differently, informs her rejection of the omniscient point of view and its rhetoric of monologic authority. Brenda R. Silver writes that "what distinguishes Woolf's perspective on traditional and cultural values from these men's is a divided consciousness, or double vision, that is inseparable from her consciousness of herself as a woman and her distrust of priestly male authority" (648). This "double vision" allows Woolf to comment upon and correct the uses and abuses of visual power that appear in New Woman and colonial adventure fiction.

In *Mrs. Dalloway*, the major targets of Woolf's criticism are dogmatic religion in the form of Miss Kilman (Clarissa's experience tells her that "religious ecstasy made people callous . . . dulled their feelings" [10]) and masculine medical authority as represented by Sir William Bradshaw and Dr. Holmes. These characters' social philanthropy is countered by their infliction of "private torture" (10) and their insensitivity to others. Holmes and Bradshaw are both blind to the suffering of shell-shocked Septimus Smith: each medical man's vision is limited by his faith in his own knowledge and by the force of his surety. These doctors are men "who mixed the vision and the sideboard; saw nothing clear, yet ruled, yet inflicted" (161). Bradshaw and Holmes have the power to impose their judgments on their patients, despite the fact that their vision is blurred, because all they see is filtered through the lenses of their own bodily health, medical fees, and British rectitude. Woolf demonstrates that the doctors can see only as well as the Regent's Park loiterers who try to decipher a skywritten advertisement. These spectators know that a plane is forming letters, and that the letters will form words, but cannot say if it is "a K, an E, a Y perhaps?" (20); they wonder, "what word was it writing?" (21). The sky watchers see that letters in the air move, shift, and drift freely, their meaning open to interpretation. The doctors do not see in this manner. They confer an incontestable diagnosis on a patient and maintain an unquestioning confidence in their own determinations.

Woolf finds this monstrous. Clarissa Dalloway has a different sort of vision: "She would not say of any one in the world now that they were this or were that . . . and she would not say of Peter, she would not say of herself, I am this, I am that" (7). Unlike the pompous self-importance and immaculate self-presentation of Hugh Whitfield—and the condescension, ostentation, and "damned insolence" that made him such "an intolerable ass" (124)—Clarissa "had the oddest sense of being herself invisible, unseen; unknown" (9). This sense of being unseen is related to her understanding that she has more than one self to see. She consciously gathers the "self" she presents to society in front of her mirror: "This was her self when some effort, some call on her to be her self, drew the parts together; she alone knew how different, how incompatible and composed so for the world only into one center, one diamond, one woman" (38). None of these incompatible selves is entirely knowable, so she does not pretend entirely to know any one else. Clarissa sees herself as unlike Miss Kilman and the doctors: "Had she ever tried to convert any one herself? Did she not wish everybody merely to be themselves?" (137).

Woolf's style, her emphasis on interior vision, also works to delegitimate the kind of visual power on display in late-Victorian fiction. Silver writes that at the end of her life, Woolf remained concerned with "the project that had occupied her throughout: the construction of a cultural narrative that would deconstruct the history and the 'traditions' that have empowered men to act like gods whose pursuit of their religions and beliefs threatened the very future of civilization itself" (647). But as we have seen, crusading feminists pursued their ends with similar zeal and righteousness. Woolf's narrative offers a corrective that is not necessarily gendered; rather, the limited point of view works against any arrogation of visual power. The course British history took at the beginning of the twentieth century—the unsatisfying outcome of the drawn-out Boer War and the devastation of World War One—caused an even more radical shift in human thought and perception than did the Post-Impressionist exhibition in or about December, 1910. As *The War of the Worlds* demonstrates, an England under attack and vulnerable must radically review its place in the world. *Mrs. Dalloway's* Peter Walsh thinks that the era directly after the war was equally important: "Those five years—1918 to 1923—had been, he suspected, somehow very important. People looked different" (77). Perhaps the difference is that people not only "looked different" but also *looked differently*. The totalizing vision was revealed as dangerous to both individual values and national safety.

In many ways, Woolf's open-eyed view of empire—her association of the imperialist desire to convert the natives with patriarchal medical practices, and her exploration of the destructive combination of militaristic and patriarchal ideology—forms a fitting conclusion to a study of New Woman and colonial adventure novels. Clarissa Dalloway provides a new vision of how to move forward in the wake of dissent from the colonies and about women's suffrage. To see as Clarissa sees, without employing the gaze of power, can counteract all those willing to say "they were this or were that"—including the imperialist who sees the native in a certain way and the New Woman who developed a more liberating, but nonetheless didactic and totalizing, vision. At the same time, as I noted in my introduction, it is important to recognize that Woolf's very repudiation of the ideas and fictional strategies of her predecessors draws significantly on the two subgenres at the center of this study. The dialog between New Woman and colonial adventure fiction—their imaginative interventions into questions of power, possession, and discursive control—opened new territory for re-imagining formulations of gender and empire.

Notes

Introduction

1. As Fraser, Green, and Johnston point out, the very term *colonization* is implicitly gendered feminine because of its close association with middle-class domesticity: Mother England and her colonies mimic the relationship of the English mother to her children. Rosemary Marangoly George explores at length how the metaphoric domestication of British foreign policy establishes the gendered authority of British women in her *The Politics of Home*.

2. This study focuses exclusively on fiction, but even a glance at the poetry of the late nineteenth century suggests that one could make similar claims about New Woman and imperial poetry. Kipling's attention to formulating "how to be a man" is congruent with some late-century women poets' new definitions of "the proper feminine" (to adapt Pykett's term). Studies of the imperial poetry of Kipling and Henty abound. The extension of the term *new woman* to poetry is fairly recent. See my "Naturally Radical: The Subversive Poetics of Dollie Radford," Ana I. Parejo Vadillo's "New Woman Poets and the Culture of the *Salon* at the *Fin de Siècle*," and Linda Hughes's introduction to *New Woman Poets: An Anthology*, which addresses the participation of women poets in the New Woman movement.

3. See Jason R. Rudy for a brief discussion of neoformalism and the recent works on Victorian poetry that have taken "literary form as a subtle and often neglected vehicle for broader cultural forces" (590), as well as Carolyn Williams's discussion of "'Genre' and 'Discourse' in Victorian Cultural Studies."

4. Talia Shaffer proposes that New Woman authors themselves manipulated this assumption in "'Nothing but Foolscap and Ink'": "Fictionalizing the New Woman allowed her to be defined in any way the author needed, at any time. It allowed Ouida and Grand to assimilate the New Woman to the powerful tradition of demonic/angelic women whose sway over the Victorian imagination Nina Auerbach has described. As a mythic icon, the New Woman evokes an extraordinary range of emotional associations, a flood of feelings which can powerfully support whatever goal the writer has channeled it towards" (45).

5. In their introduction to *The New Woman in Fiction and in Fact*, Angelique Richardson and Chris Willis identify these changing laws as "the beginnings of a new attitude toward women" (7).

Chapter 1. "A New Battle of the Books": Gender, Genre, and Imperialism

1. Sally Mitchell in "New Women, Old and New" notes that "'New Woman' had the same conflicted resonance that 'Feminist' has acquired in recent decades. . . . 'New Woman' and 'Feminist' could—and can—be claimed with pride, yet both also became terms of anathema" (581).

2. Eric Partridge's etymological analysis of "tommyrotic" confirms that this term originated in the mid-1890s from a combination of "tommyrot" (which itself likely stemmed from "tommy," meaning "bloody" like the color of the soldier's coat) and "erotic."

3. Several critics and historians, most notably J. A. Mangan and John MacKenzie, have written about the propaganda uses of boys' adventure fiction; I contend that the propaganda extended into literature read by adults.

4. Shorter New Woman narratives often violate this "rule" and are open-ended—a characteristic of many short stories. For example, Olive Schreiner's "Three Dreams in a Desert" (1891) an allegory of women's emancipation, demonstrates the slow and painful road to women's eventual liberation from masculine domination as well as her own self-imposed limits. Although Schreiner strives to assert that this brave new world will come, her utopian vision is at this point merely and literally a dream in the desert.

5. The exception to this fear of miscegenation in colonial adventure novels comes when white adventurers meet *white* women in Africa. There, as in England, the man assumes the position of authority. Indeed, the white man in Africa has more authority than he would in Britain, because the queen bows to *him* in Africa. In *King Solomon's Mines* (1885), Rider Haggard depicts a long scene in which the white queen subjects herself to Sir Henry Curtis and declares him *her* ruler. (This passage is discussed at greater length in chapter 2.) Haggard's other white queen, Ayesha, also professes her submission to a Haggard hero.

6. The hero Dick in Henty's *The Young Colonists* has a younger brother John who loves books and prefers reading to romping outdoors. This novel has no room for a boy like John, however; he drops out of the story completely after the introductory chapter. Henty's implication is that the colonies have no room for men who are book-ish and educated.

7. Hugh Stutfield's 1897 comment is typical: "the lady writer has for some years past been busily occupied in baring her soul for our benefit, and not only baring it, but dissecting it, analyzing and probing into the innermost crannies of her nature. . . . The monotony of her life, its narrowness of interest, the brutality and selfishness of man, the burden of sex, and the newly awakened consciousness of ill-usage at Nature's hands, form the principal subjects of her complaint; and the chorus of her wailings

surges up to heaven in stories, poems, and essays innumerable" ("Psychology of Feminism" 105).

8. Because of her understanding of the formative power of social conditions, the New Woman often finds herself railing against male social critics and philosophers who view the world in terms of individual action and achievement. Caird's *The Daughters of Danaus* (1894) depicts a meeting of the "Preposterous Society," the debating club formed by the precocious Fullerton children. The topic of the evening is Emerson and Fate; Ernest argues for Emerson, his sister Hadria against. While Ernest can fully embrace Emersonian self-reliance, Hadria brings practical, material circumstance to bear on philosophy and finds that "Emerson is shockingly unjust" (11): "Emerson never was a girl. . . . If he had been a girl, he would have known that conditions *do* count hideously in one's life" (14). Because of her *personal* understanding of the limitations placed on girls, over which they have no control, Hadria debunks Emerson's claim that "If the soul is strong enough it can overcome circumstances" (11). She further argues (here echoing Mill), "Girls . . . are stuffed with certain stereotyped sentiments from their infancy, and when that painful process is completed, intelligent philosophers come and smile upon the victims, and point to them as proof of the intentions of Nature regarding our sex, admirable examples of the unvarying instincts of the feminine creature" (23). Such an ideology doubly wrongs women: first by insisting on the power of individual will, then by using women's lack of individual power as proof of their inability to possess it.

9. Constance Harsh notes that newspaper reviewers often did not recognize "New Woman fiction" as a genre at all. It seems that the connection with naturalist (or, as Zola deemed it, "experimental") fiction preceded the widespread designation "New Woman" (85).

10. This literature is "effete" because it involves falling away from manly restraint and "yielding ourselves to the warmth and color of its excesses, losing our judgment in the ecstasies of the joy of life" (Waugh 210).

11. Nonetheless, in "The Decay of Lying," Wilde denigrates Haggard for being less wholehearted in his lies to his readers: "As for Mr. Rider Haggard, who really has, or had once, the makings of a perfectly magnificent liar, he is now so afraid of being suspected of genius that when he does tell us anything marvelous, he feels bound to invent a personal reminiscence, and to put it into a footnote as a kind of cowardly corroboration" (295).

12. Haggard looks forward to the day "when Naturalism has had its day, when Mr. Howells ceases to charm" ("About Fiction" 180); Clark criticizes "Mr. Howells" for trying "to dissuade this generation from having one minute's time or patience for such stories as Mr. Haggard writes" (6). Howells's prescriptions about fictions, writes Clark, are "babbling folly" and "sheer and unmixed nonsense" (6).

13. Stutfield claims that university education is responsible for the "unpleasant" books New Women write: "In particular the New Woman . . . is a victim of the universal passion for learning and 'culture,' which, when ill-digested, are apt to cause intellectual dyspepsia. With her head full of all the 'ologies and 'isms, with sex-problems and heredity, and other gleanings from the surgery and the lecture-room, there is no space left for humor, and her novels are for the most part merely pamphlets, sermons, or treatises in disguise" ("Tommyrotics" 837).

Chapter 2. "Do we speak the same language?": Contested Discourse at Home and Abroad

1. M. M. Bakhtin and Michel Foucault offer complementary definitions of "discourse" and related concepts that inform my use of the term here. For Bakhtin, discourse is the space and process where intersubjectivity is established, objects of knowledge produced, and values assigned. "Discursive genres," which are irreducibly diverse, clash and compete in the production of knowledge, and this dialogical process constitutes society (see especially 133–34). In *Discipline and Punish*, Foucault articulates the relationship between discourse and power thus: "power and knowledge directly imply one another . . . there is no power relation without the correlative constitution of a field of knowledge, nor any knowledge that does not presuppose and constitute at the same time power relations" (27). "Discursive practices" (comprising institutional bases, qualified members, and normalized production procedures) assign subject positions for their practitioners and determine their objects of knowledge.

2. Discourses of domination are riven by an irresolvable tension because they first define the other as entirely unlike the self (savage, dependent, in need of rule) and, at the same time, claim complete knowledge of this other. This knowledge/power nexus is the essence of Orientalism as Edward Said has defined it: "To have such knowledge of a thing is to dominate it, to have authority over it" (*Orientalism* 32). In this equation, knowledge is power. The equation will never balance, however, because the imperialist concomitantly posits that the value of x cannot be known: the x factor is the inscrutable other who is completely different, absolutely foreign, utterly incomprehensible.

3. See Patrick Brantlinger's discussion of John Ruskin as a "partial critic of imperialism" ("A Postindustrial Prelude" 469) for an instance of criticizing imperialism from within the terms established by colonial discourse.

4. See David Rubinstein's *Before the Suffragettes* for a treatment of the significant advances made by women in the 1890s. They propounded "types of emancipation more far-reaching than the immediate impact of the parliamentary vote could be" (xi) because they challenged attitudes toward women's capacity and chastity: the right to rational dress, education, employment; the privilege of unchaperoned travel

and participation in sports; the freedom of unfettered access to books, music, and entertainment.

5. There is far less explicit debate in the periodicals over colonial adventure novels or characters. Not only were the character types they championed farther from home and quotidian situations, readers who emulated these heroes would not have a significant impact on the British way of life. In essence, colonial adventure fiction posed less of an immediate threat to British social customs and thus was less contested. Debates over the imperial project did appear, such as the one that was printed in the pages of the *Contemporary Review* between two liberal members of Parliament, J. Lawson Walton (pro-imperialist) and R. Wallace (anti-imperialist). Their disagreement, however, did not challenge the specific valence of words or phrases, but presented different views on the topic. Neither established terms that would continue in the culture at large outside their personal debate.

6. The ubiquity of the "daughters" debate is indicated by *Punch's* contribution, "The Naughty Daughters," in which a middle-class household responds to the revolution in female manners by parodying all the debate's catchphrases.

7. Feminist "maenads" continue to be grist for the conservative mill, as when Harold Bloom speculates that Virginia Woolf is "the precursor of our current critical maenads" (31).

8. In *Backlash*, Susan Faludi reports that much the same happened in 1985 when a marriage study by Harvard and Yale researchers "proved" that among college-educated women who postponed marriage for a career, those unmarried by age 30 had a 20 percent chance of ever marrying; by 35, a 5 percent chance; by 40, a 1.3 percent chance (9). As Faludi notes, "The statistics received front-page treatment in virtually every major newspaper and top billing on network news programs and talk shows" (9), despite the fact that Jeanne Moorman, a Census Bureau demographer, debunked the numbers, the method, and the findings (11). Faludi posits that feminist backlash spurred this public punishment of women who failed to follow traditional female paths. Women who advance in their careers and postpone marriage both compete with men for jobs *and* give the lie to the image of women as romantic, relational, dependent. In fact, "The more women are paid, the less eager they are to marry. A 1982 study of three thousand singles found that women earning high incomes are almost twice as likely to *want* to remain unwed as women earning low incomes" (16).

9. Shannon Russell compares nineteenth-century emigration schemes to social sanitation: "The language of Victorian sanitary reform and the rhetoric of modern-day green politics are appropriate tools for understanding the politics of emigration. The emigrant's 'second chance for a new life' was promoted as his or her moral and social 'recycling,' with the benefit of a corresponding environmental cleanup at home once this 'shoveling out of paupers' had occurred" (46).

10. Feminists colonized the significance of these statistics to such an extent that

the small chance of a woman marrying became a primary reason for educating women to support themselves. By 1889 Grant Allen was rebutting the feminists' rebuttal of Greg without having to specifically cite any of them. He calculates the numbers to establish that there are ninety-six men for every hundred women. Allen thus finds the arguments that women must support themselves overstated. Indeed, it is "only four who need go into nunneries or study higher math" ("Plain Words on the Woman Question" 454).

11. Of course, *Heart of Darkness* specifically addresses Belgian imperialism, as Marlow travels to the Belgian Congo under the auspices of a Belgian trading company; but it is difficult to interpret the English Marlow, telling his tale in a boat on the Thames with London looming in the distance, as commenting *merely* on the Belgians' practices.

12. This seems to be one of Kurtz's admirable points in Marlow's eyes. Faced with Kurtz's death, "I was within a hair's breadth of the last opportunity for pronouncement, and I found with humiliation that probably I would have nothing to say. This is the reason why I affirm that Kurtz was a remarkable man. He had something to say" (69). While readers coming on to the seventieth page of Marlow's almost uninterrupted discourse might think he is too modest, Marlow admires Kurtz's ability to speak, even though Marlow is always affirming that his discourse is both deceitful and self-deluding.

13. This last instance seems to be Gissing's concession to propagating the species. As Mary says to Rhoda, "My dear, after all we don't desire the end of the race" (51).

14. See Hammerton on lower-middle-class female emigration, and Diamond on the FMCES.

15. He imagines women going from man to man to man, but men's sexuality is, strangely, not an issue. Nor are the prostitutes frequented by men, nor the way Grand's male characters have behaved in the past (as disease-spreading womanizers). But as this reviewer reminded us earlier, "that diamond-pointed satirist Pope . . . affirms that 'every woman is at heart a rake,' and 'most women have no character at all!'" (292).

16. This is, of course, a reversal of the prevailing law, under which it was easier for a man to end a marriage than a woman.

17. Said's caveat about Orientalist discourse is useful in this context. Orientalist knowledge *does* control the terms in which the Orient is understood, but more important is that Orientalism is a discourse in the Foucauldian sense: the network of customs, manners, knowledges, sciences, and social truths that organizes information about the East. "This is not to say that Orientalism unilaterally determines what can be said about the Orient, but that it is the whole network of interests inevitably brought to bear on (and therefore always involved in) any occasion when that peculiar entity 'the Orient' is in quest" (*Orientalism* 3).

Chapter 3. Staking Claims: Colonizing the New Woman Novel

1. Garrett Stewart is the only literary critic to have written more than a few lines on *Meeson*; he calls attention to its status as "a curious amalgam" (156) of New Woman and adventure fiction.

2. Masculinity studies are an important corollary to the study of the New Woman. For an analysis of ideologies of manliness in the context of the New Woman, imperialism, and late-century fiction, see especially Ronald Hyam's *Empire and Sexuality: The British Experience*.

3. Proponents of the New Woman cite evolutionary theory as well, but see the New Woman as a sign of progress. Frances Martin describes the "Glorified Spinster" as having evolved "from the class Spinster" (371) and notes that the New Woman marks an advance, not a decline, of the species: "An Old Maid is a woman *minus* something; the Glorified Spinster is a woman *plus* something" (374)—namely, education, self-confidence, political sensibilities, a logical mind, and a happy independence.

4. Allen appropriates J. S. Mill's formulation that patriarchal ideology and training has deformed women's nature and ability in order to blame the victim and exonerate the victimizer. He writes that "The slavishness begotten in women by the *regime* of man is what we have most to fight against, not the slave-driving instinct of the men" ("Plain Words" 458)

5. Again, imperial politics are inseparable from gender politics. Eve Sedgwick has explored the function of women in mediating relations between men in "Gender Asymmetry and Erotic Triangles." See also Elizabeth Signorotti's "Repossessing the Body: Transgressive Desire in 'Carmilla' and *Dracula*."

6. Gilbert and Gubar argue that *men* are secondary in this novel. Kallikrates was a priest of Isis (a woman); he leaves Isis to follow another woman (Amenartas); he then finds himself under Ayesha's rule and is killed by her. Leo—the reincarnation of Kallikrates—also follows Amenartas, for she is both his ancestor and the author of the artifact that brings him to Africa in search of Ayesha. Once he finds the woman his foremother sent him to destroy in revenge for killing Kallikrates, he is ruled by her, unable to control his desire for her beauty and knowledge. Despite these considerations, however, it is the men who regain center stage, and *women* who are pushed aside by the male narrator and the masculine narrative.

7. As George Stade notes in relation to *Dracula*, "We are susceptible to [Dracula] because he is already in us. . . . The primitive brain that makes Dracula what he is lies dormant even in cultured British gentlemen, but in them it is entombed in an overlay of new brain-matter generated by progressive Victorian culture. . . . It is what distinguishes Victorian gentlemen from Victorian ladies, in whom the overlay is thin" (205).

8. Arata writes that Andrew Lang, Arthur Conan Doyle, and Haggard all championed romance as antidote to effeminate modernity:
Though it has often been read by later critics as unambiguously celebrating late-Victorian masculinist ideals, the male romance is in fact deeply imbued with a sense of loss. Through this genre male middle-class writers responded, not always coherently, to their sense of disenfranchisement in the world. That this disenfranchisement was more perceived than real is indisputable. Yet the theory and practice of the male romance reveals an array of anxieties at once personal, "racial," political, and aesthetic: anxieties concerning the dissolution of masculine identity, the degeneration of the British "race," the moral collapse of imperial ideology, and the decline of the great tradition of English letters. (89)

9. Murphy notes that Ayesha also actively subverts the "mother-role" with her eugenic experiments to produce deaf-mute servants (45).

10. There are a few exceptions: Olive Schreiner's *The Story of an African Farm* is of course set in Africa, and the heroine of Schreiner's short story "The Buddhist Priest's Wife" sets out for India when she is disappointed in her life in England; Netta Syrett's "Thy Heart's Desire" is set in an unnamed colony, most likely India.

11. This unrealistic, although poetically just, rendering of Meeson's and Augusta's shipboard lives has more affinity with late-century Indian romances by women writers than with either New Woman novels or adventure romances. The typical Indian romance involved a woman sailing to India to find romance and a measure of freedom from strict British mores; Haggard's narrator opines that "A passenger-steamer is Cupid's own hot-bed" (88), and describes how "Augusta's grey eyes had been too much for Mr. Tombey [the wealthy colonist], as they had been too much for Eustace Meeson before him" (88). I discuss Indian romances at greater length in chapter 4.

12. Stewart addresses "the conscripted reader"—the ways writers induct readers into certain discursive systems by directing their attention in specific ways. He writes that both adventure tales and New Woman novels eschew direct address because "Reader apostrophe suits neither the tall tale that is credible only if free of all rhetorical posturing nor the psychosocial exemplum too rigorous for the ruses of persuasion" (153–54). Haggard's consistent use of direct address here exemplifies the "genre trouble" that vexes his narrative enterprise in *Meeson*.

13. The bound volume of *Meeson* was published by Spencer Blackett, who bought out J. and R. Maxwell's publishing business.

Chapter 4. "Aboriginal" Interventions: The New Woman Adventure Novel

1. Although I believe *On the Face of the Waters* has been consistently undervalued in the critical literature, I am skeptical of the hagiographic impulse among Steel's early commentators, which for decades obscured the imaginative complexity of her

best work. Daya Patwardhan describes her monograph, *A Star of India: Flora Annie Steel, Her Works and Times*, as "a tribute" to Steel. Indeed, Patwardhan writes that Steel "was not a mere author. She mixed with ordinary humanity, the average men and women of India of her time, in the various capacity of a social reformer, medical advisor and practical educationist. Her natural gifts of intelligence, tenderness, sympathy and charm enabled her to understand the philosophy and religious ideology of India. . . . Indeed, Mrs. Steel's work reveals the heart and soul of India as seen by a sensitive, sympathetic British woman" (2).

2. Both of these statements appear in the publisher's notices advertising *On the Face of the Waters*, found at the end of *In the Permanent Way* (1898 reprint).

3. Gottlob Schreiner, Olive's father, was a German citizen who traveled to Africa with a British missionary society. According to First and Scott, Gottlob "continued all his life to feel alien, not as a white missionary in Africa but as a German attached to an English mission society" (45). Olive's presentation of national views that range beyond England may well have been influenced by her father's national identity as well as his sense of alienation.

4. Whether Schreiner's depiction of native Africans reveals her unexamined racism, or whether Schreiner is depicting the harsh truth of British and Boer attitudes toward African natives is much at issue. See Gerson for a summary of divergent critical opinion.

5. The essays in Strobel and Chaudhuri's *Western Women and Imperialism* address precisely this issue.

6. And not just for nonpolitical reasons, as Steel's critics often suggest. The discontent had been fostered for some time, from the annexation of Oude, to the public shackling of soldiers and the rumors of animal fats in the cartridges. Indeed, Steel opens the novel with the aftermath of the Oude annexation to show discontent among Indian people of all castes. Soma reveals that sepoys are especially disillusioned by the move: "Now that Oude was annexed, [the British] took away [from the sepoys] the extra leave due to foreign service" (31). Soma tells Jim that "the current jest" in the regiments is "that the maps were tinted red—i.e. shown to be British territory—by savings stolen from the sepoy's pocket" (31).

7. This exploding of the sexual double standard—Steel's implicit argument that "fallen" women are as worthwhile, honorable, and decent as their "fallen" male partners—also aligns *On the Face of the Waters* with New Woman novels.

8. Singh uses "Anglo-Indian" in the late nineteenth century sense, meaning British citizens living in India (not, as it tends to used now, persons with mixed Indian/British heritage). For the sake of clarity and consistency, I will adopt this usage throughout the chapter.

9. Perhaps because the majority are written by women, Singh tars Indian romances with the same brush that critics have often applied to New Woman novels: they

have "little sense of style, are poor in characterization and plot construction, and occasionally suffer from a propagandist tendency"(4).

10. In *Rule of Darkness* Brantlinger devotes a chapter, "The Well at Cawnpore: Literary Representations of the Indian Mutiny of 1857," to Indian Mutiny novels, which were enormously popular at the end of the century. He reports that over fifty Indian Mutiny novels were published in the last twenty years of the nineteenth century. Jenny Sharpe categorizes *On the Face of the Waters* as "Indian Mutiny fiction" (85), but places Mutiny fiction within the wider framework of colonial adventure novels.

11. Erlton's highly colloquial speech—using the term "oner at thinking" to indicate that Kate is a singularly thoughtful person—reveals his similarity to Kipling's Tommy Atkins: blunt, unpretentious, unrefined.

12. An excellent example of the adventure novel's naturalization and aggrandizement of violence comes from *Dracula*. Arthur Goldaming is instructed by the vampire hunter Van Helsing to kill the vampire who was once his fiancée:

"Take this stake in your left hand, ready to place the point over the heart, and the hammer in your right".... Arthur took the stake and the hammer, and when once his mind was set on action his hands never trembled nor even quivered. ... Then he struck with all his might.... He looked like a figure of Thor as his untrembling arm rose and fell, driving deeper and deeper the mercy-bearing stake, whilst the blood from the pierced heart welled and spurted up around it. His face was set, and high duty seemed to shine through it; the sight gave us courage. (191–92)

After Arthur thanks Van Helsing for the rest they have given Lucy, "the Professor and I sawed the top off the stake, leaving the point of it in the body. Then we cut off the head and filled the mouth with garlic. We soldered up the leaden coffin, screwed on the coffin lid, and gathering up our belongings, came away" (193). The rationality of their action, the inevitably of the narrative, the surety of their virtue—all of these elements work together to justify this act of extreme violence and, indeed, represent it as an act of deliverance. The reader is given no scope to picture a different scenario—one in which, perhaps, vampires represent an advance on human mortality and weakness and allay British fears of degenerative decline.

13. Unaccountably, Saunders uses this passage to establish that Steel's novel is a "typical adventure tale" in which "the presence of women and children on the frontier provides the men with justification for any behavior" (312).

14. Steel's short fiction provides further evidence of how she refutes the soldierly adventure aesthetic. Nathaniel Craddock, in her story "The King's Well" (1897), is a British soldier hiding from insurgent sepoys during the Mutiny. He is aided by an Indian woman who judges him as an individual rather than as part of a hated group: the British Army. When British troops return to take the village, she is bringing Crad-

dock supplies. The overeager British troops shoot and kill her. Not only do they "*kill somebody*," they kill a civilian woman who has helped a British soldier.

15. Sharpe mentions the New Woman, but does not argue for the status of *On the Face of the Waters* as New Woman novel: "Although Steel restores English women to the colonial historiography from which they are absent, she writes her story according to gender issues that were current at the time of the novel's writing. . . . My own interest in Steel's Mutiny novel lies less in demonstrating a faithfulness to the past than in reading how the past is made to accommodate the 'new Woman' of the post-Mutiny era" (88).

16. I do not claim, however, that Alice "becomes a model for Steel of appropriate female behavior" (308) as Saunders does.

17. Kate Flint identifies one of the aims of New Woman fiction as generating and consolidating this type of community. The letters received by Sarah Grand, George Egerton, Mona Caird, and Emma Brooke "testify to their popularity among woman readers, and to the influence of their work in the growing feminist movement. The 'New Woman' fiction, far more even than the sensation novels earlier in the century, may be said to have created and consolidated a community of woman readers" (305).

Chapter 5. "Unhand Her!": Possession and Property

1. Caird's argument famously prompted 27,000 responses when the *Daily Telegraph* requested correspondence on the subject "Is Marriage a Failure?"

2. Feminists frequently deployed the figure of the prostitute in their fight against compulsory marriage. Customs and laws that make it difficult for single women to support themselves, argue Frances Power Cobbe and Olive Schreiner (among others), force women to marry merely for support, essentially prostituting themselves for money. Cobbe writes: "Is it not to the conclusion that to make it woman's *interest* to marry, to force her, by barring out every means of self-support and all fairly remunerative labor, to look to marriage as her sole chance of competency, is precisely to drive her into one of those sinful and unhappy marriages" ("What Shall We Do?" 238). Schreiner's *Woman and Labor* (1909) revealed her belief that the vast majority of European sexual relationships—in marriage or in prostitution—were determined or influenced by the financial power of the male (First and Scott 272). Even though feminists exploited the connection between prostitution and marriage for their own ends, the association has a strong antiwoman component. As Jan Cohn points out, women's exclusion from the public sphere "reduced women's economic function to her role in the marriage market," thus making marriage "her only real economic resource; and marriage to a man socially and economically her superior, her only real chance for upward mobility, her only recourse to power. But such a marriage,

however desirable it might in fact have been, was publicly denigrated; romantic love insisted that marriage be based on emotional rather than economic considerations" (8).

3. These early critical works generally focused on canonical—that is, male—authors. Except for George Eliot, New Woman writers analyzed in these studies are men: Thomas Hardy, George Meredith, George Moore, George Gissing, and occasionally Grant Allen.

4. *Deronda*'s critique of marriage is not limited to Alcharisi's sentiments. But although the novel features in Gwendolyn a strong female protagonist (as do *Middlemarch* and *The Mill on the Floss*), and although it demonstrates the consequences of Grandcourt's "empire of fear" (395), *Daniel Deronda* still does not affect a New Woman novel's critique of marriage. While Gwendolyn's marriage is deplored and deplorable, it is not so much the institution that is evil as the man she marries. One senses that Deronda's and Mirah's marriage will not reproduce the injustice of Gwendolyn's and Grandcourt's.

5. The encounter between Deronda and his mother exemplifies the paradox of nationalism identified by Anne McClintock: the family as a metaphor for the nation offers a single genesis narrative of national history and unity; at the same time, the family as an institution is dehistoricized and excluded from national power.

6. A "Hill-Top Novel," according to Allen's introduction to *The British Barbarians*, "is one which raises a protest in favor of purity" (vii). He further has decided "to add the words, 'A Hill-top Novel,' to every one of my stories and solely for the sake of embodying and enforcing my own opinions" (xi) because so often, editors and publishers refuse his books or insist on certain emendations before agreeing that they are fit for a mixed audience. When answering the question of why he does not merely write "deliberate treatises" (xiv) read only by wise men who will not be harmed by the radical ideas therein, he answers: "because wise men are wise already; it is the boys and girls of a community who stand most in need of suggestion and instruction. Women, in particular, are the chief readers of fiction; and it is women whom one mainly desires to arouse to interest in profound problems by the aid of this vehicle" (xv). Allen is a good patriarch: he will guide and inform women of what they need to know and what they should think on various topics.

7. The critique of custom in *The British Barbarians* (Ingledew says that being "brought up" to think in a certain way is "a very queer substitute indeed for thinking" [87]) does not seem to pertain to Allen's own sentiments regarding women. In "Plain Words on the Woman Question" he writes, "being a man, I, of course, take it for granted that the first business of a girl is to be pretty" (455).

8. Even though there is a nineteenth-century ideal of sacrifice for men—to their country, for instance, as displayed in *Daniel Deronda*—it is not generally a sacrifice made to women.

9. Deirdre David addresses Elizabeth Barrett Browning's father's pathological need to regulate his daughter thus: "she declared to Browning that 'the evil is in the system' which sanctions paternal enforcement of filial submission by that 'most dishonoring of necessities, the necessity of living.' In terms of her career as a political intellectual, the most significant connection she makes between the patriarchal 'system' and society is to be found in her association of domestic and socialistic tyranny" (134).

10. Edith Simcox argued that men have excelled over women in all the intellectual arts for one very good reason. In a proto-Woolfian formulation, she writes that the great male thinkers' time to think and to write "was secured by the industry of wives and slaves, and any latent aptitude their sisters might have had for religion or philosophy was sacrificed to the necessity for grinding corn or looking after the maids" (586). Moreover, the primitive division of labor confined women to the domicile and cut them off from the "educational influences of power and free association with powerful equals" (588).

11. Thompson and Wheeler describe this situation thus: "The restraints on adult daughters it is true are not, like those of the mothers, imposed by law, but simply those of education, custom and public opinion, engendering such a moral and physical persecution in case of disobedience as renders the vain permission of law a dead letter. Had a positive law sanctioned these restraints on adult daughters, we should be told that this law was the preserver, *for their own happiness*, of the morals of daughters, and similar disgusting and insulting hypocrisy" (43).

12. The very concept of "home," writes Rosemary George, is enmeshed in sexual politics: "The word 'home' immediately connotes the private sphere of patriarchal hierarchy, gendered self-identity, shelter, comfort, nurture and protection" (1).

13. The tribe is made up of light-skinned Africans. The "good" queen Nyleptha and her educated kin are as fair as the Brits. The "bad" queen Sorais and the manual laborers unsurprisingly (given Haggard's imperial politics) have significantly darker coloring.

Conclusion. The Territory Ahead: Wilde, Wells, Woolf

1. Similarities among such diverse literary forms can be understood in terms of "repeatable materiality" as defined by Foucault in *The Archeology of Knowledge* (107). This is the process by which a discursive formation can be dispersed, redistributed, and transformed from one realm to another. It is *repeatable* in that the same logics of language move from one domain to another; it is *material* in its real-life function of forming meaning and defining subjectivity. Visual power functions in precisely this way, informing diverse narratives as well as forming modes of identity.

2. Other critics of the genre merely acknowledge science fiction's "mongrel origins in Victorian fiction's sub-genres" (Ellis and Garnett 3).

3. The narrator obsesses on this theme; just paragraphs earlier he says: "You ought to settle down and marry like other women, not go wandering about the world to India and China and Italy, and God knows where" (89).

4. In this sense she is anticipating Michel Foucault's *Discipline and Punish*, in which Foucault applies Jeremy Bentham's model of the Panopticon to modes of surveillance and ideological regulation more generally. As Foucault explains, the major effect of the Panopticon is "to induce in the inmate a state of conscious and permanent visibility that assures the automatic functioning of power. So to arrange things that the surveillance is permanent in its effects, even if it is discontinuous in its action; that the perfection of power should tend to render its actual exercise unnecessary" (*Discipline* 201).

5. Ann Heilmann suggests that New Woman authors also anticipated some of Woolf's social diagnoses, especially the need for a woman to create a public female self through the appropriation of private space (291). Like Woolf, New Woman writers realized women's need for rooms of their own.

Works Cited

A.M.F.R. "A Letter from London." Review of *She*. *Literary World* (5 March 1887): 72–73.

Abel, Elizabeth. "Narrative Structure(s) and Female Development: The Case of *Mrs. Dalloway*." *The Voyage In: Fictions of Female Development*. Ed. Elizabeth Abel, Marianne Hirsch, and Elizabeth Langland. Hanover: University Press of New England, 1983. 161–85.

Allen, Grant. *The British Barbarians: A Hill-Top Novel*. London: John Lane, 1895.

———. "The Monopolist Instinct." *Post-Prandial Philosophy*. London: Chatto and Windus, 1894. 79–86.

———. "Plain Words on the Woman Question." *Fortnightly Review* 52 (1889): 448–58.

———. "The Romance of the Clash of Races." *Post-Prandial Philosophy*. London: Chatto and Windus, 1894. 70–78.

———. *The Woman Who Did*. 1895. New York: Oxford University Press, 1995.

Amos, Sarah M. "The Evolution of the Daughters." *Contemporary Review* 115 (1894): 515–20.

"An Anglo-Indian Novelist: Interview with Mrs. F. A. Steel." *American Monthly Review of Reviews* 16 (1897): 348–49.

Arata, Stephen. *Fictions of Loss in the Victorian Fin de Siècle: Identity and Empire*. Cambridge: Cambridge University Press, 1996.

Ardis, Ann. *New Women, New Novels: Feminism and Early Modernism*. New Brunswick, N.J.: Rutgers University Press, 1990.

Armstrong, Nancy. *Desire and Domestic Fiction: A Political History of the Novel*. New York: Oxford University Press, 1987.

Bakhtin, M. M. *Speech Genres and Other Late Essays*. Trans. Vern W. McGee. Ed. Caryl Emerson and Michael Holquist. Austin: University of Texas Press, 1986.

Barry, William. "The Strike of a Sex." *Quarterly Review* 179 (1894): 289–318.

Bhabha, Homi K. *The Location of Culture*. New York: Routledge, 1994.

Billington, Louis, and Rosamund Billington. "'A Burning Zeal for Righteousness': Women in the British Anti-Slavery Movement, 1820–1860." *Equal or Different: Women's Politics 1800–1914*. Ed. Jane Rendall. Oxford: Basil Blackwell, 1987. 82–111.

Bishop, William Henry. "Mr. Kipling's Work, So Far." *Forum* 19 (1894): 476–83.

Bland, Lucy. "The Married Woman, the 'New Woman' and the Feminist: Sexual Politics of the 1890s." *Equal or Different: Women's Politics 1800–1914*. Ed. Jane Rendall. Oxford: Basil Blackwell, 1987. 141–64.

Blankley, Elyse. "'Beyond the Talent of Knowing.'" *Critical Essays on Gertrude Stein.* Ed. Michael Hoffman. Boston: Hall, 1986.

Bloom, Harold. "Feminism as the Love of Reading." *Raritan: A Quarterly Review* 14.2 (1994): 29–42.

Brandon, Ruth. *The New Women and the Old Men: Love, Sex, and the Woman Question.* London: Secker and Warburg, 1990.

Brantlinger, Patrick. "A Postindustrial Prelude to Postcolonialism: John Ruskin, William Morris, and Gandhism." *Critical Inquiry* 22 (Spring 1996): 466–85.

———. *Rule of Darkness: British Literature and Imperialism, 1830–1914.* Ithaca, N.Y.: Cornell University Press, 1988.

Brontë, Charlotte. *Jane Eyre.* 1847. Ed. Richard J. Dunn. New York: Norton, 1987.

Brown, Herbert E. *Betsey Jane on the New Woman.* Chicago: C. H. Kerr, 1897.

Burdett, Carolyn. *Olive Schreiner and the Progress of Feminism: Evolution, Gender, Empire.* London: Palgrave, 2001.

Burton, Antoinette. *Burdens of History: British Feminists, Indian Women, and Imperial Culture, 1865–1915.* Chapel Hill: University of North Carolina Press, 1994.

Burton, Richard. "The Persistence of Romance." *The Dial* 15 (1893): 380–81.

Caird, Mona. *The Daughters of Danaus.* 1894. New York: Feminist Press, 1989.

———. "A Defense of the So-called 'Wild Women.'" *The Nineteenth Century* 31 (1892): 811–29.

———. "Marriage." 1888. *The Morality of Marriage, and Other Essays on the Status and Destiny of Woman.* London: G. Redway, 1897.

———. "The Morality of Marriage." 1890. *Prose by Victorian Women: An Anthology.* Ed. Andrea Broomfield and Sally Mitchell. New York: Garland, 1996. 566–82.

Cholmondeley, Mary. *Red Pottage.* 1899. Ed. Elaine Showalter. London: Virago, 1985.

Chrisman, Laura. "The Imperial Unconscious? Representations of Imperial Discourse." *Critical Quarterly* 32 (1990): 38–58.

Clark, Samuel M. "Mr. Haggard's Romances." *The Dial* 8 (1887): 5–7.

Cobbe, Frances Power. *The Duties of Women: A Course of Lectures.* Boston: George H. Ellis, 1881.

———. "What Shall We Do with Our Old Maids?" 1862. *Prose by Victorian Women: An Anthology.* Ed. Andrea Broomfield and Sally Mitchell. New York: Garland, 1996. 236–61.

———. "Wife Torture in England." 1878. *Prose by Victorian Women: An Anthology.* Ed. Andrea Broomfield and Sally Mitchell. New York: Garland, 1996. 292–333.

Cohn, Jan. *Romance and the Erotics of Property: Mass-Market Fiction for Women.* Durham, N.C.: Duke University Press, 1988.

Conrad, Joseph. *Heart of Darkness*. 1902. Ed. Robert Kimbrough. 3rd ed. New York: Norton, 1988.

Crackenthorpe, B. A. "The Revolt of the Daughters." *Nineteenth Century* 35 (1894): 23–31.

———. "The Revolt of the Daughters: A Last Word on 'the Revolt.'" *Nineteenth Century* 35 (1894): 424–29.

Cuffe, Kathleen. "A Reply from the Daughters." *Nineteenth Century* 35 (1894): 437–42.

Cunningham, Gail. *The New Woman and the Victorian Novel*. London: Macmillan Press, 1978.

Darwin, Charles. *The Descent of Man*. 2 vols. London: John Murray, 1871.

David, Deirdre. *Intellectual Women and Victorian Patriarchy: Harriet Martineau, Elizabeth Barrett Browning, George Eliot*. Ithaca, N.Y.: Cornell University Press, 1987.

"Declaration of Sentiments and Resolutions, Seneca Falls." 1848. *Feminism: The Essential Historical Writings*. Ed. Miriam Schneir. New York: Random House, 1972. 76–82.

Devlin, Kimberly. "The Eye and the Gaze in *Heart of Darkness*: A Symptomological Reading." *Modern Fiction Studies* 40 (1994): 711–35.

Diamond, Marion. "Maria Rye's Journey: Metropolitan and Colonial Perceptions of Female Emigration." *Imperial Objects: Essays on Victorian Women's Emigration and the Unauthorized Imperial Experience*. Ed. Rita S. Kranidis. New York: Twayne, 1998. 126–42.

Dickens, Charles. "A Bundle of Emigrants' Letters." 1850. *Charles Dickens' Uncollected Writings from Household Words, 1850–1859*. Vol. 1. Ed. Harry Stone. Bloomington: Indiana University Press, 1968. 85–96.

———. *Dombey and Son*. 1848. New York: Penguin, 1985.

Dixon, Ella Hepworth. *The Story of a Modern Woman*. 1894. London: Merlin Press, 1990.

Dowling, Linda. "The Decadent and the New Woman in the 1890s." *Nineteenth Century Fiction* 33 (March 1979): 434–53.

Egerton, George. "Virgin Soil." *Keynotes* and *Discords*. Ed. Martha Vicinus. London: Virago, 1983. 145–62.

Eliot, George. *Daniel Deronda*. 1876. Ed. Graham Handley. Oxford: Clarendon, 1984.

———. *Middlemarch*. 1872. Ed. Bert G. Hornback. New York: Norton, 1977.

———. *The Mill on the Floss*. 1860. Ed. Carol T. Christ. New York: Norton, 1994.

Ellis, R. J., and Rhys Garnett. Introduction to *Science Fiction Roots and Branches: Contemporary Critical Approaches*. Ed. R. J. Ellis and Rhys Garnett. New York: St. Martin's, 1990. 1–6.

Ellmann, Mary. *Thinking About Women*. New York: Harvest, 1968.

"The Fall of Fiction." *Fortnightly Review* 50 (1888): 324–36.

Faludi, Susan. *Backlash: The Undeclared War Against American Women*. New York: Anchor, 1991.

Fanon, Franz. "On National Culture." *Colonial Discourse and Post-Colonial Theory*. Ed. Patrick Williams and Laura Chrisman. New York: Columbia University Press. 36–52.

Faymonville, Carmen. "'Waste Not, Want Not': Even Redundant Women Have Their Uses." *Imperial Objects: Essays on Victorian Women's Emigration and the Unauthorized Imperial Experience*. Ed. Rita S. Kranidis. New York: Twayne, 1998. 64–84.

Fernando, Lloyd. *"New Women" in the Late Victorian Novel*. University Park: Penn State University Press, 1977.

First, Ruth, and Ann Scott. *Olive Schreiner: A Biography*. New York: Schocken, 1980.

Flint, Kate. *The Woman Reader, 1837–1914*. Oxford: Clarendon Press, 1994.

Fortnightly Review 52 (1889).

Foucault, Michel. *The Archeology of Knowledge and the Discourse on Language.* Trans. A. M. Sheridan Smith. New York: Pantheon, 1972.

———. *Discipline and Punish: The Birth of the Prison*. Trans. Alan Sheridan. New York: Vintage, 1978.

———. *The History of Sexuality*. Trans. Robert Hurley. Vol. 1: An Introduction. New York: Vintage, 1990.

Fraser, Hillary, Stephanie Green, and Judith Johnston. *Gender and the Victorian Periodical*. Cambridge: Cambridge University Press, 2003.

Frye, Northrup. "Excerpt from *Anatomy of Criticism.*" *Theory of the Novel: A Historical Approach*. Ed. Michael McKeon. Baltimore: Johns Hopkins University Press, 2000. 5–13.

George, Rosemary Marangoly. *The Politics of Home: Postcolonial Relocations and Twentieth-Century Fiction*. Cambridge: Cambridge University Press, 1996.

Gerson, Carole. "Wild Colonial Girls: New Women of the Empire, 1883–1901." *Journal of Commonwealth and Post Colonial Studies* 3 (Fall 1995): 61–77.

Gilbert, Sandra, and Susan Gubar. *No Man's Land: The Place of the Woman Writer in the Twentieth Century*. Vol. 2: *Sexchanges*. New Haven: Yale University Press, 1989.

Gissing, George. *New Grub Street*. 1891. Ed. John Goode. New York: Oxford, 1993.

———. *The Odd Women*. 1893. New York: Norton, 1971.

Grand, Sarah. *The Heavenly Twins*. 1893. Ann Arbor: University of Michigan Press, 1992.

———. "The New Aspect of the Woman Question." 1894. *Prose by Victorian Wom-*

en: An Anthology. Ed. Andrea Broomfield and Sally Mitchell. New York: Garland, 1996. 660–66.

———. "The New Woman and the Old." 1898. *Prose by Victorian Women: An Anthology.* Ed. Andrea Broomfield and Sally Mitchell. New York: Garland, 1996. 668–76.

Green, Martin. *Dreams of Adventure, Deeds of Empire.* New York: Basic, 1979.

Greenberger, Allen J. *The British Image of India: A Study in the Literature of Imperialism, 1880–1960.* London: Oxford University Press, 1969.

Greg, W. R. "Why Are Women Redundant?" *National Review* 14 (1862): 434–60.

Haggard, H. Rider. "About Fiction." *Contemporary Review* 51 (1887): 172–80.

———. *Allan Quartermain.* 1887. London: Collins, 1955.

———. *Allan's Wife.* 1889. London: Macdonald, 1951.

———. *Ayesha: The Return of She.* 1905. North Hollywood, Calif.: Newcastle, 1977.

———. *Cetywayo and His White Neighbors.* 1882. New York: AMS Press, 1983.

———. *Jess.* 1887. Berkeley Heights, N.J.: Wildside Press, 2000.

———. *King Solomon's Mines.* 1885. Ed. Dennis Butts. Oxford: Oxford University Press, 1989.

———. *Mr. Meeson's Will.* 1888. New York: Arno Press, 1976.

———. *She: A History of Adventure.* 1887. Ed. Daniel Karlin. Oxford: Oxford University Press, 1991.

Halberstam, Judith. *Skin Shows: Gothic Horror and the Technology of Monsters.* Durham, N.C.: Duke University Press, 1995.

Hammerton, A. James. "'Out of Their Natural Station': Empire and Empowerment in the Emigration of Lower-Middle-Class Women." *Imperial Objects: Essays on Victorian Women's Emigration and the Unauthorized Imperial Experience.* Ed. Rita S. Kranidis. New York: Twayne, 1998. 143–69.

Harper, Charles. *Revolted Women: Past, Present, and to Come.* London: Elkin Matthews, 1894.

Harris, Jose. *Private Lives, Public Spirit: Britain 1870–1914.* Harmondsworth, England: Penguin, 1994.

Harsh, Constance. "Reviewing New Woman Fiction in the Daily Press: The *Times,* the *Scotsman,* and the *Daily Telegraph.*" *Victorian Periodicals Review* 34 (2001): 79–96

Haweis, M. E. "The Revolt of the Daughters: Daughters and Mothers." *Nineteenth Century* 35 (1894): 430–36.

Heilmann, Ann. "Feminist Resistance, the Artist and 'A Room of One's Own' in New Woman Fiction." *Women's Writing* 2 (1995): 291–308.

Helsinger, Elizabeth, William Veeder, and Robin Lauterbach Sheets. *The Woman*

Question: Society and Literature in Britain and America, 1837–1883. 3 vols. Chicago: University of Chicago Press, 1989.

Hemery, Gertrude. "The Revolt of the Daughters. An Answer by One of Them." *Westminster Review* 141 (1894): 679–81.

Henty, G. A. *The Young Colonists.* New York: Mershon, 1880.

Howells, William Dean. "Editor's Easy Chair." *Harper's New Monthly Magazine* 74 (1887): 475–81.

———. "Editor's Study." *Harper's New Monthly Magazine* 74 (1887): 482–86.

———. "Editor's Study." *Harper's New Monthly Magazine* 74 (1887): 824–29.

Hughes, Linda K., ed. *New Woman Poets: An Anthology.* London: 1890s Society, 2001.

Hughes, Linda K., and Michael Lund. *The Victorian Serial.* Charlottesville: University Press of Virginia, 1991.

Hyam, Ronald. *Empire and Sexuality: The British Experience.* Manchester, England: Manchester University Press, 1992.

"The 'Imperialism' of Kipling and Stevenson." *American Monthly Review of Reviews* 19 (1899): 466–67.

James, Henry. "The Art of Fiction." 1884, 1888. *The Art of Criticism: Henry James on the Theory and the Practice of Fiction.* Ed. William Veeder and Susan M. Griffin. Chicago: University of Chicago Press, 1986. 165–95.

Jameson, Fredric. *The Political Unconscious: Narrative as a Socially Symbolic Act.* Ithaca, N.Y.: Cornell University Press, 1981.

Jeune, May. "The Revolt of the Daughters." *Fortnightly Review* 55 (1894): 267–76.

Kaplan, Sydney Janet. *Feminine Consciousness in the Modern British Novel.* Urbana: University of Illinois Press, 1975.

Kersley, Gillian. *Darling Madame: Sarah Grand and Devoted Friend.* London: Virago, 1983.

Kipling, Rudyard. *Kim.* 1901. Ed. Alan Sandison. Oxford: Oxford University Press, 1987.

———. "The Man Who Would Be King." 1888. *The Mark of the Beast and Other Stories.* New York: Signet, 1964. 216–51.

Lang, Andrew. "Realism and Romance." *Contemporary Review* 52 (1887): 683–93.

Ledger, Sally. *The New Woman: Fiction and Feminism at the Fin de Siècle.* New York: Manchester University Press, 1997.

Lee, Vernon. [Violet Paget]. "Gospels of Anarchy." *Prose by Victorian Women: An Anthology.* Ed. Andrea Broomfield and Sally Mitchell. New York: Garland, 1996. 712–29.

LeGallienne, Richard. *Grant Allen.* New York: Tucker, 1900.

Linton, Eliza Lynn. "Nearing the Rapids." 1894. *Prose by Victorian Women: An An-*

thology. Ed. Andrea Broomfield and Sally Mitchell. New York: Garland, 1996. 378–86.

———. "The Wild Women as Politicians." *The Nineteenth Century* 30 (1891): 79–88.

Locke, John. *Two Treatises of Government.* 1690. Ed. Peter Laslett. Student ed. Cambridge: Cambridge University Press, 1988.

Lyall, A. C. "The Anglo-Indian Novelist." *Edinburgh Review* 190 (1899): 415–39.

MacKenzie, John M. *Propaganda and Empire: The Manipulation of British Public Opinion, 1880–1960.* Manchester, England: Manchester University Press, 1984.

Macpherson, C. B. *The Political Theory of Possessive Individualism: Hobbes to Locke.* Oxford: Oxford University Press, 1962.

Mangan, J. A. *The Games Ethic and Imperialism: Aspects of the Diffusion of an Ideal.* New York: Viking, 1986.

Martin, Frances. "The Glorified Spinster." *Macmillan's* 58 (1888): 371–76.

Martineau, Harriet. From *Society in America.* 1837. *Prose by Victorian Women: An Anthology.* Ed. Andrea Broomfield and Sally Mitchell. New York: Garland, 1996. 68–75.

McClintock, Anne. *Imperial Leather: Race, Gender, and Sexuality in the Imperial Contest.* New York: Routledge, 1995.

Mew, Charlotte. "An Open Door." 1903. *Collected Poems and Prose.* Ed. Val Warner. London: Virago, 1982. 127–45.

———. "A White Night." 1903. *Daughters of Decadence: Women Writers of the Fin-de-Siècle.* Ed. Elaine Showalter. New Brunswick, N.J.: Rutgers University Press, 1993. 118–38.

Meyer, Susan. *Imperialism at Home: Race and Victorian Women's Fiction.* Ithaca: Cornell University Press, 1996.

Mill, John Stuart. "The Subjection of Women." 1869. *Mill.* Ed. Alan Ryan. New York: Norton, 1997. 133–213.

Mitchell, Sally. "The New Woman, Old and New." *Victorian Literature and Culture* 27 (1999): 579–88.

Moore, Augustus M. "Rider Haggard and 'The New School of Romance.'" *Time* 16 (May 1887): 513–24.

Moore, George. "Literature at Nurse: Or, Circulating Morals: A Polemic on Victorian Censorship." 1885. Ed. Pierre Coustillas. Atlantic Highlands, N.J.: Humanities Press, 1976.

Murphy, Patricia. *Time Is of the Essence: Temporality, Gender, and the New Woman.* Albany: SUNY Press, 2001.

My Trivial Life and Misfortunes. By a Plain Woman. New York: G. P. Putnam's Sons, 1883.

The National Vigilance Association. "Pernicious Literature." 1889. *Document of Modern Literary Realism*. Ed. George J. Becker. Princeton: Princeton University Press, 1964. 350–83.

"The Naughty Daughters." *Punch* 106 (27 January 1894): 42.

Nelson, Carolyn Christensen, ed. *A New Woman Reader: Fiction, Articles, Drama of the 1890s*. Peterborough, Ontario: Broadview Press, 2001.

Newton, Judith. "Making and Remaking History: Another Look at 'Patriarchy.'" *Tulsa Studies in Women's Literature* 3 (1984): 125–41.

Noble, James Ashcroft. "The Fiction of Sexuality." *Contemporary Review* 67 (1895): 490–98.

Nordau, Max. *Degeneration*. 1895. Lincoln: University of Nebraska Press, 1993.

"The Novel of the Mutiny." *New Review* 16 (1897): 78–83.

Nunokawa, Jeff. *The Afterlife of Property: Domestic Security and the Victorian Novel*. Princeton: Princeton University Press, 1994.

Oakley, Ann. *Subject Women*. New York: Pantheon, 1981.

Parry, Benita. *Delusions and Discoveries: Studies on India in the British Imagination, 1880–1930*. Berkeley and Los Angeles: University of California Press, 1972.

Partridge, Eric. *The Routledge Dictionary of Historical Slang*. Abr. Jacqueline Simpson. London: Routledge, 1973.

Patwardhan, Daya. *A Star of India: Flora Annie Steel, Her Works and Times*. Poona, India: Griha Prakashan, 1963.

Paxton, Nancy. "Complicity and Resistance in the Writings of Flora Annie Steel and Annie Besant." *Western Women and Imperialism: Complicity and Resistance*. Ed. Nupur Chauduri and Margaret Strobel. Bloomington: Indiana University Press, 1992. 158–76.

Pykett, Lyn. *The Improper Feminine: The Women's Sensation Novel and the New Woman Writing*. New York: Routledge, 1992.

Rabine, Leslie. *Reading the Romantic Heroine: Text, History, Ideology*. Ann Arbor: University of Michigan Press, 1985.

"Radcliffe College." *The Dial* 15 (1893): 380.

Ren, Michele. "The Return of the Native: Hardy's Arabella, Agency, and Abjection." *Imperial Objects: Essays on Victorian Women's Emigration and the Unauthorized Imperial Experience*. Ed. Rita S. Kranditis. New York: Twayne, 1998. 108–25.

Review of *In the Permanent Way*. By Flora Annie Steel. *The Critic* 32 (June 1898): 398–99.

Richardson, Angelique, and Chris Willis. Introduction to *The New Woman in Fiction and in Fact: Fin de Siècle Feminisms*. Ed. Angelique Richardson and Chris Willis. London: Palgrave, 2001. 1–38.

Richardson, LeeAnne Marie. "Naturally Radical: The Subversive Poetics of Dollie Radford." *Victorian Poetry* 38 (Spring 2000): 109–24.

Rubinstein, David. *Before the Suffragettes: Women's Emancipation in the 1890s*. Brighton: Harvester, 1986.

Rudy, Jason R. "On Cultural Neoformalism, Spasmodic Poetry, and the Victorian Ballad." *Victorian Poetry* 41 (2003): 590–96.

Ruskin, John. *Sesame and Lilies*. 1865. New York: Chelsea House, 1983.

Russell, Shannon. "Recycling the Poor and Fallen: Emigration Politics and the Narrative Resolutions of *Mary Barton* and *David Copperfield*." *Imperial Objects: Essays on Victorian Women's Emigration and the Unauthorized Imperial Experience*. Ed. Rita S. Kranidis. New York: Twayne, 1998. 43–63.

Said, Edward W. *Culture and Imperialism*. New York: Vintage, 1993.

———. *Orientalism*. New York: Pantheon, 1978.

Sanders, Valerie. *Eve's Renegades: Victorian Anti-Feminist Women Novelists*. New York: St. Martin's Press, 1996.

Saunders, Rebecca. "Gender, Colonialism, and Exile: Flora Annie Steel and Sara Jeannette Duncan in India." *Women's Writing in Exile*. Ed. Mary Lynn Broe and Angela Ingram. Chapel Hill: University of North Carolina Press, 1989. 303–24.

Schmitt, Cannon. *Alien Nation: Nineteenth-Century Gothic Fictions and English Nationality*. Philadelphia: University of Pennsylvania Press, 1997.

Schreiner, Olive. "The Buddhist Priest's Wife." *Daughters of Decadence: Women Writers of the Fin-de-Siècle*. Ed. Elaine Showalter. New Brunswick, N.J.: Rutgers University Press, 1993. 84–97.

———. "Life's Gifts." 1890. *Daughters of Decadence: Women Writers of the Fin-de-Siècle*. Ed. Elaine Showalter. New Brunswick, N.J.: Rutgers University Press, 1993. 317.

———. *The Story of an African Farm*. 1883. Ed. Joseph Bristow. Oxford: Oxford University Press, 1992.

———. "Three Dreams in a Desert." 1890. *Daughters of Decadence: Women Writers of the Fin-de-Siècle*. Ed. Elaine Showalter. New Brunswick, N.J.: Rutgers University Press, 1993. 308–16.

———. *Woman and Labor*. New York: Frederick A. Stokes, 1911.

Sedgwick, Eve Kosofsky. "Gender Asymmetry and Erotic Triangles." *Between Men: English Literature and Male Homosocial Desire*. New York: Columbia University Press, 1985. 21–27.

Senf, Carol A. "*Dracula*: Stoker's Response to the New Woman." *Victorian Studies* 26 (Autumn 1982): 33–49.

Shaffer, Talia. "'Nothing but Foolscap and Ink': Inventing the New Woman." *The New Woman in Fiction and in Fact: Fin-de-Siècle Feminisms*. Ed. Angelique Richardson and Chris Willis. London: Palgrave, 2001. 39–52.

Sharpe, Jenny. *Allegories of Empire: The Figure of Woman in the Colonial Text.* Minneapolis: University of Minnesota Press, 1993.

Showalter, Elaine. *A Literature of Their Own: British Women Novelists from Bronte to Lessing.* Expanded ed. Princeton: Princeton University Press, 1999.

———. *Sexual Anarchy: Gender and Culture at the Fin de Siècle.* New York: Viking, 1990.

Signorotti, Elizabeth. "Repossessing the Body: Transgressive Desire in 'Carmilla' and *Dracula.*" *Criticism* 38 (Fall 1996): 607–32.

Silver, Brenda R. "Virginia Woolf: Cultural Critique." *The Gender of Modernism: A Critical Anthology.* Ed. Bonnie Kime Scott. Bloomington: Indiana University Press, 1990. 646–58.

Simcox, Edith Jemima. "The Capacity of Women." 1887. *Prose by Victorian Women: An Anthology.* Ed. Andrea Broomfield and Sally Mitchell. New York: Garland, 1996. 584–97.

Singh, Bhupal. *A Survey of Anglo-Indian Fiction.* 1934. London: Curzon Press, 1975.

Smith, Alys W. Pearsall. "A Reply from the Daughters." *Nineteenth Century* 35 (1894): 443–50.

Spencer, Kathleen L. "Purity and Danger: *Dracula*, the Urban Gothic, and the Late Victorian Degeneracy Crisis." *ELH* 59 (1992): 197–225.

Spivak, Gayatri Chakravorty. "Three Women's Texts and a Critique of Imperialism." *Critical Inquiry* 12 (1985): 243–61.

Spurr, David. *The Rhetoric of Empire: Colonial Discourse in Journalism, Travel Writing, and Imperial Administration.* Durham, N.C.: Duke University Press, 1993.

Stacy, Enid. "A Century of Women's Rights." *Forecasts for the Coming Century by a Decade of Writers.* Ed. Edward Carpenter. Manchester, England: Labour Press, 1897.

Stade, George. "Dracula's Women." *Partisan Review* 53 (1986): 200–215.

Stead, W. T. "The Novel of the Modern Woman." *Review of Reviews* 10 (1894): 64–74.

Steel, Flora Annie. *The Garden of Fidelity: Being the Autobiography of Flora Annie Steel, 1847–1929.* London: Macmillan, 1930.

———. "The King's Well." *In the Permanent Way and Other Stories.* 1897. London: William Heinemann, 1898. 150–64.

———. *On the Face of the Waters.* New York: Macmillan, 1897.

Steel, Flora Annie, and Grace Gardiner. *The Complete Indian Housekeeper and Cook: Giving the Duties of Mistress and Servants, the General Management of the House and Practical Recipes for Cooking in All its Branches.* 2nd ed. Edinburgh: Frank Murray, 1890.

Stevenson, Robert Louis. *The Ebb-Tide.* 1894. London: Everyman/J. M. Dent, 1994.

————. "A Humble Remonstrance." 1884. *R. L. Stevenson on Fiction: An Anthology of Literary and Critical Essays*. Ed. Glenda Norquay. Edinburgh: Edinburgh University Press, 1999. 80–91.

Stewart, Garrett. *Dear Reader: The Conscripted Audience in Nineteenth-Century British Fiction*. Baltimore: Johns Hopkins University Press, 1996.

Stoker, Bram. *Dracula*. 1897. Ed. Nina Auerbach and David J. Skal. New York: Norton, 1997.

Strobel, Margaret, and Nupur Chaudhuri, eds. *Western Women and Imperialism: Complicity and Resistance*. Bloomington: Indiana University Press, 1992.

Stubbs, Patricia. *Women and Fiction: Feminism and the Novel, 1880–1920*. Sussex: Harvester Press, 1979.

Stutfield, Hugh E. M. "The Psychology of Feminism." *Blackwood's* 161 (1897): 104–17.

————. "Tommyrotics." *Blackwood's* 157 (1895): 833–45.

Syrett, Netta. "Thy Heart's Desire." *A New Woman Reader: Fiction, Articles, and Drama of the 1890's*. Ed. Carolyn Christensen Nelson. Peterborough, Ontario: Broadview, 2000. 52–69.

Tate, Trudi. *Modernism, History and the First World War*. Manchester, England: Manchester University Press, 1998.

Taylor, Helen. "The Ladies Petition." 1867. *Prose by Victorian Women: An Anthology*. Ed. Andrea Broomfield and Sally Mitchell. New York: Garland, 1996. 464–81.

Thackeray, William Makepeace. *Vanity Fair*. 1847. New York: Norton, 1994.

Thompson, William, and Anna Wheeler. *Appeal of One Half the Human Race, Women, Against the Pretensions of the Other Half, Men*. 1825. Bristol: Thoemmes Press, 1994.

Vadillo, Ana I. Parejo. "New Woman Poets and the Culture of the *Salon* at the *Fin de Siècle*." *Women: A Cultural Review* 10 (1999): 22–34.

Wallace, R. "The Seamy Side of 'Imperialism.'" *Contemporary Review* 75 (1899): 782–99.

Walton, J. Lawson. "Imperialism." *Contemporary Review* 75 (1899): 305–10.

Ward, Mrs. Humphrey. *Marcella*. 1894. New York: Penguin, 1985.

Waugh, Arthur. "Reticence in Literature." *The Yellow Book* 1 (1894): 201–19.

Wells, H. G. *The Invisible Man*. 1897. New York: Dover, 1992.

————. *The War of the Worlds*. 1898. Ed. David Y. Hughes. Oxford: Oxford University Press, 1995.

Wilde, Oscar. "The Critic as Artist." 1891. *The Artist as Critic: Critical Writings of Oscar Wilde*. Ed. Richard Ellmann. Chicago: University of Chicago Press, 1982. 341–408.

————. "The Decay of Lying." 1891. *The Artist as Critic: Critical Writings of Oscar*

Wilde. Ed. Richard Ellmann. Chicago: University of Chicago Press, 1982. 290–320.

———. *Lady Windermere's Fan*. 1892. *The Importance of Being Ernest and Other Plays*. Ed. Richard Allen Cave. New York: Penguin, 2000. 1–64.

———. "The Picture of Dorian Gray." 1890. *The Picture of Dorian Gray and Other Stories*. Ed. Paul Montazzoli. New York: Barnes and Noble, 1995. 3–241.

Williams, Carolyn. "'Genre' and 'Discourse' in Victorian Cultural Studies." *Victorian Literature and Culture* 27 (1999): 517–20.

Williams, Harold. *Modern English Writers: Being a Study of Imaginative Literature 1890–1914*. London: Sedgwick and Jackson, 1918.

Williams, Raymond. *Culture and Society, 1780–1950*. 1958. New York: Columbia University Press, 1983.

Willis, Chris. "'Heaven defend me from political or highly-educated women!': Packaging the New Woman for Mass Consumption." *The New Woman in Fiction and in Fact: Fin de Siècle Feminisms*. Ed. Angelique Richardson and Chris Willis. London: Palgrave, 2001. 53–65.

Wilt, Judith. "The Imperial Mouth: Imperialism, the Gothic, and Science Fiction." *Journal of Popular Culture* 14 (1981): 618–28.

Wollstonecraft, Mary. *A Vindication of the Rights of Women*. 1792. Ed. Carol H. Poston. 2nd ed. New York: Norton, 1988.

Woolf, Virginia. "Modern Fiction." *The Common Reader*. 1925. New York: Harcourt, Brace, 1957. 150–58.

———. *Mrs. Dalloway*. 1925. New York: Harcourt Brace, 1997.

———. "Professions for Women." *The Death of the Moth and Other Essays*. London: Hogarth Press, 1942. 235–42.

Zola, Emile. "Naturalism in the Theater." 1880. *Documents of Modern Literary Realism*. Ed. George J. Becker. Princeton: Princeton University Press, 1964. 197–229.

Index

LeeAnne M. Richardson is assistant professor of English at Georgia State University in Atlanta, where she researches and teaches courses in late-Victorian British literature and culture.